AN INDEX
TO THE POEMS
OF
OGDEN NASH

by

Lavonne Axford

The Scarecrow Press, Inc.
Metuchen, N.J.   1972

Library of Congress Cataloging in Publication Data

Axford, Lavonne B
    An index to the poems of Ogden Nash.

    1. Nash, Ogden, 1902-1971--Concordances.
I. Title.
PS3527.A637Z49 1972   811'.5'2   72-7266
ISBN 0-8108-0547-2

PREFACE

Several years ago, while engaged in a research project related to the organization of a university library catalog, I had the opportunity to use the library at the University of Illinois in Urbana. One evening, after several grueling hours at the public catalog, I suddenly had the illusion that I was living a scene from one of Ogden Nash's more imaginative poems which took place after hours in the American History Museum in New York. Before the bedazzled eyes of a visitor who had fallen asleep and gotten locked into the building, the great skeletons of a variety of pre-historic reptiles were swirling through a series of gay mazurkas and polkas. As the intruder witnessed this bizarre scene, he suddenly became aware of a small reptilian skeleton at his feet, which looked up at him and remarked with a toothy grin, "there is some virtue in being extinct."

This line seemed to serve as a catalyst which began to pull together the paper on which I was working. With the confidence born of 20 years of reference experience, I dashed off to the reference collection to locate the poem which had sprung to mind. Four frustrating hours later, I finally located it after a laborious search through book after book of Nash's collected works. The problem was that while many of Nash's poem had titles which facilitated identifying their contents, many did not. For instance, the poem for which I had searched so long had the totally unhelpful title of "Next." It was at this point that it occurred to me that a KWOC index to Nash's poems, utilizing augmented titles, might be a useful reference work. Had such an index been available I could have quickly located "Next" by looking under descriptors such as 'mazurka' or 'brontosaurus.'

The index is organized in the following manner. Each book or individual issue of a periodical in which one of Nash's poems appeared has a distinctive symbol. For instance, The Private Dining Room and Other New Verse (Boston, Little Brown; 1952), has the symbol (5). The April, 1970 issue of Travel and Camera, in which "Have Caesar, or Boadicea's Revenge" appeared, has the symbol (*).

A title can have more than one symbol. For instance, the poem "Funebral Reflection" has 6, EYZ89h, indicating that it appeared in six different publications. In the case where a title has multiple symbols they are sequenced as follows, capital letters, arabic numerals, lower case letters, random symbols. Lower case letters indicate children's poems. In order to find where a poem was published, it is necessary to check the symbol index. The need to have multiple locations illustrates the fact that Nash published many of his poems several times; occasionally, the same poem even appears under different titles. No attempt was made to indicate every place a given poem appears, but an attempt has been made to give the user several choices.

A special note of appreciation is due Judith Stipandic for keypunching the entries and for help in editing the final manuscript.

INDEX OF SYMBOLS

A   Nash, Ogden. <u>There's Always Another Windmill.</u> Decorated by John Alcorn. Boston: Little, Brown, 1968.

B   _____. <u>Marriage Lines, Notes of a Student Husband.</u> Illustrated by Isadore Seltzer. Boston: Little, Brown, 1964.

C   _____. <u>Free Wheeling.</u> Illustrated by O. Soglow. New York: Simon & Schuster, 1931.

D   _____. <u>The Primrose Path.</u> Illustrated by O. Soglow. New York: Simon & Schuster, 1935.

E   _____. <u>Hard Lines.</u> Illustrated by O. Soglow. New York: Simon & Schuster, 1931.

F   _____. <u>Happy Days.</u> Illustrated by O. Soglow. New York: Simon & Schuster, 1933.

G   _____. <u>The Bad Parents' Garden of Verse.</u> Illustrated by Reginald Birch. New York: Simon & Schuster, 1936.

H   <u>Life Magazine</u>, 65: 75-81, December 13, 1968.

J   <u>The New Yorker</u>, 44: 24, July 6, 1968.

K   <u>The New Yorker</u>, 44: 30, December 21, 1968.

L   <u>Holiday Magazine</u>, 44: 136, November, 1968.

M   <u>The New Yorker</u>, 44: 28, August 17, 1968.

N   <u>Travel and Camera</u>, 32: 60-1, September, 1969.

O   <u>The New Yorker</u>, 45: 36, April 5, 1969.

P   <u>The New Yorker</u>, 45: 36, February 22, 1969.

Q   <u>The New Yorker</u>, 45: 36, June 14, 1969.

R   <u>The New Yorker</u>, 45: 44, February 14, 1970.

S   <u>The New Yorker</u>, 45: 34, March 8, 1969.

T   <u>The New Yorker</u>, 45: 48, April 26, 1969.

U   <u>McCalls'</u>, 97: 131, February, 1970.

V   <u>Life Magazine</u>, 66: 1, January 24, 1969.

W   Nash, Ogden. <u>Bed Riddance; a Posy for the Indisposed.</u> Boston: Little, Brown, 1969.

X   <u>Holiday Magazine</u>, 47: 22, April, 1970.

Y   Nash, Ogden.   The Selected Verse of Ogden Nash.   New York: Modern Library, 1946.

Z   _____ .   Verses From 1929 On.   New York: Modern Library, 1959.

1   Nash, Ogden.   The Face Is Familiar;   The Selected Poems of Ogden Nash.   Boston: Little, Brown, 1940.

2   _____ .   Good Intentions.   Boston: Little, Brown, 1942.

3   _____ .   Versus.   Boston: Little, Boston, 1949.

4   _____ .   I'm a Stranger Here Myself.   Boston: Little, Brown, 1935.

5   _____ .   The Private Dining Room and Other New Verses.   Boston: Little, Brown, 1952.

6   _____ .   You Can't Get There From Here.   Boston: Little, Brown, 1957.

7   _____ .   Everyone but Thee, Me and Thee.   Boston: Little, Brown, 1962.

8   _____ .   Many Long Years Ago.   Boston: Little, Brown, 1945.

9   _____ .   Family Reunion.   Boston: Little, Brown, 1950.

a   Cole, William (ed.).   Humorous Poetry for Children.   New York: World Publishing Co., 1955.

b   Nash, Ogden (ed.).   The Moon Is Shining Bright as Day.   Philadelphia: Lippincott, 1953.

c   Cole, William (ed.).   Story Poems Old and New.   New York: World Publishing Co., 1957.

d   Love, Katherine Isabel (comp.).   Little Laughter.   New York: Crowell, 1957.

e   Plotz, Helen (comp.).   Untune the Sky.   New York: Crowell, 1957.

f   Ferris, Helen Josephine (comp.).   Favorite Poems Old and New.   New York: Doubleday, 1957.

g   Johnson, Edna, Sickels, Evelyn R., and Sayers, Frances Clarke.   Anthology of Childrens' Literature.   3rd ed.   New York: Houghton, 1959.

h   Plotz, Helen.   Imagination's Other Place.   New York: Crowell, 1955.

j   Nash, Ogden.   Everybody Ought to Know.   Philadelphia: Lippincott, 1961.

k   Smith, J.A. (comp.).   Looking Glass Book of Verse.   New York: Random House, 1959.

ℓ   Brewton, Sarah Westbrook and John E. (comps.).   Birthday Candles Burning Bright.   New York: Macmillan, 1960.

m   McDonald, G.D.   Way of Knowing.   New York: Crowell, 1959.

n   Thompson, B.J. (ed.).   Pocketful of Poems.   New York: Oxford Book Co., 1954.

o   Adshead, Gladys L., and Duff, Annis (comps.).   Inheritance of Poetry.   New York: Houghton, 1948.

p   Nash, Ogden.   A Boy Is a Boy; the Fun of Being a Boy.   Pictures by Arthur Shilstone.   New York: Franklin Watts, 1960.

q   _____. The Cruise of the Aardvark. Pictures by Wendy Watson. Philadelphia: Lippincott, 1967.

r   _____. The New Nutcracker Suite and Other Innocent Verses. New York: Little, Brown, 1961.

s   _____. Parents Keep Out: Elderly Poems for Youngerly Readers. New York: Little, Brown, 1951.

t   _____. Mysterious Ouphe. Illustrated by Frank Darling. Eau Claire: E. M. Hale, 1967.

u   _____. Custard the Dragon and the Wicked Knight. New York: Little, Brown, 1961.

v   _____. The Christmas that Almost Wasn't. New York: Little, Brown, 1957.

w   _____. The Animal Garden. Drawings by Hilary Knight. New York: M. Evans, 1965.

x   _____. The Untold Adventures of Santa Claus. Illustrated by Walter Lorraine. Boston: Little, Brown, 1962.

y   _____. Custard the Dragon. Pictures by Linell Nash. Boston: Little, Brown, 1961.

&   Ladies' Home Journal, 87: 65, May, 1970.

-        Atlantic, 225: 66, June, 1970.

*   Travel and Camera, 33: 35, April, 1970.

Nash, Ogden. Santa Go Home: a Case History for Parents. New York: Little, Brown, 1967.

$ Saturday Review, 54: 20, May 8, 1971.

INDEX
TO THE POEMS
OF
OGDEN NASH

AGING
PREFACE TO THE PAST/AGING/BACHELOR/GRANDPA/CHILDREN   Z6
CROSSING THE BORDER/AGING   BWZ6
OLD IS FOR BOOKS/AGING   Z6
THE VOLUBLE WHEEL CHAIR/AGING   Z5
DON'T LOOK NOW, BUT THERE'S SOMETHING BEHIND THE CURTAIN/ADVENTURE/GREENHORNS/AGING   7
AGONISTES
SAMSON AGONISTES/BATH/CHILL   YZ29
AGREEING
SEEING EYE TO EYE IS BELIEVING/AGREEING   Z2
AH
PRIDE GOETH BEFORE A RAISE, OR AH, THERE, MRS. CADWALLADER-SMITH!/SOCIALITES/POISE   FZ8
AH, WHO?/PHILOPROGENTIVE   E
AHEAD
GO AHEAD, IT WILL DO YOU GOOD OR HER EYES ARE MUCH BIGGER THAN HIS STOMACH/WIFE/HUSBAND/EAT   WZ6
GO AHEAD, LOOK, AND LISTEN/TRAINS   2
AID
DARKEST HALF HOUR; TOO EARLY IS THE TIME FOR ALL GOOD GUESTS TO COME TO THE AID OF A PARTY   A
AIMEE
AIMEE MCPHERSON   D
AIR
HAND ME DOWN MY OLD SCHOOL SLIDING PADS OR THERE'S HINT OF STRAWBERRY LEAVES IN THE AIR   5
AIRPLANES
NO, YOU BE A LONE EAGLE/AIRPLANES/FLYING   E
HOW HIGH IS UP? A SORT OF CHANTEY/AIRPLANES/FLYING   5
AIRY
AIRY, AIRY, QUITE CONTRARY/GRANDFATHER'S JOURNAL   A
ALARMS
DON'T SIT UNDER THE FAMILY TREE/ALARMS/NASH/SCRAM   7
ALAS
A VISITOR FROM PORLOCK, BUT, ALAS, NO XANADU/TRUISMS/THOUGHTS   A
ALBUM
STAMP TOO BIG FOR LETTER, MUST BE FOR ALBUM/POSTMASTER   A
ALDEN
THE ENTRAPMENT OF JOHN ALDEN/PILGRIMS   A
ALFRED
PERMISSIVE PICTURES PRESENTS "HAPPY HALLOWEEN, EVERYBODY" AN ALFRED HITCHCOCK PRODUCTION   A
ALGONQUIANS
THE WENDIGO/CANNIBAL/ALGONQUIANS   WZ5
ALIAS
ALIAS AND MELISANDE OR, GAMMON ME ONCE, GAMMON ME TWICE,/PUBLISHING   7
ALIEN
PERIOD PERIOD; PERIOD I/INNOCENT/ACCUSED; PERIOD II/ALIEN/HUMAN   Z6
ALIVE
IF HE WERE ALIVE TODAY, MAYHAP, MR. MORGAN WOULD SIT ON THE MIDGET'S LAP/BANKER   A
ROLL OVER AND PLAY ALIVE, WHO SAYS YOU CAN'T TEACH AN OLD DOG TIRESOME TRICKS/KIPLING/JOKE   5
ALL
AWAY FROM IT ALL/MONASTERY   Z4
OH, DID YOU GET THE TICKETS? BECAUSE I DON'T THINK I'LL GO, AFTER ALL/WOMEN/DECISIONS   4
DING DONG, TOOT TOOT, ALL ABOARD!/TRAINS   D
ALL, ALL ARE GONE, THE OLD FAMILIAR QUOTATIONS   Z5
IT ALL DEPENDS ON WHO YOU ARE/FAME/PUBLICITY   D8
WITHOUT ALL DUE RESPECT/OTTO KAHN/PUBLICITY   C
WE'LL ALL FEEL BETTER BY WEDNESDAY/MONDAY/WEEKENDS   3
THE WRONGS OF SPRING OR, NO ALL FOOLS' DAY LIKE AN ALL OLD FOOLS' DAY/BIRTHDAY   A
ALL GOOD AMERICANS GO TO LAROUSSE OR, I DON'T PRETEND TO BE MOLIERE THAN THOU/FRENCH   A
DARKEST HALF HOUR; TOO EARLY IS THE TIME FOR ALL GOOD GUESTS TO COME TO THE AID OF A PARTY   A
IMPRESSIONS OF SUBURBIA BY ONE WHO HAS NEVER BEEN THERE, OR ALL I KNOW IS WHAT I SEE IN ADS   7
THE ETERNAL VERNAL OR IN ALL MY DREAMS MY FAIR FACE BEAMS/SPRING   Z3
ALL OF THE PLEASURE AND NONE OF THE RESPONSIBILITY? LEAVES FROM GRANDFATHER'S SUMMER JOURNAL A
MERRY CHRISTMAS, YOU-ALL OR WHO FORGOT SAVANNAH?/CARDS/ARTISTS   5
WHO WANTS TO TRAVEL ALL OVER EUROPE AND SEE NOTHING BUT A LOT OF AMERICAN TOURISTS? I DO   6
OH, STOP BEING THANKFUL ALL OVER THE PLACE/GRACE OF GOD   DYZ18
ALL QUIET ALONG THE POTOMAC EXCEPT THE LETTER G/WASHINGTON/KISSINGER/KIPLINGER   7
DON'T CRY, DARLING, IT'S BLOOD ALL RIGHT/CHILDREN/BLOODTHIRSTY   DGZ89
WHEN YOU SAY THAT, SMILE! OR ALL RIGHT THEN, DON'T SMILE/UPHILL FIGHTS   FYZ18
NO BUSKIN, ALL SOCK, MAKES LAUGHINSTOCK/MOUSETRAP/MEAT-GRINDER/HUSBAND   A
LINES INDITED WITH ALL THE DEPRAVITY OF POVERTY/RICH   EYZ8
AND LO! HONORE'S NAME LED ALL THE REST/BALZAC/LITERATURE   Q
PROCRASTINATION IS ALL THE TIME/TORPOR/SLOTH   Z189
NO TROUBLE AT ALL, IT'S AS EASY AS FALLING OFF A LOGGERHEAD/HOSTS/COCKTAILS   S
ALL'S
ALL'S BRILLIG IN TIN PAN ALLEY/POPULAR SONGS   Z6
ALL'S NOEL THAT ENDS NOEL OR, INCOMPATIBILITY IS THE SPICE OF CHRISTMAS/SHOPPING   7

3

ALLEN
    MEL ALLEN, MEL ALLEN, LEND ME YOUR CLICHE/BASEBALL/PITCHERS/MACTIVITY   6
ALLERGY
    THE EMANCIPATION OF MR. POPLIN OR SKOAL TO THE SKIMMERLESS/ALLERGY/HAT-CHECK   Z6
    ALLERGY IN A COUNTRY CHURCHYARD/HAYFEVER   2
    ALLERGY MET A BEAR   Y4
ALLEY
    ALL'S BRILLIG IN TIN PAN ALLEY/POPULAR SONGS   Z6
    TIN PAN ALLEY; GOOD NIGHT, SWEET MIND/WINTER WONDERLAND/SONGS   9
    TIN PAN ALLEY; I SAW EUTERPE KISSING SANTA CLAUS/DREAMS   Z6
    PEACOCK ALLEY-OOP/WALDORF ASTORIA HOTEL   C
ALLIGATOR
    THE PURIST/SCIENTIST/ALLIGATOR   YZ49a
ALLOW
    ALLOW ME, MADAM, BUT IT WON'T HELP/WOMEN/COATS   YZ2
ALMA
    ALMA MATTER 67, MIND AGGIES 3/BOOKSELLERS/LIQUOR-DEALERS/MONEY   C
ALMOST
    THE CHRISTMAS THAT ALMOST WASN'T?/NICKOLAS/LULLAPAT/HEROES   V
    WHAT ALMOST EVERY WOMAN KNOWS SOONER OR LATER/HUSBANDS   BDYZ89
    PEEKABOO, I ALMOST SEE YOU/MIDDLE-AGE/GLASSES   WZ5
ALONE
    PLEASE LEAVE FATHER ALONE/FATHER'S DAY/MOTHER'S DAY   DGZ8
    LOVE ME BUT LEAVE MY DOG ALONE/MR. BEAMINGTON/POPULARITY   Z5
    LEAVE ME ALONE, AND THE WORLD IS MINE/AUTOMOBILES/RADIOS   D
ALONG
    ALL QUIET ALONG THE POTOMAC EXCEPT THE LETTER G/WASHINGTON/KISSINGER/KIPLINGER   7
    HOW TO GET ALONG WITH YOURSELF OR I RECOMMEND SOFTENING OF THE OUGHTERIES/FAULTS/TOLERANCE   Z5
ALREADY
    IT WOULD HAVE BEEN QUICKER TO WALK OR DON'T TELL ME WE'RE THERE ALREADY/TAXI/PAYING   Z6
ALSO
    IT'S ALWAYS JUNE IN JANUARY, ALSO VICE VERSA/SUMMER   A
ALWAYS
    THERE'S ALWAYS AN UBBLEBUB/MATCHMAKING/PARTIES   Z2
    IT'S ALWAYS APPLEBLOSSOM TIME, UNFORTUNATELY   4
    THERE'LL ALWAYS BE A WAR BETWEEN THE SEXES/HUSBANDS/WIVES   Z6
    WHAT'S IT LIKE OUTSIDE? OR ITS ALWAYS FAIR WEATHER UNLESS SOMEBODY SAYS IT ISN'T   T
    WHAT'S IN A NAME? SOME LETTER I ALWAYS FORGET/SPELLING   Z5
    IT'S ALWAYS JUNE IN JANUARY, ALSO VICE VERSA/SUMMER   A
    ALWAYS MARRY AN APRIL GIRL   BZ3
    I ALWAYS SAY A GOOD SAINT IS NO WORSE THAN A BAD COLD/VALENTINE   F8
    I ALWAYS SAY THERE'S NO PLACE LIKE NEW YORK IN THE SUMMER/COTTAGES   Z6
    AND THAT'S WHY I ALWAYS TAKE THE OAKLAND FERRY TO BEVERLY HILLS/TRAIN STATIONS   6
    GOD BLESS THE GIDEONS OR THERE'S ALWAYS THE KING JAMES VERSION/HOTEL/BOOKS   A
AM
    I AM FULL OF PREVIOUS EXPERIENCE/NEWSPAPERMEN   Z3
    TO A SMALL BOY STANDING ON MY SHOES WHILE I AM WEARING THEM   CGY9
    OH SHUCKS, MA'AM, I MEAN EXCUSE ME/GIRLS/PROFANITY   Z3
    AT LEAST I'M NOT THE KIND OF FOOL WHO SOBS; WHAT KIND OF FOOL AM I?   X
AMANDA
    DON'T BE CROSS, AMANDA   BZ6
AMATEUR
    BOOP-BOOP-ADIEUP, LITTLE GROUP!/AMATEUR THEATER   Z4
    DO, DO, DO WHAT YOU DONE, DONE, DONE BEFORE, BEFORE, BEFORE/APPLAUSE/AMATEUR THEATER   YZ2
AMBITIOUS
    THE STRANGE CASE OF THE AMBITIOUS CADDY/GOLF   Z4
AMBULANCE
    HI-HO THE AMBULANCE-O/STREETS/WHEELS/FEET   Z5
AMERICA
    CIVILIZATION IS CONSTANT VEXATION/AMERICA/EUROPE/BARBARIANS   D
    DON'T SELL AMERICA SHORT/STOCK MARKET   F
    COLUMBUS/AMERICA   Z4
    LOOK WHAT YOU DID, CHRISTOPHER/COLUMBUS/AMERICA   FZ8
AMERICAN
    WHO WANTS TO TRAVEL ALL OVER EUROPE AND SEE NOTHING BUT A LOT OF AMERICAN TOURISTS? I DO.   6
    HEY, HEY FOR THE AMERICAN WAY/REPUBLICANS/DEMOCRATS   5
    MEMORANDUM TO AMERICAN WOMANHOOD, OR LINES FOR A FASHION PAGE   F
AMERICANS
    AMERICANS WILL BE AMERICANS/EUROPE   D
    ALL GOOD AMERICANS GO TO LAROUSSE OR, I DON'T PRETEND TO BE MOLIERE THAN THOU/FRENCH   A
AMOEBA
    MR. JUDD AND HIS SNAIL, A SORRY TALE/AMOEBA/RACING   A

BACK
       I'LL CALL YOU BACK LATER/WRITERS   C
       THE BACK OF MINE HAND TO MINE HOST/HOTEL   7
       PUT BACK THOSE WHISKERS, I KNOW YOU/NEW YEAR   Z2
       AN EXILED IRAQI WENT BACK   A
       PAPERBACK, WHO MADE THEE? DOST THOU KNOW WHO MADE THEE?/PAPYRUS-BACK   A

BACKBITERS
       HUSH, HERE THEY COME/BACKBITERS/GOSSIP/FRANKNESS   Z18

BACKSTROKE
       AND DON'T FORGET WEIGHT-LIFTING, SHOTPUTTING, AND THE LADIES' JUNIOR BACKSTROKE CHAMPIONSHIP   7

BACKWARD
       BACKWARD, TURN BACKWARD, O COMMENTATOR, IN THY FLIGHTS/BASEBALL   A
       MY TRIP DAORBA/EUROPE/TRAVELING/BACKWARD   Z5
       NOW YOU SEE IT, NOW I DON'T/TRAINS/RIDING FOREWARD/BACKWARD   YZ2

BAD
       I ALWAYS SAY A GOOD SAINT IS NO WORSE THAN A BAD COLD/VALENTINE   F8

BAEDEKER
       EVERYBODY WANTS TO GET INTO THE BAEDEKER/GEOGRAPHY/TRAVELING   Z5

BAFFLED
       THE STRANGE CASE OF THE BAFFLED HERMIT/OLIPHANT   D1

BAITERS
       JACK DO-GOOD-FOR-NOTHING, A CURSORY NURSERY TALE FOR TOT-BAITERS/BEFRIENDING   7

BALL
       THE SENDING OF THE PENS/BALL-POINT PENS   7

BALLENTINE
       THE STRANGE CASE OF MR. BALLENTINE'S VALENTINE   Z4

BALLET
       JUST ONE MORE PLEA TO THE SULTAN OF THE METROPULTAN/BALLET/METROPOLITAN   C

BALLETRAMUS
       SHALL WE DANCE? BEING THE CONFESSIONS OF A BALLETRAMUS   7

BALLROOM
       WALTZ OF THE FLOWERS/BALLROOM/DANCE   r

BALTIMORE
       SPRING COMES TO BALTIMORE OR CHRISTMAS COMES MORE PROMPTLY   3

BALZAC
       AND LO! HONORE'S NAME LED ALL THE REST/BALZAC/LITERATURE   Q

BAN
       INVOCATION (SMOOT PLANS TARIFF BAN ON IMPROPER BOOKS-NEWS ITEMS)/PORNOGRAPHY   EYZ18

BANKER
       MA, WHAT'S A BANKER? OR HUSH, MY CHILD   DZ18
       THE BANKER'S SPECIAL/COMMUTERS   3
       ANYBODY FOR MONEY? OR JUST BRING YOUR OWN BASKET/BANKER   Z6
       IF HE WERE ALIVE TODAY, MAYHAP, MR. MORGAN WOULD SIT ON THE MIDGET'S LAP/BANKER   A

BANKERS
       BANKERS ARE JUST LIKE ANYBODY ELSE, EXCEPT RICHER/MONEY   Z4

BANKS
       NO CONFORMITY TO ENORMITY, THE BIGGER THEY ARE THE HARDER I FALL/CARS/STAMPS/BANKS   7

BANQUET
       THE BANQUET/BOSANQUET   Z4

BANTU
       DO YOU PLAN TO SPEAK BANTU? OR ABBREVIATION IS THE THIEF OF SANITY   Z6

BARBARIANS
       CIVILIZATION IS CONSTANT VEXATION/AMERICA/EUROPE/BARBARIANS   D

BARBER
       I'LL GET ONE TOMORROW/BARBER/HAIRCUT   Y49

BARCALOW
       MR. BARCALOW'S BREAKDOWN/TACT/VISITING   Z4

BARGAIN
       THE BARGAIN/SAINT IVES/SEVEN LIVES   6
       TO BARGAIN, TOBOGGAN, TO-WHOO!/SAVING MONEY   4

BARK
       HARK! HARK! THE PARI-MUTUELS BARK/HORSE RACING/BETTING   4
       HARK, HARK, THE LARKS DO BARK/SHELLEY/HAMMERSTEIN   A

BARMAIDS
       BARMAIDS ARE DIVINER THAN MERMAIDS/FISH/OCEAN/SWIMMING   Z4

BARMECIDE
       MR. BURGESS, MEET MR. BARMECIDE/NATURE STORIES/YOWLER THE BOBCAT   Z6

BARNYARD
       BARNYARD COGITATIONS/DUCK/CHICKEN/LAMB/TURKEY/PIGEON   G

BARTENDER
       HOW DO YOU SAY HA-HA IN FRENCH?/BARTENDER   Z3

BAS
       A BAS BEN ADHERN/REPRODUCTION/FELLOW MAN   EYZ8

BASEBALL

      MEL ALLEN, MEL ALLEN, LEND ME YOUR CLICHE/BASEBALL/PITCHERS/MACTIVITY   6
      LINE-UP FOR YESTERDAY: AN ABC OF BASEBALL IMMORTALS   3
      BABE, JUST BABE/RUTH/BASEBALL   D
      COEFFICIENTS OF EXPANSION/BASEBALL   T
      BACKWARD, TURN BACKWARD, O COMMENTATOR, IN THY FLIGHTS/BASEBALL   A
      DECLINE AND FALL OF A ROMAN UMPIRE/BASEBALL   7
      STICKS AND STONES MAY BREAK THEIR BONES, BUT NAMES WILL LOSE A SPONSOR/BASEBALL   A

BASKET

      ANYBODY FOR MONEY? OR JUST BRING YOUR OWN BASKET/BANKER   Z6

BAT

      THE BAT   Z5

BATH

      SAMSON AGONISTES/BATH/CHILL   YZ29

BATHING

      CLEANLINESS IS NEXT TO CATASTROPHE/BATHING/HISTORY   D
      DON'T LOOK NOW/BATHING SUITS/FIGURES   YZ8
      AND THREE HUNDRED AND SIXTY-SIX IN LEAP YEAR/SHAVING/BATHING   Z2

BATHTUBS

      SPLASH!/BATHTUBS/SHOWERS   Z4

BEACH

      THE MOOSE ON THE BEACH/GEESE   A
      PRETTY HALCYON DAYS/BEACH/OCEAN   DYZ8
      BIRTHDAY ON THE BEACH   WZ6
      OCEAN, KEEP RIGHT ON ROLLING/BEACH   D
      SEASIDE SERENADE/OCEAN BREEZE/BEACH   GYZ89

BEAMINGTON

      LOVE ME BUT LEAVE MY DOG ALONE/MR. BEAMINGTON/POPULARITY   Z5

BEAMS

      THE ETERNAL VERNAL OR IN ALL MY DREAMS MY FAIR FACE BEAMS/SPRING   Z3

BEAR

      ADVENTURES OF ISABEL/BEAR/WITCH/GIANT/DOCTOR   G89a
      DON'T GRIN OR YOU'LL HAVE TO BEAR IT/HUMOR/POINT-OF-VIEW   Z14
      GRIN AND BEAR LEFT/DIRECTIONS   Z3
      ALLERGY MET A BEAR   Y4
      EXIST, PURSUED BY A BEAR   Z6

BEARD

      THE LIFE OF THE PARTY/ARTIE/BEARD/HUMOR   FYZ8

BEASTS

      BEASTS, MEN AND GODS   D

BEAT

      BEAT THAT LIGHT!/AUTOMOBILES/FATALITIES/HORSES   D

BEATEN

      THE STRANGE CASE OF MR. GOODBODY OR A TEAM THAT WON'T BE BEATEN, CAN'T BE BEATEN/CLICHES   D1

BEATER

      COME, COME, KEROUAC. MY GENERATION IS BEATER THAN YOURS/PROGRESS   7

BEAUTY

      I'LL TAKE A BROMIDE, PLEASE/BEAUTY/TRUTH   D

BECAME

      AND SO MANHATTAN BECAME AN ISLE OF JOY/INDIANS   A
      WHAT'S IN NAME OR I WONDER WHAT BECAME OF JOHN AND MARY   Z6

BECAUSE

      OH, DID YOU GET THE TICKETS? BECAUSE I DON'T THINK I'LL GO, AFTER ALL/WOMEN/DECISIONS   4
      I'M GLAD YOU ASKED THAT QUESTION, BECAUSE IT SHOWS YOU IN YOUR TRUE COLORS/REMEMBERING   7

BECOMES

      ELECTRA BECOMES MORBID/HAIR   FYZ8

BED

      GET UP, FELLOWS, IT'S TIME TO GO TO BED/FISH/ANCESTORS   2
      HAVE YOU TRIED STAYING AWAKE? OR THEY'LL FIND A WAY TO STOP THAT, TOO/BED-BOARD   WZ3
      I'LL BE UP IN A MINUTE/BED   4

BEEFBURGER

      THE BEEFBURGER/HAMBURGER   7

BEEN

      HOW LONG HAS THIS BEEN GOING ON? OH, QUITE LONG/BETTING/HORSE-RACING   Z18
      IT WOULD HAVE BEEN QUICKER TO WALK OR DON'T TELL ME WE'RE THERE ALREADY/TAXI/PAYING   Z6
      IMPRESSIONS OF SUBURBIA BY ONE WHO HAS NEVER BEEN THERE OR, ALL I KNOW IS WHAT I SEE IN ADS   7
      A POTTED WATCH NEVER BOILS OR, MAYBE THAT'S WHAT THEY'VE BEEN TRYING TO PROVE/WRISTWATCH   7

BEES

      THE BIRD TO THE BEES   D

BEFORE
        DO, DO, DO WHAT YOU DONE, DONE, DONE BEFORE, BEFORE, BEFORE/APPLAUSE/AMATEUR THEATER   YZ2
        PRIDE GOETH BEFORE A RAISE, OR AH, THERE, MRS. CADWALLADER-SMITH!/SOCIALITES/POISE   FZ8
        SONG BEFORE BREAKFAST/CHARACTER   Z4
        PLEASE REMIND ME BEFORE I FORGET/MEMORY   R
BEFRIENDING
        JACK DO-GOOD-FOR-NOTHING, A CURSORY NURSERY TALE FOR TOT-BAITERS/BEFRIENDING   7
BEGGAR
        THE BEGGAR (AFTER WILLIAM BLAKE)   F1
BEGINNER
        THE BEGINNER'S GUIDE TO THE OCEAN   YZ29
BEGINNINGLESS
        CHAT AT THE END OF A BEGINNINGLESS SUMMER/WOMB/DAMPNESS   A
BEHIND
        MAYBE YOU CAN'T TAKE IT WITH YOU, BUT LOOK WHAT HAPPENS WHEN YOU LEAVE IT BEHIND/MONEY   Z5
        DON'T LOOK NOW, BUT THERE'S SOMETHING BEHIND THE CURTAIN/ADVENTURE/GREENHORNS/AGING   7
        HAVE A SEAT BEHIND THE POTTED PALM, SIR/TRAVEL/ARRIVAL/GROOMING   Z5
BEING
        A BOY IS A BOY; THE FUN OF BEING A BOY   p
        THE CALENDAR-WATCHERS OR WHAT'S SO WONDERFUL ABOUT BEING A PATRIARCH?/AGE   Z5
        THE STRANGE CASE OF MR. WOODS FRUSTRATION/BEING FIRST   Z6
        THE PANDIT OR, PERHAPS WE WERE WRONG ABOUT THAT, BUT AS LONG AS WE'RE BEING FRANK   7
        OH, STOP BEING THANKFUL ALL OVER THE PLACE/GRACE OF GOD   DYZ18
        SHALL WE DANCE? BEING THE CONFESSIONS OF A BALLETRAMUS   7
BELIEVE
        THEY WON'T BELIEVE, ON NEW YEAR'S EVE, THAT NEW YEAR'S DAY WILL COME WHAT MAY/HANGOVER   BZ5
        RAINY DAY/CHILDREN'S GAMES/MAKE-BELIEVE   G89
BELIEVING
        SEEING EYE TO EYE IS BELIEVING/AGREEING   Z2
BELLS
        JANGLE BELLS/SNOW   Z4
BEN
        A BAS BEN ADHERN/REPRODUCTION/FELLOW MAN   EYZ8
BENCH
        A MINT OF PHRASES OR, A TEAM IS AS STRONG AS ITS BENCH/ORATORS/ELOQUENCE   7
BENDER
        I MAY BE WRONG/BENDER   E
BENEDICT
        HOLLANDAISE/ASPERAGUS/EGGS BENEDICT   7
BENJAMIN
        BENJAMIN/GIRL/CONNECTICUT   8
BENTLEY
        A POSEY FOR EDMUND CLERICHEW BENTLEY/POETS   3
BERLITZ
        CHACUN A' SON BERLITZ/FRENCH   Z6
BERNARR
        BERNARR MACFADDEN/BODIES/EXERCISE   E
BERTRAND
        YOU ARE OLD, FATHER BERTRAND/TRIALS/RUSSELL   A
BESSEMER
        NO WOE IS GOSSAMER TO MR. BESSEMER/PESSIMISTS   Z6
BEST
        NATURE KNOWS BEST/MORNING/RISING   Z4
        A DOG'S BEST FRIEND IS HIS ILLITERACY/CLICHES   Z5
        SOME OF MY BEST FRIENDS ARE CHILDREN   FGYZ89
        COUSIN EUPHEMIA KNOWS BEST OR PHYSICIAN, HEAL SOMEBODY ELSE/CURES   WZ
BET
        YOU BET TRAVEL IS BROADENING   Z3
BETA
        THE QUACK FROWN SOX LUMPS OVEN THE... OR, FAREWELL, PHI BETA KAFKA/SECRETARIES   A
BETES
        AUTRES BETES, AUTRES MOEURS/FISH/TURTLE   E
BETTER
        WE'LL ALL FEEL BETTER BY WEDNESDAY/MONDAY/WEEKENDS   3
        TO A LADY PASSING TIME BETTER LEFT UNPASSED/CARDS/SOLITAIRE   BZ4
BETTERS
        REFLECTION ON THE PHYSICAL TASTES OF OUR INTELLECTUAL BETTERS/UNIVERSITIES   C
BETTING
        TURNS IN A WORM'S LANE/BETTING/SPORTS   FYZ18
        HOW LONG HAS THIS BEEN GOING ON? OH, QUITE LONG/BETTING/HORSE-RACING   Z18
        HARK! HARK! THE PARI-MUTUELS BARK/HORSE RACING/BETTING   4
        WEATHER CLEAR, TRACK FAST, HORSES PHOOIE!/BETTING   D

11

BETTS
> MR. BETTS'S MIND A KINGDOM IS/FORGET/MEMORY   Z5

BETWEEN
> BETWEEN BIRTHDAYS   r
> THERE'LL ALWAYS BE A WAR BETWEEN THE SEXES/HUSBANDS/WIVES   Z6
> RING OUT THE OLD, RING IN THE NEW, BUT DON'T GET CAUGHT IN BETWEEN; FIRST CHIME; SECOND CHIME Z6

BEVERLY
> AND THAT'S WHY I ALWAYS TAKE THE OAKLAND FERRY TO BEVERLY HILLS/TRAIN STATIONS 6

BEWARE
> BEWARE THE IDES OF MARCH, OR BROTHER, CAN YOU SPARE AN IDE?   D

BEYOND
> FOR DOCTOR WARREN ADAMS, WHO KINDLY BOUND THE AUTHOR FOR BEYOND HIS DESERTS/TATTOOED 2

BIB
> LINES TO BE EMBROIDERED ON A BIB OR, CHILD IS FATHER OF THE MAN, BUT NOT FOR QUITE A WHILE Z39

BIBBIDI
> WHAT IS BIBBIDI-BOBBIDI-BOO IN SANSCRIT?/FRENCH   Z5

BICARBONATE
> ELEGY IN A CITY SHAMBLES/BICARBONATE/SLEEP   D

BIG
> STAMP TOO BIG FOR LETTER, MUST BE FOR ALBUM/POSTMASTER   A
> THE BIG TENT UNDER THE ROOF/CIRCUS   GYZ89
> EVERYBODY'S MIND TO ME A KINGDOM IS OR, A GREAT BIG WONDERFUL WORLD IT'S/PUNS   Z5

BIGGER
> GO AHEAD, IT WILL DO YOU GOOD OR HER EYES ARE MUCH BIGGER THAN HIS STOMACH/WIFE/HUSBAND/EATS WZ6
> THEIR STOMACH IS BEGGER THAN YOUR EYES/GRANDFATHER'S JOURNAL   A
> NO CONFORMITY TO ENORMITY, THE BIGGER THEY ARE THE HARDER I FALL/CARS/STAMPS/BANKS 7

BILLBOARDS
> LATHER AS YOU GO/BILLBOARDS/ACCIDENTS/ADVERTISING   Z29
> SONG OF THE OPEN ROAD/BILLBOARDS/TREE   FYZ189n

BILLED
> WHO CALLED THAT PIED-BILLED GREBE A PODILYMBUS PODICEPS PODICEPS?/BIRD   A

BILLS
> THE SECOND MONTH IT'S NOT ITEMIZED/BILLS/DESK   Z3
> THE MIDDLE OF THE MONTH/BILLS   Z49
> OLD DOCTOR VALENTINE TO HIS ONLY MILLIONAIRE/BILLS   5

BIOGRAPHY
> BRIEF LIVES IN NOT SO BRIEF/GOSSIP/BIOGRAPHY/JOHN AUBREY   7
> THE NON BIOGRAPHY OF A NOBODY/MINOR LITERARY FIGURE   A

BIOLOGICAL
> BIOLOGICAL REFLECTION/GIRL/CHEEKS/PAINT   EYZ18

BIRD
> THE SWALLOW/BIRD   r
> THE PHOENIX/BIRD/EUGENICS   CZ89
> CAPERCAILLIE, AVE ATQUE VAILLIE/BIRD SONGS   7
> THE BIRD TO THE BEES   D
> UP FROM THE EGG: THE CONFESSIONS OF A NUTHATCH AVOIDER/BIRD WATCHERS   WZ6
> WHO CALLED THAT PIED-BILLED GREBE A PODILYMBUS PODICEPS PODICEPS?/BIRD   A
> HIGH, LOW THE COMEDY: A LAST WINTER'S TALE/BIRD/CAT $

BIRDIE
> WAITING FOR THE BIRDIE/PHOTOGRAPHERS   Y4

BIRDIES
> BIRDIES, DON'T MAKE ME LAUGH/CHILDREN/QUARRELING   G19

BIRDS
> THE BIRDS/SINGS   Z5
> PROGNOSTICATIONS ARE FOR THE BIRDS: LAY OFF ME, PLEASE WHILE I EAT MY WORDS/FOOTBALL/COLTS V
> THE GRACKLE/BIRDS   Z29
> TWO AND ONE ARE A PROBLEM/BIRDS   YZ18
> WHO CALLED THAT ROBIN A PICCOLO PLAYER/BIRDS   Z3

BIRDSONG
> THE STRANGE CASE OF THE WISE CHILD/PENDLETON BIRDSONG/FATHER   D1

BIRTH
> BIRTH COMES TO THE ARCHBISHOP/UNMARRIED MOTHER   EYZ8

BIRTHDAY
> ONE, TWO, BUCKLE MY SHOE/BIRTHDAY/DAUGHTER   DG89 l
> NOT GEORGE WASHINGTON'S, NOT ABRAHAM LINCOLN'S, BUT MINE/BIRTHDAY/THIRTY-EIGHT/CAREER Z2
> CONFESSION TO BE TRACED ON A BIRTHDAY CAKE   BZ3
> WASHINGTON'S BIRTHDAY EVE   Y14
> ADMONITORY LINES FOR THE BIRTHDAY OF AN OVER-ENERGETIC CONTEMPORARY   A
> BIRTHDAY ON THE BEACH   WZ6
> A BIRTHDAY THAT NEVER WAS: A FEBRUARY FANTASY/JOHN WILKES BOOTH/LINCOLN/WASHINGTON 6

BIRTHDAY
  HYMN TO THE SUN AND MYSELF/BIRTHDAY   E
  THE PARTY/BIRTHDAY   FYZ9
  LINES TO BE SCRIBBLED ON SOMEBODY ELSE'S THIRTIETH MILESTONE/BIRTHDAY   Z4
  THE WRONGS OF SPRING OR, NO ALL FOOLS' DAY LIKE AN ALL OLD FOOLS'DAY/BIRTHDAY   A
BIRTHDAYS
  BETWEEN BIRTHDAYS   a
BISCUIT
  PLEASE PASS THE BISCUIT/DOG/SPANGLE   YZ29
BISHOP
  JOHN PEEL, SHAKE HANDS WITH 37 MAMAS; BISHOP DE WOLFE GREETS 37 DEBUTANTES ON LONG ISLAND   A
BIT
  THIS IS GOING TO HURT JUST A LITTLE BIT/DENTISTS   W4
BITE
  DON'T BITE THE HAND THAT PUTS ITS FOOT IN YOUR MOUTH/TAMMANY/OCTOPUS   7
BITES
  MAN BITES DOG DAYS/SUMMER/ITCH   WZ14
BIZ
  CAESAR KNIFED AGAIN OR CULTURE BIZ GETS HEP, BOFFS PROFS/COLLEGE TEACHING   Z6
BLACK
  HEARTS AND FLOWERS OR WHAT I KNOW ABOUT BOLIVAR BLACK/GENEROSITY/LOANS   DZ8
BLACKMAILING
  THE STRANGE CASE OF THE BLACKMAILING DOVE/DAINGERFIELD   Z4
BLAKE
  EPITAPH FOR AN EXPLORER/WILLIAM BLAKE/TIGER   3
  THE BEGGAR (AFTER WILLIAM BLAKE)   F1
BLANCH
  ONE WESTERN, TO GO/BLANCH/RANCH   A
BLANKETS
  COMPLAINT TO FOUR ANGELS/SLEEP/BLANKETS   WZ49
BLESS
  GOD BLESS THE GIDEONS OR THERE'S ALWAYS THE KING JAMES VERSION/HOTEL/BOOKS   A
BLIGHT
  THE STRANGE CASE OF THE BLIGHT THAT FAILED/GREAT-AUNT/WRATH   6
BLISSFUL
  THE BLISSFUL DREAM OF MR. FARR/MARRIAGE/WIFE   3
BLOOD
  DON'T CRY, DARLING, IT'S BLOOD ALL RIGHT/CHILDREN/BLOODTHIRSTY   DGZ89
BLOODTHIRSTY
  DON'T CRY, DARLING, IT'S BLOOD ALL RIGHT/CHILDREN/BLOODTHIRSTY   DGZ89
BLOWS
  THAR SHE BLOWS/WIND/MARCH/TAXES   3
BLUE
  BABY, WHAT MAKES THE SKY BLUE/CHILDREN/INGENUOUS/PARENTS   19
  HERE'S TO YOU, LITTLE BOY BLUE/SLEEP/DREAMS   2
  ROLL ON, THOU DEEP AND DARK BLUE COPY WRITER-ROLL/HEMINGWAY/MOVIES   Z3
  ROLL ON, THOU DEEP AND DARK BLUE SYLLABLES, ROLL ON/METROPOLITAN OPERA/MILTON CROSS   A
BOADICEA
  HAVE CAESAR, OR BOADICEA'S REVENGE/TRAVEL   *
BOARD
  SPLINTERS FROM THE FESTIVE BOARD   A
  HAVE YOU TRIED STAYING AWAKE? OR THEY'LL FIND A WAY TO STOP THAT, TOO/BED-BOARD   WZ3
BOB
  HOW TO TELL A QUAIL FROM A PARTRIDGE/BOB WHITE   D
BOBBIDI
  WHAT IS BIBBIDI-BOBBIDI-BOO IN SANSCRIT?/FRENCH   Z5
BOBCAT
  MR. BURGESS, MEET MR. BARMECIDE/NATURE STORIES/YOWLER THE BOBCAT   Z6
BODER
  IF A BODER MEET A BODER, NEED A BODER CRY? YES/FORBODINGS/AFTBODINGS   A
BODIES
  BERNARR MACFADDEN/BODIES/EXERCISE   E
BOFFS
  CAESAR KNIFED AGAIN OR CULTURE BIZ GETS HEP, BOFFS PROFS/COLLEGE TEACHING   Z6
BOG
  A PRINCESS WHO LIVED NEAR A BOG/FROG   A
BOILED
  REFLECTION ON A COMMON MISAPPREHENSION/LADIES/HARD-BOILED/FREUD   C1
BOILS
  A WATCHED EXAMPLE NEVER BOILS/THUNDERSTORM   GZ189
  A POTTED WATCH NEVER BOILS OR, MAYBE THAT'S WHAT THEY'VE BEEN TRYING PROVE/WRISTWATCH   7

13

BOLIVAR
      HEARTS AND FLOWERS OR WHAT I KNOW ABOUT BOLIVAR BLACK/GENEROSITY/LOANS   DZ8
BOND
      A PARABLE FOR SPORTS WRITERS/SOCIETY COLUMNISTS, BOND SALESMEN AND POETS/PUBLISHING BOOKS   FZ8
BONDS
      NO BONDS TODAY   2
BONES
      STICKS AND STONES MAY BREAK MY BONES, BUT NAMES WILL BREAK MY HEART/INDIVIDUAL DIGNITY   7
      STICKS AND STONE MAY BREAK THEIR BONES, BUT NAMES WILL LOSE A SPONSOR/BASEBALL   A
BONUS
      GOODBYE, OLD YEAR, YOU OAF, OR WHY DON'T THEY PAY THE BONUS?/NEW YEAR'S EVE   DYZ8
BOO
      BOO/MOSQUITO   2
      WHAT IS BIBBIDI-BOBBIDI-BOO IN SANSCRIT?/FRENCH   Z5
BOOJUM
      THE SNARK WAS A BOOJUM WAS A PRAWN/SANTIAGO   Z6
BOOK
      YOUR LEAD, PARTNER, I HOPE WE'VE READ THE SAME BOOK/BRIDGE/CARDS   Z6
      THE THIRD JUNGLE BOOK/PYGMY/POLYGAMY   Y2
      OUR NUMBER'S IN THE BOOK/TELEPHONE SOLICITATION   D
      THE BOOK OF JOB   7
      THE BOOK OF PROVERBS: A WORD TO HUSBANDS/MARRIAGE/ARGUMENTS   7
      O TEMPORA, OH-OH!/NEWSPAPERS/BOOK-REVIEWS/EROTICA   A
BOOKS
      OLD IS FOR BOOKS/AGING   Z6
      THE TROUBLE WITH SHAKESPEARE YOU REMEMBER HIM/BOOKS/DESERT ISLAND/AGATHA CHRISTIE   6
      THE MAN ON THE SHELF/CHILDREN'S BOOKS/DESERT ISLAND   6
      HAVE YOU READ ANY GOOD BOOKS TOMORROW?   7
      INVOCATION (SMOOT PLANS TARIFF BAN ON IMPROPER BOOKS-NEWS ITEMS)/PORNOGRAPHY   EYZ18
      A PARABLE FOR SPORTS WRITERS, SOCIETY COLUMNISTS, BOND SALESMEN AND POETS/PUBLISHING BOOKS   FZ8
      BOD BLESS THE GIDEONS FOR THERE'S ALWAYS THE KING JAMES VERSION/HOTEL/BOOKS   A
BOOKSELLERS
      ALMA MATTER 67, MIND AGGIES 3/BOOKSELLERS/LIQUOR-DEALERS/MONEY   C
      ASIDE TO THE TRADE/BOOKSELLERS   F
BOOKSTORE
      LECTURER IN BOOKSTORE/AUTOGRAPHING   Z5
BOOP
      BOOP-BOOP-ADIEUP, LITTLE GROUP!/AMATEUR THEATER   Z4
BOOT
      TABOO TO BOOT/ITCH/SCRATCH   WYZ189
BOOTH
      A BIRTHDAY THAT NEVER WAS: A FEBRUARY FANTASY/JOHN WILKES BOOTH/LINCOLN/WASHINGTON   6
BORDER
      CROSSING THE BORDER/AGING   BWZ6
BOREDOM
      HAPPY DAYS, ELMER/DISASTER/BOREDOM/NEWS   FY8
      JUDGEMENT DAYS/PARENTS/CHILDREN/BOREDOM   GYZ89
      THE STRANGE CASE OF MR. DONNYBROOK'S BOREDOM   BWZ4
BORES
      EH?/DEAFNESS/BORES   7
      THE GRYNCH/BORES   5
      I KNOW EXACTLY WHO DROPPED THE OVERALLS IN MRS. MURPHY'S CHOWDER/BORES   Z6
      LONG TIME NO SEE, 'BY NOW'/MR. LATOUR/BORES   5
      WILL YOU HAVE YOUR TEDIUM RARE OR MEDIUM?/BORES   Z3
BORN
      M.C. LOVES TV OR A PERSONALITY IS BORN/HAM/EGO   5
      THERE'S A HOST BORN EVERY MINUTE/WEEKENDS/GUESTS   D1
      CONFESSIONS OF A BORN SPECTATOR/ATHLETES   4
      NEVER WAS I BORN TO SET THEM RIGHT/VEXATION   A
BORROWING
      POLONIUS, YES, POLONIUS, NO/HAMLET/BORROWING/LOANING   5
BOSANQUET
      THE BANQUET/BOSANQUET   Z4
BOSS
      SONGS FOR A BOSS NAMED MR. LINTHICUM   E
      TWO SONGS FOR A BOSS NAMED MR. LONGWELL   Z8
BOTANIST
      BOTANIST, AROINT THEE! OR, HENBANE BY ANY OTHER NAME   A
BOTTLENECK
      ILL-MET BY FLOURESCENCE/HOUSES/BOTTLENECK GAVOTTE   A

BROMIDE
I'LL TAKE A BROMIDE, PLEASE/BEAUTY/TRUTH   D
BRONCHITIS
A RIDE ON THE BRONXIAL LOCAL/BRONCHITIS   14
BRONTOSAURUSES
NEXT!/MUSEUM OF NATURAL HISTORY/BRONTOSAURUSES/FOSSIL/POLKA/MOZURKAS   WZ5
BRONX
GEOGRAPHICAL REFLECTION/BRONX   E
BRONXIAL
A RIDE ON THE BRONXIAL LOCAL/BRONCHITIS   14
BROODING
FROM A MANHATTAN TOMB/BROODING/LACKADAISICLE   CWYZ8
BROOKLYNESE
THE GREEKS HAD A WORD FOR IT, SO WHY SPEAK ENGLISH/DIALECTS/SOUTHERN/BROOKLYNESE 6
BROTHER
I YIELD TO MY LEARNED BROTHER/PROFESSIONALS/LAWYER/DOCTOR/MORTITIAN   DWZ18
BEWARE THE IDES OF MARCH, OR BROTHER, CAN YOU SPARE AN IDE?   D
BROW
JUST HOW LOW CAN A HIGHBROW GO WHEN A HIGHBROW LOWERS HIS BROW   7
BRUISES
DEAR GODMOTHER, I HOPE SHE BRUISES EASY!/FAIRY/APRIL FOOL   4
BRUNCH
NOT EVEN FOR BRUNCH/COINED WORDS/GLADIOLUS/CUCUMBER/CHRYSANTHEMUM/CANTALOUPE   Z3
BUCK
THE OUTCOME OF MR. BUCK'S SUPERSTITION/LUCK   Z3
BUCKET
THE COMIC SPIRIT NEVER SAY DIE, SAY KICK THE BUCKET   6
BUCKLE
ONE, TWO, BUCKLE MY SHOE/BIRTHDAY/DAUGHTER   DG89ℓ
BUDDY
KINDLY UNHITCH THAT STAR, BUDDY/SUCCESS/FAILURE   DYZ18
BUDS
SING A SONG OF TASTE BUDS/WINE SNOB/GIN SNOB   7
TASTE BUDS, EN GARDE/FROZEN STRAWBERRIES   A
BUFFALO
I HAPPEN TO KNOW/BUFFALO/SEAL/LOCUST   Z29
THE STRANGE CASE OF CLASHING CULTURES/ANGLOPHILE/BUFFALO   7
BUGLER
EDOUARD/MACDOUGAL/BUGLER/FRUGAL   Z8d
BUGS
GOODBYE, BUGS   Z2
THE STRANGE CASE OF THE ENTOMOLOGIST'S HEART/BUGS   Z3
BULBUL
FLOW GENTLY, SWEET ETYMOLOGY, ORNITHOLOGY, AND PENOLOGY/NIGHTINGALE/PERSION/BULBUL 5
BULFINCH
FABLES BULFINCH FORGOT: NARCISSUS AND THE TREACHEROUS VOWEL/SPEAKING   A5
BULGONIA
THE STRANGE CASE OF THE TSAR'S SUPERIORITY COMPLEX/BULGONIA   4
BULLETIN
A BULLETIN HAS JUST COME IN/DISEASE/ANIMALS   Z2
BUND
HOMEWARD BUND/MOTH   Y29
BURGESS
MR. BURGESS, MEET MR. BARMECIDE/NATURE STORIES/YOWLER THE BOBCAT   Z6
BURN
I BURN MONEY/MILLIONAIRE   Z2
BURNING
THERE ARE MORE WAYS TO ROAST A PIG THAN BURNING THE HOUSE DOWN/CIGARETTE LIGHTERS Z3
BURNS
THE LOUSE/ROBERT BURNS   2
EVERYTHING'S HAGGIS IN HOBOKEN OR, SCOTS WHA HAE HAE/ROBERT BURNS   Z5
BURNT
WHO TAUGHT CADDIES TO COUNT? OR A BURNT GOLFER FEARS THE CHILD   Z3
BUS
ARE YOU SAVING THIS SEAT FOR ANYONE OR YES, BUT WHAT'S THE USE?/BUS   D
BUSES
THE BUSES HEADED FOR SCRANTON   Z6
BUSINESS
MERRY N.R.A. AND HAPPY FISCAL YEAR/BUSINESS   F
BUSKIN
NO BUSKIN, ALL SOCK, MAKES LAUGHINSTOCK/MOUSETRAP/MEAT-GRINDER/HUSBAND   A

16

BUSTS
     VIVA VAMP, VALE VAMP/BUSTS/LIPSTICK/MASCARA   7

BUSY
     A BRIEF GUIDE TO RHYMING OR, HOW BE THE LITTLE BUSY DOTH?/ENGLISH/PLURAL   Z6

BUSYBODIES
     A WORD TO BUSYBODIES   B

BUTTERFLIES
     THE LEPIDOPTERIST/BUTTERFLIES   5

BUTTON
     NEVER MIND THE OVERCOAT, BUTTON UP THAT LIP/GOSSIP   Z6
     JUST PRESS THE BUTTON, THE BUTTON-HOLE IS REALLY A DEEPFREEZE/APPLIANCES   5

BUY
     WHO'LL BUY MY LINGUAL? OR YOU PRONOUNCE PLUIE, LOUIE/FRENCH   6
     LET ME BUY THIS ONE/RICH/MONEY   4

BYRD
     ADMIRAL BYRD   E

CAD
     YOU CAD, WHY DON'T YOU CRINGE?/KNAVE/COWARD   18

CADDIES
     WHO TAUGHT CADDIES TO COUNT? OR A BURNT GOLFER FEARS THE CHILD   Z3

CADDY
     THE STRANGE CASE OF THE AMBITIOUS CADDY/GOLF   Z4

CADWALLADER
     PRIDE GOETH BEFORE A RAISE, OR AH, THERE, MRS. CADWALLADER-SMITH!/SOCIALITES/POISE   FZ8

CAESAR
     CAESAR KNIFED AGAIN OR CULTURE BIZ GETS HEP, BOFFS PROFS/COLLEGE TEACHING   Z6
     HAVE CAESAR, OR BOADICEA'S REVENGE/TRAVEL   *

CAFE
     OUR CITY, OUR CITIZENS/VILLAGE/GOLD COAST/PRESS CAFE/THEATER   7

CAKE
     CONFESSION TO BE TRACED ON A BIRTHDAY CAKE   B

CALCUTTA
     ARTHUR/CALCUTTA/SNORING   WZ18a

CALDER
     BABY, IT'S CALDER INSIDE/MOBILES/ART   5

CALENDAR
     ONE THIRD OF A CALENDAR/WINTER/ILLNESS/CHILDREN   WYZ189
     THE CALENDAR-WATCHERS OR WHAT'S SO WONDERFUL ABOUT BEING A PATRIARCH?/AGE   Z5
     POEMS TO BE PINNED TO THE CALENDAR   D

CALF
     THE CALF   9

CALL
     THERE'S A LAW, ISN'T THERE? OR I CAN CALL YOU NAMES BUT DON'T CALL ME NAMES/LIBEL   5
     I'LL CALL YOU BACK LATER/WRITERS   C

CALLED
     A THOUGHT ON THE MANNER OF THOSE WHO STRIVE TO ACHIEVE THE MANNER CALLED HEMINGWAY/WRITERS   C
     I DIDN'T SAY A WORD OR WHO CALLED THAT PICCOLO PLAYER A FATHER?/HEARING/VOICE/LOUDNESS   Z5
     WHO CALLED THAT PIED-BILLED GREBE A PODILYMBUS PODICEPS PODICEPS?/BIRD   A
     WHO CALLED THAT ROBIN A PICCOLO PLAYER/BIRDS   Z3

CALLING
     CALLING SPRING VII-MMMC/MYSTERIES/ROMAN-NUMERALS/PUBLISHERS   Z5
     WHO SHALL I SAY IS CALLING?/NAMES/PSUEDONYMS   2

CALLIOPE
     PEDIATRIC REFLECTION/INFANT/CALLIOPE   EGYZ89

CAME
     WHICH CAME FIRST, OBEISANCE OR OBESITY/PLATE-WATCHERS/WEIGHT-WATCHERS   7

CAMEL
     MOROCCO/MARRAKECH/CAMEL   7
     THE CAMEL   GYZ89d

CAN
     JUST HOW LOW CAN A HIGHBROW GO WHEN A HIGHBROW LOWERS HIS BROW   7
     YOU CAN BE A REPUBLICAN, I'M A GERONTOCRAT/FRIENDS/AGE   WZ5
     THERE'S A LAW, ISN'T THERE? OR I CAN CALL YOU NAMES BUT DON'T CALL ME NAMES/LIBEL   5
     A MAN CAN COMPLAIN, CAN'T HE? (A LAMENT FOR THOSE WHO THINK OLD)   AW
     HOW CAN ECHO ANSWER WHAT ECHO CANNOT HEAR?/VOICE/WIFE   B7
     LET GEORGE DO IT, IF YOU CAN FIND HIM   D8
     TWO GOES INTO TWO ONCE, IF YOU CAN GET IT THERE/SQUARE PEG/ROUND HOLE   5
     I CAN HARDLY WAIT FOR THE SANDMAN/DREAMS   WZ6
     CAN I GET YOU A GLASS OF WATER? OR PLEASE CLOSE THE GLOTTIS AFTER YOU/COUGHING   Z6
     BEWARE THE IDES OF MARCH, OR BROTHER, CAN YOU SPARE AN IDE?   D
     THE STRANGE CASE OF MR GOODBODY OR A TEAM THAT WON'T BE BEATEN, CAN'T BE BEATEN/CLICHES   D1

CHAMPIONS
    CHAMPIONS AND CHIMPIONS/FOOTBALL/HUSHMOUTH/MCGUNN/APES
CHAMPIONSHIP
    AND DON'T FORGET WEIGHT-LIFTING, SHOTPUTTING, AND THE LADIES' JUNIOR BACKSTROKE CHAMPIONSHIP   7
CHANGE
    CHANGE HERE FOR WICHITA FALLS OR, HAS ANYBODY SEEN MY WANDERLUST?/TRAVEL   Z5
CHANNEL
    A CAUTION TO HILLBILLY SINGERS, HARPISTS, HARPOONISTS, CHANNEL-SWIMMERS, PEOPLE FIRST IN
        LINE FOR WORLD SERIES TICKETS/FAME   5
CHANT
    RAVEN, DON'T STAY AWAY FROM MY DOOR - A CHANT FOR APRIL FIRST   FZ8
CHANTEY
    HOW HIGH IS UP? A SORT OF CHANTEY/AIRPLANES/FLYING   5
CHARACTER
    SONG BEFORE BREAKFAST/CHARACTER   Z4
CHARADES
    WHAT'LL WE DO NOW, OR, I'M AFRAID I KNOW OR, GOOD OLD JUST PLAIN CHARADES, FAREWELL/GAMES   2
    THE QUEEN IS IN THE PARLOR/GAMES/CHARADES   Z4
CHARGEACCOUNT
    THE FRIENDLY TOUCH/CHARGEACCOUNT/LETTER   Z4
CHARLES
    CHARLES AND ANNE LINDBERGH   D
CHARM
    LIMERICK TWO/LADY/GUAM/CHARM/MAUGHAM   5
CHART
    NOTES FOR THE CHART IN 306/HOSPITAL   A
CHAT
    CHAT AT THE END OF A BEGINNINGLESS SUMMER/WOMB/DAMPNESS   A
CHAUFFEURS
    MAY I DRIVE YOU HOME, MRS. MURGATROYD/AUTOMOBILES/CHAUFFEURS   DY1
CHECK
    THE EMANCIPATION OF MR. POPLIN OR SKOAL TO THE SKIMMERLESS/ALLERGY/HAT-CHECK   Z6
CHEEKS
    BIOLOGICAL REFLECTION/GIRL/CHEEKS/PAINT   EYZ18
CHEF
    THE CHEF HAS IMAGINATION OR, IT'S TOO HARD TO DO IT EASY/LETTUCE/SALAD DRESSING   5
CHERUB
    THE CHERUB   Z3
CHICKEN
    BARNYARD COGITATIONS/DUCK/CHICKEN/LAMB/TURKEY/PIGEON   G
    EXPERIMENT DEGUSTATORY/RATTLESNAKE MEAT/CHICKEN   A
CHILD
    FIRST CHILD ... SECOND CHILD   3
    IT IS INDEED SPINACH/CHILD/GROWN-UP   4
    THE STRANGE CASE OF THE WISE CHILD/PENDLETON BIRDSONG/FATHER   D1
    HOW THE RHINOCEROS GOT ITS HIDE OR THE CONFESSIONS OF COUNT MOWGLI DE SADE/CHILD/READING   3
    EPISTLE TO THE OLYMPIANS/PARENTS/CHILD/SIZE   G89
    OUR CHILD DOESN'T KNOW ANYTHING OR THANK GOD!   DGZ8
    OUR CHILD DOESN'T KNOW ANYTHING OR THANK HEAVEN   9
    ODE TO C.B.E., PRACTICALLY THE ONLY NEW MALE CHILD I KNOW OF   G9
    LINES TO BE EMBROIDERED ON A BIB OR, THE CHILD IS FATHER OF THE MAN, BUT NOT FOR QUITE A
        WHILE   Z39
    THE CHILD IS FATHER TO THE MAN, BUT WITH MORE AUTHORITY/CHORES/PARENTS   Z5
    'MY CHILD IS PHLEGMATIC,,,' - ANXIOUS PARENT   CGYZ89
    THE MAN IS FATHER OF THE CHILD, OR BUT HE NEVER QUITE GETS USED TO IT   9
    TO THE CHILD WHO'S FARTHER FROM THE MANNERS OR, HOW TO BE YOUNG GRACEFULLY   7
    A CHILD'S GUIDE TO PARENTS   GZ89
    MA, WHAT'S A BANKER? OR HUSH, MY CHILD   DZ18
    WHO TAUGHT CADDIES TO COUNT? OR A BURNT GOLFER FEARS THE CHILD   Z3
CHILDHOOD
    POSIES FROM A SECOND CHILDHOOD OR HARD HOW GAFFER DO CHAFFER   Z6
CHILDREN
    ANIMAL GARDEN/ABIDON/PETS/CHILDREN   W
    DON'T CRY, DARLING, IT'S BLOOD ALL RIGHT/CHILDREN/BLOODTHIRSTY   DG789
    JUDGEMENT DAY/PARENTS/CHILDREN/BOREDOM   GYZ89
    SONG TO BE SUNG BY THE FATHER OF INFANT FEMALE CHILDREN/BOYS/MARRIAGE   YZ189
    SONG TO BE SUNG BY THE FATHER OF SIX-MONTHS-OLD FEMALE CHILDREN/BOYS/MARRIAGE   FG
    A CAROL FOR CHILDREN/CHRISTMAS   GYZ89o
    LITTLE FEET/CHILDREN/GENIUS/FAMILIES   GZ89
    THE ABSENTEES/CHILDREN/HOME   Z6
    THE PARENT/CHILDREN/IGNORE   FGZ89

DAUGHTER

    IN WHICH THE POET IS ASHAMED BUT PLEASED/DAUGHTER/FATHER DGYZ89

    A GOOD PARENT'S GARDEN OF VISION; THE DREAM; THE NIGHTMARE; THE AWAKENING/DAUGHTER FGZ89

    DADDY'S HOME, SEE YOU TOMORROW/BOYFRIEND/DAUGHTER Z6

    ONE, TWO, BUCKLE MY SHOE/BIRTHDAY/DAUGHTER DG89ℓ

DAWES

    THE BOY WHO LAUGHED AT SANTA CLAUS/JABEZ DAWES 29c

DAY

    THE WRONGS OF SPRING OR, NO ALL FOOLS'S DAY LIKE AN ALL OLD FOOLS'S DAY/BIRTHDAY A

    RAINY DAY/CHILDREN'S GAMES/MAKE-BELIEVE G89

    MIRIAM'S LUCKY DAY/DELIRIUM Z4

    LADIES DAY/GAMBLING 4

    PLEASE LEAVE FATHER ALONE/FATHER'S DAY/MOTHER'S DAY DGZ8

    AS I WAS SAYING TO SAINT PAUL JUST THE OTHER DAY/OPSIMATHY/LIFE 7

    JUDGEMENT DAY/PARENTS/CHILDREN/BOREDOM GYZ89

    IS TOMORROW REALLY ANOTHER DAY? OR NO MORE OF THE SAME, PLEASE 3

    ELECTION DAY IS A HOLIDAY/VOTING FZ8

    EVERY DAY IS MONDAY/WEEKDAYS Z4

    THE DAY OF THE LOCUST OR, WHOSE WEDDING IS THIS ANYWAY?/GUESTS A

    A DAY ON A CRUISE OR, WHAT A DAY. WHAT A CRUISE./SHIPS 7

    THEY WON'T BELIEVE, ON NEW YEAR'S EVE, THAT NEW YEAR'S DAY WILL COME WHAT MAY/HANGOVER BZ5

    EPILOGUE TO MOTHER'S DAY, WHICH IS TO BE PUBLISHED ON ANY DAY BUT MOTHER'S DAY Z4

    MIDSUMMER'S DAYMARE/JUNE/LONGEST DAY Z14

    PLEASE LEAVE FATHER ALONE/FATHER'S DAY/MOTHER'S DAY DGZ8

DAYMARE

    MIDSUMMER'S DAYMARE/JUNE/LONGEST DAY Z14

DAYS

    PRETTY HALCYON DAYS/BEACH/OCEAN DYZ8

    MAN BITES DOG DAYS/SUMMER/ITCH WZ14

    EHEU! FUGACES OR, WHAT A DIFFERENCE A LOT OF DAYS MAKE/YOUTH/MIDDLE-AGE WZ5

    THERE WERE GIANTS IN THOSE DAYS OR MAYBE THERE WEREN'T ANECDOTES Z3

    HAPPY DAYS, ELMER/DISASTER/BOREDOM/NEWS FY8

DE

    THEY DON'T READ DE QUINCEY IN PHILLY OR CINCY/MURDER A

    HOW THE RHINOCEROS GOT ITS HIDE OR THE CONFESSIONS OF COUNT MOWGLI DE SADE/CHILD/READING 3

    THE LITERARY SCENE/DE SADE/SPILLANE/SITWELL Z6

    JOHN PEEL, SHAKE HANDS WITH 37 MAMAS; BISHOP DE WOLFE GREETS 37 DEBUTANTES ON LONG ISLAND A

DEAD

    THE STRANGE CASE OF THE DEAD DIVORCEE/MINT JULEP Z4

    PAVANE FOR A DEAD DOLL OR, THE PAIN IN GRANDFATHER'S NECK/PAPER DOLLS 7

    HOW MANY MILES TO THE DEAD LETTER OFFICE/POSTAGE STAMPS A

    SO THIS IS WASHINGTON OR DEAD MEN RESENT NO TALES/PROHIBITION D

    THE ONLY GOOD INDIAN IS A DEAD PUBLIC RELATIONS COUNSELLOR/INTERVIEWS D

DEAFNESS

    EH?/DEAFNESS/BORES 7

DEALERS

    ALMA MATTER 67, MIND AGGIES 3/BOOKSELLERS/LIQUOR-DEALERS/MONEY C

DEAR

    FATHER, DEAR FATHER, GO JUMP IN THE LAKE OR, YOU'RE COSTLIER THAN YOU THINK/PARENTS/SUPPORT Z5

    DEAR GODMOTHER, I HOPE SHE BRUISES EASY!/FAIRY/APRIL FOOL 4

    I CAN'T HAVE A MARTINI, DEAR, BUT YOU TAKE ONE/DIETING WZ6

    MY DEAR, HOW DID YOU EVER THINK UP THIS DELICIOUS SALAD? DYZ18

DEATH

    DEATH ON THE NINETEENTH HOLE/MADEMOISELLE FROM ARMENTIERS/AFFAIRS F8

    OLD MEN/DEATH EYZ8j

DEBT

    FIRST PAYMENT DEFERRED/DEBT/CREDIT Z18

DEBUNKING

    IT OUGHT TO BE HISTORY, OR DON'T SAY IT ISN'T SO/DEBUNKING D

DEBUTANTES

    JOHN PEEL, SHAKE HANDS WITH 37 MAMAS;BISHOP DE WOLFE GREETS 37 DEBUTANTES ON LONG ISLAND A

DECEMBER

    CONFOUND YOU, DECEMBER TWENTY-SIXTH, I APOLOGIZE/CHRISTMAS Z3

DECISIONS

    OH, DID YOU GET THE TICKETS? BECAUSE I DON'T THINK I'LL GO, AFTER ALL/WOMEN/DECISIONS 4

    SUPPOSE HE THREW IT IN YOUR FACE/TIPPING/DECISIONS YZ29

DECLINE

    DECLINE AND FALL OF A ROMAN UMPIRE/BASEBALL 7

DEEP

    ROLL ON, THOU DEEP AND DARK BLUE COPY WRITER-ROLL/HEMINGWAY/MOVIES Z3

    ROLL ON, THOU DEEP AND DARK BLUE SYLLABLES, ROLL ON/METROPOLITAN OPERA/MILTON CROSS A

DEEPFREEZE
     JUST PRESS THE BUTTON, THE BUTTON-HOLE IS REALLY A DEEPFREEZE/APPLIANCES   5
DEFERRED
     FIRST PAYMENT DEFERRED/DEBT/CREDIT   Z18
DEGUSTATORY
     EXPERIMENT DEGUSTATORY/RATTLESNAKE MEAT/CHICKEN   A
DELAWARE
     UNTOLD ADVENTURES OF SANTA CLAUS/WASHINGTON/DELAWARE/REVOLUTION   x
DELAYS
     LONG LIVE DELAYS OF ANCIENT ROME/PROCRASTINATION   D
DELICIOUS
     MY DEAR, HOW DID YOU EVER THINK UP THIS DELICIOUS SALAD?   DYZ18
DELIRIUM
     MIRIAM'S LUCKY DAY/DELIRIUM   Z4
DELVED
     CORRECTION: EVE DELVED AND ADAM SPAN/GARDEN CLUB/LADIES   Z5
DEMOCRATES
     HEY, HEY FOR THE AMERICAN WAY/REPUBLICANS/DEMOCRATES   5
DEMOCRATS
     LOVE UNDER THE REPUBLICANS (OR DEMOCRATS)/MARRIAGE/ECONOMY   BEZ8
     VIVE LE POSTMASTER GENERAL/REPUBLICANS/DEMOCRATS   F8
DENTISTS
     NATURAL REFLECTION/DENTISTS   E
     THIS IS GOING TO HURT JUST A LITTLE BIT/DENTISTS   W4
DEPARTMENT
     WE WOULD REFER YOU TO OUR SERVICE DEPARTMENT, IF WE HAD ONE/APPLIANCES   Z3
DEPENDS
     IT ALL DEPENDS ON WHO YOU ARE/FAME/PUBLICITY   D8
DEPRAVITY
     LINES INDITED WITH ALL THE DEPRAVITY OF POVERTY/RICH   EYZ8
     I SPY OR THE DEPRAVITY OF PRIVACY/PUBLICITY   Z6
DESCENDANTS
     PILGRIM'S PROGRESS/THANKSGIVING/MAYFLOWER/DESCENDANTS   D
DESERT
     THE TROUBLE WITH SHAKESPEARE YOU REMEMBER HIM/BOOKS/DESERT ISLAND/AGATHA CHRISTIE   6
     THE MAN ON THE SHELF/CHILDREN'S BOOKS/DESERT ISLAND   6
DESERTS
     FOR DOCTOR WARREN ADAMS, WHO KINDLY BOUND THE AUTHOR FOR BEYOND HIS DESERTS/TATTOOED   2
DESERVES
     ONE GOOD HOARDER DESERVES ANOTHER/TIRES   2
DESIGN
     IT'S A GRAND PARADE IT WILL BE, MODERN DESIGN/SAINT PATRICK   YZ2
DESK
     THE SECOND MONTHS IT'S NOT ITEMIZED/BILLS/DESK   Z3
DETECTIVE
     DON'T GUESS, LET ME TELL YOU/DETECTIVE STORIES   YZ18
     THE SPINSTER DETECTIVE   3
DETECTIVES
     MACBETH HATH MURDERED SLEEP? OR DON'T MAKE ME LAUGH/DETECTIVES   F8
DETROIT
     DETROIT, SPARE THAT WHEEL!/AUTOMOBILES/HORSEPOWER   6
DEVIL
     WHEN THE DEVIL WAS SICK COULD HE PROVE IT?/SYMPTOMS   WZ18
DEVOTEE
     AN ENTHUSIAST IS A DEVOTEE IS A ROOTER OR, MR. HEMINGWAY, MEET MR. STENGEL   Z6
DIALECTS
     THE GREEKS HAD A WORD FOR IT, SO WHY SPEAK ENGLISH/DIALECTS/SOUTHERN/BROOKLYNESE   6
DIARY
     THE UNSEEING EYE: THE TRAVEL DIARY OF A NON-OBSERVER   7
DICKINSON
     THE CHIPMUNK/EMILY DICKINSON   Z5
DICTATORSHIP
     RECIPE FOR A DICTATORSHIP   4
DICTIONARIES
     TO EE IS HUMAN/DICTIONARIES/MR. WEBSTER/MR. MERRIAM   Z6
     WHERE THERE'S A WILL, THERE'S VELLEITY/VOLITION/DICTIONARIES/WORDS   YZ4
DID
     DID SOMEONE SAY 'BABIES?'   CG19
     WHO DID WHICH? OR WHO INDEED?/KNOWLEDGE/FACTS   WZ3
     MY DEAR, HOW DID YOU EVER THINK UP THIS DELICIOUS SALAD?   DYZ18

DID
OH, DID YOU GET THE TICKETS? BECAUSE I DON'T THINK I'LL GO, AFTER ALL/ WOMEN/DECISIONS   4
LOOK WHAT YOU DID, CHRISTOPHER/COLUMBUS/AMERICA   FZ8
DIDN'T
I DIDN'T SAY A WORD OR WHO CALLED THAT PICCOLO PLAYER A FATHER?/HEARING/VOICE/LOUDNESS   Z5
DIE
THE COMIC SPIRIT NEVER SAY DIE, SAY KICK THE BUCKET   6
OLD DOCTOR VALENTINE TO HIS SON/LIVE/DIE   5
DIED
NO WONDER OUR FATHERS DIED/HOUSES/PLUMBING/FURNACES   YZ4
DIET
CURL UP AND DIET/LADIES/WEIGHT   WZ4
I'LL STAY OUT OF YOUR DIET IF YOU'LL STAY OUT OF MINE   2
DIETING
I CAN'T HAVE A MARTINI, DEAR, BUT YOU TAKE ONE/DIETING   WZ6
DIETS
JUST A PIECE OF LETTUCE AND SOME LEMON JUICE, THANK YOU/DIETS   FY
DIFFERENCE
EHEU! FUGACES OR, WHAT A DIFFERENCE A LOT OF DAYS MAKE/YOUTH/MIDDLE-AGE   WZ5
DIGNITY
STICKS AND STONES MAY BREAK MY BONES, BUT NAMES WILL BREAK MY HEART/INDIVIDUAL DIGNITY   7
DIGS
HE DIGS, HE DUG, HE HAS DUG/GARDEN   Z3
DING
DING DONG, TOOT TOOT, ALL ABOARD!/TRAINS   D
DINING
THE PRIVATE DINING ROOM/DATING/LAVENDAR/TAFFETA   Z5
DINNER
THE ABSENTEES/TURKEY DINNER/GRAVY/CRANBERRIES   Z29
ONE NIGHT IN OZ/DINNER PARTY/ENEMIES   YZ2
TELL ME NO FIBLETS, WHERE ARE THE GIBLETS/GRAVY/TURKEY DINNER   A
DIRECTIONS
GRIN AND BEAR LEFT/DIRECTIONS   Z3
DIRGE
A NECESSARY DIRGE/PERVERSITY/HUMANITY   Z4
DISAPPOINTMENT
THE STRANGE CASE OF MR. FORTAGUE'S DISAPPOINTMENT/INNISFREE   Z4
DISASTER
HAPPY DAYS, ELMER/DISASTER/BOREDOM/NEWS   FY8
PRAYER AT THE END OF A ROPE/DISASTER/JAMS   YZ14
DISASTERS
WHAT'S HECUBA TO HIM? A ONE-MINUTE CLOSE-UP/TV REPORTING DISASTERS   A
DISEASE
A BULLETIN HAS JUST COME IN /DISEASE/ANIMALS   Z2
DISEASES
I'M TERRIBLY SORRY FOR YOU, BUT I CAN'T HELP LAUGHING/DISEASES   WZ4
DISH
THE SPOON RAN AWAY WITH THE DISH?/TV COMMERCIALS/DISWASHING   7
ISN'T THAT A DAINTY DISH? NO!/COCKTAILS/GADGETS   Z14
DISHONORABLE
WRONG-HEADED/DISHONORABLE   E
DISHWASHING
THE SPOON RAN AWAY WITH THE DISH?/TV COMMERCIALS/DISHWASHING   7
DISKJOCKEY
YOU CAN'T TELL THE HIT PARADE WITHOUT A DRUM MAJORETTE/DISKJOCKEY   5
DISPASSIONATE
THE PASSIONATE PAGAN AND THE DISPASSIONATE PUBLIC, A TRAGEDY OF THE MACHINE AGE/SPRING   FYZ8
DISPRAISE
LINES IN DISPRAISE OF DISPRAISE/ANALYZING   E
DISTRESS
SUCH AN OLD THEME, BUT SUCH FRESH DISTRESS/CULTURE   C
DISTRESSED
LINES WRITTEN TO CONSOLE THOSE LADIES DISTRESSED BY THE LINES "MEN SELDOM MAKE PASSES"/GLASSES EG
DISTRIBUTION
THE SONG OF SONGS/WEALTH/DISTRIBUTION   4
DITHERERS
SONG FOR DITHERERS   WZ4
DIVINER
BARMAIDS ARE DIVINER THAN MERMAIDS/FISH/OCEAN/SWIMMING   Z4
DIVORCEE
THE STRANGE CASE OF THE DEAD DIVORCEE/MINT JULEP   Z4

DOWN
     THERE ARE MORE WAYS TO ROAST A PIG THAN BURNING THE HOUSE DOWN/CIGARETTE LIGHTERS   Z3
     HAND ME DOWN MY OLD SCHOOL SLIDING PADS OR THERE'S HINT OF STRAWBERRY LEAVES IN THE AIR   5
     UP THE WALDORF, DOWN ON THE FARM/FARMER/CITYDWELLER   D
     RAPUNZEL, RAPUNZEL, LET'S LET DOWN OUR HAIR/WITS   Z6
     DOWN THE MOUSEHOLE, AND WHAT SCIENCE MISSED THERE/MARRIAGE/APOLOGY   WZ2
     I'LL WRITE THEIR NUMBER DOWN WHEN WE GET HOME/WORDS/SOCIAL-LIFE   Z2
     SLOW DOWN, MR. GANDERONK, YOU'RE LATE/GOLF   Z2
     THE LOST CAUSE/SLOGAN/CROWDS/SIT DOWN   4

DRAGON
     CUSTARD THE DRAGON AND THE WICKED KNIGHT/BRAVERY/COWARDICE   u
     CUSTARD THE DRAGON/BRAVERY/COWARDISE   y
     THE TALE OF CUSTARD THE DRAGON/BRAVERY/COWARDICE   GZ89f

DRAGONS
     DRAGONS ARE TOO SELDOM/MONSTERS/MYTHOLOGY/SEA-SERPENTS   DYZ8

DRAWBRIDGE
     POOR MR. STRAWBRIDGE/DRAWBRIDGE   Z14

DREADS
     MRS. PURVIS DREADS ROOM SERVICE OR, MR. PURVIS DREADS IT, TOO/HOTEL   Z3

DREAM
     MY MY; MY DREAM/HAIR; MY CONSCIENCE   Z6
     DREAM OF INNOCENT ORGIES/STAGE-DOOR-JOHNNY   J
     THE BLISSFUL DREAM OF MR. FARR/MARRIAGE/WIFE   3
     A GOOD PARENT'S GARDEN OF VISION; THE DREAM; THE NIGHTMARE; THE AWAKENING/DAUGHTER   FGZ89
     LIMERICK THREE/RISING SUN/DREAM   5
     MY DREAM   B

DREAMS
     SWEET DREAMS/SLEEP   r
     THE STRANGE CASE OF THE GIRL O' MR. SPONSOON'S DREAMS/RUN-OVER   Z4
     PIPE DREAMS/PLUMBER/SUMMER COTTAGE   Z4
     THE ETERNAL VERNAL OR IN ALL MY DREAMS MY FAIR FACE BEAMS/SPRING   Z3
     OLD DOCTOR VALENTINE FOR ONCE DREAMS OF WEALTH/BRA/PEPS-OO-LA-LA/BOUNCE   5
     SIGMUND FREUD/DREAMS   D
     HERE'S TO YOU, LITTLE BOY BLUE/SLEEP/DREAMS   2
     I CAN HARDLY WAIT FOR THE SANDMAN/DREAMS   Z6
     TIN PAN ALLEY; I SAW EUTERPE KISSING SANTA CLAUS/DREAMS   Z6

DRESS
     ESSAY ON WOMAN/DRESS   4

DRESSES
     PAJAMAS, HUH? OR DRESSES WERE SO NICE/PANTS   C

DRESSING
     APPREHENSION/DRESSING/GRANDFATHER'S JOURNAL   A
     THE CHEF HAS IMAGINATION OR, IT'S TOO HARD TO DO IT EASY/LETTUCE/SALAD DRESSING   5

DRINK
     I WANT A DRINK OF WATER, BUT NOT FROM THE THERMOS/FATHERS/TRIPS   Z2
     A DRINK WITH SOMETHING IN IT/COCKTAILS   DYZ8
     YOU'LL DRINK YOUR ORANGE JUICE AND LIKE IT, COMRADE/CYPRUS/SOVIET UNION   7

DRIVE
     DRIVE SLOW, MAN CHORTLING, OR, APRIL, 1941/NEW CAR   2
     MAY I DRIVE YOU HOME, MRS. MURGATROYD/AUTOMOBILES/CHAUFFEURS   DY1

DRIVER
     WHAT STREET IS THIS, DRIVER?/SIXTH-AVENUE EL/NEW YORKER   2
     THE STRANGE CASE OF THE PLEASING TAXI-DRIVER   Z4

DRIVERS
     PRESENTING DOCTOR FELL/DRIVERS   2

DRIVING
     THE AZORES/DRIVING   7

DROP
     THE DROP OF A HAT/WOMEN   Z14

DROPPED
     I KNOW EXACTLY WHO DROPPED THE OVERALLS IN MRS. MURPHY'S CHOWDER/BORES   Z6

DRUM
     YOU CAN'T TELL THE HIT PARADE WITHOUT A DRUM MAJORETTE/DISKJOCKEY   5

DRUNKS
     IT MUST BE THE MILK/INFANT/DRUNKS   GZ189

DRUSILLA
     DRUSILLA/QUARRY/SOIREE   Z8

DUCK
     BARNYARD COGITATIONS/DUCK/CHICKEN/LAMB/TURKEY/PIGEON   G
     THE DUCK   Y89b
     THE HUNTER/DUCK   Z39j

EIGHT
        NOT GEORGE WASHINGTON'S, NOT ABRAHAM LINCOLN'S, BUT MINE/BIRTHDAY/THIRTY-EIGHT/CAREER   Z2
        ONE TIMES ONE IS EIGHT/GRANDFATHER'S JOURNAL   A
        THE EIGHT O'CLOCK PERIL/BREAKFAST   Z4
EINE
        EINE KLEINE NASHMUSIK/MOZART   L
EITHER
        MACHINERY DOESN'T ANSWER, EITHER, BUT YOU AREN'T MARRIED TO IT/WIVES/KNITTING   GZ89
EL
        WHAT STREET IS THIS, DRIVER?/SIXTH-AVENUE EL/NEW YORKER   2
ELASTIC
        ASPIC/ELASTIC   7
ELECTION
        ELECTION DAY IS A HOLIDAY/VOTING   FZ8
ELECTRA
        ELECTRA BECOMES MORBID/HAIR   FYZ8
        THE SELF-EFFACEMENT OF ELECTRA THORNE/ACTRESSES   Z6
ELEGY
        ELEGY IN A CITY SHAMBLES/BICARBONATE/SLEEP   D
ELEPHANTS
        ELEPHANTS HAVEN'T GOT ANYTHING TO FORGET/MANKIND   D
ELEVATORS
        DO SPHINXES THINK?/FINGERNAILS/ELEVATORS   Z4
ELMER
        HAPPY DAYS, ELMER/DISASTER/BOREDOM/NEWS   FY8
ELOQUENCE
        A MINT OF PHRASES OR, A TEAM IS AS STRONG AS ITS BENCH/ORATORS/ELOQUENCE   7
ELSE
        COUSIN EUPHEMIA KNOWS BEST OR PHYSICIAN, HEAL SOMEBODY ELSE/CURES   WZ3
        ANYBODY ELSE HATE NICKYNAMES?   Z6
        BANKERS ARE JUST LIKE ANYBODY ELSE, EXCEPT RICHER/MONEY   Z4
        SO DOES EVERYBODY ELSE, ONLY NOT SO MUCH/ANECDOTES/REPEATING   Z2
        LINES TO BE SCRIBBLED ON SOMEBODY ELSE'S THIRTIETH MILESTONE/BIRTHDAY   Z4
EMANCIPATION
        THE EMANCIPATION OF MR. POPLIN OR SKOAL TO THE SKIMMERLESS/ALLERGY/HAT-CHECK   Z6
EMBROIDERED
        LINES TO BE EMBROIDERED ON A BIB OR, THE CHILD IS FATHER OF THE MAN, BUT NOT FOR QUITE A WHILE Z39
EMBROIDERY
        MADEIRA/WINERIES/EMBROIDERY   7
EMILY
        I WANT TO SIT NEXT TO EMILY/CONVERSATION   D
        THE CHIPMUNK/EMILY DICKINSON   Z5
EMMET
        THE EMMET/ANT   Z7
EN GARDE
        TASTE BUDS, EN GARDE/FROZEN STRAWBERRIES   A
ENCYCLOPEDIA
        ENCYCLOPEDIA BRITANNICA/WRITERS   C
END
        LINES FOR A SUMMER'S END/HEAT/MANHATTAN   F8
        ON WAKING TO THE THIRD RAINY MORNING OF A LONG WEEK END/HOUSE GUEST   Z3
        CHAT AT THE END OF A BEGINNINGLESS SUMMER/WOMB/DAMPNESS   A
        PRAYER AT THE END OF A ROPE/JAMS/DISASTER   YZ14
ENDING
        THE HAPPY ENDING OF MR. TRAIN/MR. SLOAN/MR. RHODES   Z5
ENDORSEMENTS
        I HAVE USED IT FOR YEARS/ADVERTISING/ENDORSEMENTS   F8
ENDS
        IF I HAD THE WINGS OF A HELICOPTER OR HALL'S MILLS THAT ENDS MILLS/QUESTIONS/ANSWERS   6
        ALL'S NOEL THAT ENDS NOEL OR, INCOMPATIBILITY IS THE SPICE OF CHRISTMAS/SHOPPING   7
ENEMIES
        ONE NIGHT IN OZ/DINNER PARTY/ENEMIES   YZ2
ENERGETIC
        ADMONITORY LINES FOR THE BIRTHDAY OF AN OVER-ENERGETIC CONTEMPORARY   A
ENGLAND
        ENGLAND EXPECTS/ENGLISHMEN   YZ4
        IF THERE WERE NO ENGLAND, 'COUNTRY LIFE' WOULD INVENT IT/HOUSES   A
        ETHNOLOGICAL REFLECTION/BREAKFAST/ENGLAND   E
ENGLISH
        SIC SEMPER MR. SHERMAN'S TEMPER OR KINDLY PLACE YOUR ORDER IN ENGLISH/COCKTAILS   6
        LAMENTS FOR A DYING LANGUAGE/ENGLISH/COINED WORDS   7

EVE
　　CORRECTION: EVE DELVED AND ADAM SPAN/GARDEN CLUB/LADIES　　　　　Z5
　　LAMENT ON THE EVE OF PARTING/ABEL/SERVANT　　　　　YZ2
　　THEY WON'T BELIEVE, ON NEW YEAR'S EVE, THAT NEW YEAR'S DAY WILL COME WHAT MAY/HANGOVER　　BZ5
　　WASHINGTON'S BIRTHDAY EVE　　　　　Y14
　　GOOD RIDDANCE, BUT NOW WHAT?/NEW YEAR'S EVE　　　　　WZ39
　　GOODBYE, OLD YEAR, YOU OAF, OR WHY DON'T THEY PAY THE BONUS?/NEW YEAR'S EVE　　DYZ8
EVEN
　　NOT EVEN FOR BRUNCH/COINED WORDS/GLADIOLUS CUCUMBER/CHRYSANTHEMUM/CANTALOUPE　　Z3
　　EVERYBODY LOVES A BRIDE, EVEN THE GROOM/WEDDING　　　　　5
　　WE HAVE MET THE SASSENACHS AND THEY ARE OURS; EVEN THE YEAR IS NOW MCMLXIV/MCLUHAN/MCKUEN　　P
　　I NEVER EVEN SUGGESTED IT/QUARRELS/MARRIAGE　　　　　BYZ18
EVENING
　　THE EVENING OUT/WOMEN/LATE　　　　　YZ4
EVER
　　MY DEAR, HOW DID YOU EVER THINK UP THIS DELICIOUS SALAD?　　　　　DYZ18
EVERY
　　EVERY DAY IS MONDAY/WEEKDAYS　　　　　Z4
　　THERE'S A HOST BORN EVERY MINUTE/WEEKENDS/GUESTS　　　　　D1
　　WHAT ALMOST EVERY WOMAN KNOWS SOONER OR LATER/HUSBANDS　　　　　BDYZ89
　　WHAT EVERY WOMAN KNOWS SOONER OR LATER/HUSBANDS　　　　　1
EVERYBODY
　　A CAUTION TO EVERYBODY/AUK/MAN/FLY/WALK/THINK　　　　　Z5
　　EVERYBODY EATS TOO MUCH ANYHOW/AUTOMOBILES/TRAVEL/LUNCH　　　　　YZ149
　　SO DOES EVERYBODY ELSE, ONLY NOT SO MUCH/ANECDOTES/REPEATING　　　　　Z2
　　EVERYBODY HAS AN UNCLE　　　　　9
　　EVERYBODY LOVES A BRIDE, EVEN THE GROOM/WEDDING　　　　　5
　　EVERYBODY MAKES POETS　　　　　Z4
　　EVERYBODY TELLS ME EVERYTHING/NEWS　　　　　Z18
　　EVERYBODY WANTS TO GET INTO THE BAEDEKER/TRAVELING/GEOGRAPHY　　　　　Z5
　　MERRY CHRISTMAS, NEARLY EVERYBODY!　　　　　4
　　PERMISSIVE PICTURES PRESENTS 'HAPPY HALLOWEEN, EVERYBODY' AN ALFRED HITCHCOCK PRODUCTION　　A
EVERYBODY'S
　　EVERYBODY'S FULL OF CARBONACEOUS MATERIAL OBTAINED BY THE IMPERFECT COMBUSTION OF WOOD　　A
　　EVERYBODY'S MIND TO ME A KINGDOM IS OR, A GREAT BIG WONDERFUL WORLD IT'S/PUNS　　Z5
EVERYTHING
　　EVERYBODY TELLS ME EVERYTHING/NEWS　　　　　Z18
　　MONEY IS EVERYTHING　　　　　C8
EVERYTHING'S
　　EVERYTHING'S HAGGIS IN HOBOKEN OR, SCOTS WHA HAE HAE/ROBERT BURNS　　　　　Z5
EXACTLY
　　I KNOW EXACTLY WHO DROPPED THE OVERALLS IN MRS. MURPHY'S CHOWDER/BORES　　　　　Z6
EXAMPLE
　　A WATCHED EXAMPLE NEVER BOILS/THUNDERSTORM　　　　　GZ189
EXCEPT
　　I DON'T MEAN US, EXCEPT OCCASIONALLY/LIFE/PESSIMISM　　　　　Y2
　　BANKERS ARE JUST LIKE ANYBODY ELSE, EXCEPT RICHER/MONEY　　　　　Z4
　　ALL QUIET ALONG THE POTOMAC EXCEPT THE LETTER G/WASHINGTON/KISSINGER/KIPLINGER　　7
EXCUSE
　　HEARTS OF GOLD OR A GOOD EXCUSE IS WORSE THAN NONE/APOLOGIES/REMORSE　　　　　FYZ8
　　OH, SHUCKS, MA'AM, I MEAN EXCUSE ME/GIRLS/PROFANITY　　　　　Z3
EXECUTIVES
　　THERE'S MORE TIME AT THE TOP, OR I WANT TO SEE MR. MURGATROYD/EXECUTIVES/ASSISTANTS　　D
EXERCISE
　　BERNARR MAC FADDEN/BODIES/EXERCISE　　　　　E
EXILED
　　AN EXILED IRAQI WENT BACK　　　　　A
EXIST
　　EXIST, PURSUED BY A BEAR　　　　　Z6
EXPANSION
　　COEFFICIENTS OF EXPANSION/BASEBALL　　　　　T
EXPECTS
　　ENGLAND EXPECTS/ENGLISHMEN　　　　　YZ4
EXPERIENCE
　　THE VOICE OF EXPERIENCE/LECTURES/HUSBANDS　　　　　BYZ29
　　I AM FULL OF PREVIOUS EXPERIENCE/NEWSPAPERMEN　　　　　Z3
　　EXPERIENCE TO LET　　　　　Z3
　　SONGS OF EXPERIENCE　　　　　A
EXPERIMENT
　　EXPERIMENT DEGUSTATORY/RATTLESNAKE MEAT/CHICKEN　　　　　A
　　THERE IS NO DANGER LINE/SCIENTIST/EXPERIMENT　　　　　D
EXPLANATION
　　A BRIEF EXPLANATION OF WOMEN　　　　　2
EXPLORER
　　EPITAPH FOR AN EXPLORER/WILLIAM BLAKE/TIGER　　　　　3

FLOURESCENCE
        ILL-MET BY FLOURESCENCE/HOUSES/BOTTLENECK GAVOTTE   A
FLOW
        FLOW GENTLY, SWEET ETYMOLOGY, ORNITHOLOGY, AND PENOLOGY/NIGHTINGALE/PERSION/BULBUL   5
FLOWERS
        WALTZ OF THE FLOWERS/BALLROOM/DANCE   r
        THE SOLITUDE OF MR. POWERS/FLOWERS/ARRANGING   BZ6
        HEARTS AND FLOWERS OR WHAT I KNOW ABOUT BOLIVAR BLACK/GENEROSITY/LOANS   DZ8
FLOWERY
        MAX SCHLING, MAX SCHLING, LEND ME YOUR GREEN THUMB; A CATALOG OF FLOWERY CATALOGUES   Z5
FLUNKED
        IT WAS NOT I WHO POSED FOR RODIN OR WHY I FLUNKED PHILOSOPHY IV/THINKING/FRENCH   5
FLUTES
        THE FLUTES/TOOTS   r
FLY
        A CAUTION TO EVERYBODY/AUK/MAN/FLY/WALK/THINK   Z5
        THE FLY   YZ29f
FLYING
        HOW HIGH IS UP? A SORT OF CHANTEY/AIRPLANES/FLYING   5
        NO, YOU BE A LONE EAGLE/AIRPLANES/FLYING   E
FOLKS
        REMEMBER THE OLD FOLKS AT HOME/GIFTS/HOLIDAYS   C8
FOOD
        THE CLEAN PLATTER/FOOD   DZ8
FOOL
        AT LEAST I'M NOT THE KIND OF FOOL WHO SOBS; WHAT KIND OF FOOL AM I?   X
        DEAR GODMOTHER, I HOPE SHE BRUISES EASY!/FAIRY/APRIL FOOL   4
FOOLS
        THE WRONGS OF SPRING OR, NO ALL FOOLS' DAY LIKE AN ALL OLD FOOLS' DAY/BIRTHDAY   A
FOOT
        DON'T BITE THE HAND THAT PUTS ITS FOOT IN YOUR MOUTH/TAMMANY/OCTOPUS   7
FOOTBALL
        PROGNOSTICATIONS ARE FOR THE BIRDS: LAY OFF ME, PLEASE, WHILE I EAT MY WORDS/FOOTBALL/COLTS B
        CHAMPIONS AND CHIMPIONS/FOOTBALL/HUSHMOUTH MCGUNN/APES   7
        COLTS IS THE NAME, FOOTBALL'S THE GAME   H
        ONE MAN'S MEED IS ANOTHER MAN'S OVEREMPHASIS/COLLEGE FOOTBALL   Z4
FOOTNOTE
        WHILE HOMER NODDED: A FOOTNOTE TO THE ILIAD/ZEUS/ANTISCRUPULOS   A
FOR
        I'M A PLEASURE TO SHOP FOR/PRESENTS/CHRISTMAS   Z5
        SONGS FOR A BOSS NAMED MR. LINTHICUM   E
        TWO SONGS FOR A BOSS NAMED MR. LONGWELL   Z8
        PAVANE FOR A DEAD DOLL OR, THE PAIN IN GRANDFATHER'S NECK/PAPER DOLLS   7
        RECIPE FOR A DICTATORSHIP   4
        NOTES FOR A DOCUMENTARY IN SEARCH OF A SPONSOR/TV   A
        LAMENTS FOR A DYING LANGUAGE/ENGLISH/COINED WORDS   7
        MEMORANDUM TO AMERICAN WOMANHOOD, OR LINES FOR A FASHION PAGE   F
        FOR A GOOD DOG   Z3
        A PLEA FOR A LEAGUE OF SLEEP   Z49
        LINES FOR A SUMMER'S END/HEAT/MANHATTAN   F8
        SONG FOR A TEMPERATURE OF A HUNDRED AND ONE/GRIPPE/INFLUENZA   FWYZ89
        STAMP TOO BIG FOR LETTER, MUST BE FOR ALBUM/POSTMASTER   A
        DARKEST HALF HOUR; TOO EARLY IS THE TIME FOR ALL GOOD GUESTS TO COME TO THE AID OF A PARTY A
        EPITAPH FOR AN EXPLORER/WILLIAM BLAKE/TIGER   3
        TUNE FOR AN ILL-TEMPERED CLAVICHORD/YANKAKEE   Z5
        FOR ANY IMPROBABLE SHE/COURTSHIP   E
        ARE YOU SAVING THIS SEAT FOR ANYONE OR YES, BUT WHAT'S THE USE?/BUS   D
        RAVEN, DON'T STAY AWAY FROM MY DOOR - A CHANT FOR APRIL FIRST   FZ8
        FOR DOCTOR WARREN ADAMS, WHO KINDLY BOUND THE AUTHOR FOR BEYOND HIS DESERTS/TATTOOED   2
        SANTA GO HOME: A CASE HISTORY FOR PARENTS   #
        OLD IS FOR BOOKS/AGING   Z6
        NOT EVEN FOR BRUNCH/COINED WORDS/GLADIOLUS/CUCUMBER/CHRYSANTHEMUM/CANTALOUPE   Z3
        CAT NAPS ARE TOO GOOD FOR CATS   Z49
        A CAROL FOR CHILDREN/CHRISTMAS   GYZ89o
        SONG FOR DITHERERS   WZ4
        A POSEY FOR EDMUND CLERICHEW BENTLEY/POETS   3
        UNCALLED-FOR EPITAPH   F
        DON'T LOOK FOR THE SILVER LINING, JUST WAIT FOR IT/SERENDIPITY   Z5
        I SUPPOSE THE GREEKS HAD A COMMERCIAL FOR IT OR, HAIL, SOLON. HOW'S THY COLON/TV   7
        THE GREEKS HAD A WORD FOR IT, SO WHY SPEAK ENGLISH/DIALECTS/SOUTHERN/BROOKLYNESE   6

41

GAMMON
    ALIAS AND MELISANDE OR, GAMMON ME ONCE, GAMMON ME TWICE,/PUBLISHING   7
GANDER
    THE GANDER/GOOSE   Z29
    WATER FOR THE GANDER/THIRST/CHILDREN   29
GANDERDONK
    SLOW DOWN, MR GANDERDONK, YOU'RE LATE/GOLF   Z2
GARDE
    TASTE BUDS, EN GARDE/FROZEN STRAWBERRIES   A
GARDEN
    ANIMAL GARDEN/ABIDON/PETS/CHILDREN   W
    CORRECTION: EVE DELVED AND ADAM SPAN/GARDEN CLUB/LADIES   Z5
    A GOOD PARENT'S GARDEN OF VISION; THE DREAM; THE NIGHTMARE; THE AWAKENING/DAUGHTER   FGZ89
    HE DIGS, HE DUG, HE HAS DUG/GARDEN   Z3
GARRISON
    A CRUSADER'S WIFE SLIPPED FROM THE GARRISON   A
GARTER
    A KNIGHT OF THE GARTER LONG HENCE   A
GAUGUIN
    AS GAUGUIN SAID TO SADIE THOMPSON, YOU PRONOUNCE IT, I'LL PAINT IT/SAMOA   7
GAUNTLET
    GOODBYE NOW OR PARDON MY GAUNTLET/REFINED/JANET   6
GAVOTTE
    ILL-MET BY FLOURESCENCE/HOUSES/BOTTLENECK GAVOTTE   A
GAY
    ROULETTE US BE GAY/GAMBLING   D1
GEDDONDILLO
    GEDDONDILLO/NONSENSE/VERSE   Y29
GEESE
    THE MOOSE ON THE BEACH/GEESE   A
GENEALOGICAL
    GENEALOGICAL REFLECTION/MCTAVISH/LAVISH   EYZ18
GENERAL
    VIVE LE POSTMASTER GENERAL/REPUBLICANS/DEMOCRATS   F8
    THOUGHTS THOUGHT WHILE RESTING COMFORTABLY IN PHILLIPS HOUSE, MASSACHUSETTS GENERAL HOSPITAL   A
GENERATION
    COME, COME, KEROUAC. MY GENERATION IS BEATER THAN YOURS/PROGRESS   7
GENEROSITY
    HEARTS AND FLOWERS OR WHAT I KNOW ABOUT BOLIVAR BLACK/GENEROSITY/LOANS   DZ8
GENIUS
    LITTLE FEET/CHILDREN/GENIUS/FAMILIES   GZ89
GENTLEMEN
    THE GENTLEMEN LADY'S MAID/GRANDFATHER'S JOURNAL   A
GENTLY
    FLOW GENTLY, SWEET ETYMOLOGY, ORNITHOLOGY, AND PENOLOGY/NIGHTINGALE/PERSION/BULBUL   5
GEOGRAPHICAL
    GEOGRAPHICAL REFLECTION/BRONX   E
GEOGRAPHY
    EVERYBODY WANTS TO GET INTO THE BAEDEKER/TRAVELING/GEOGRAPHY   Z5
GEORGE
    LET GEORGE DO IT, IF YOU CAN FIND HIM   D8
    NOT GEORGE WASHINGTON'S, NOT ABRAHAM LINCOLN'S, BUT MINE/BIRTHDAY/THIRTY-EIGHT/CAREER   Z2
    WATCHMAN, WHAT OF THE FIRST FIRST LADY?/MRS. GEORGE WASHINGTON   CYZ8
GERM
    THE GERM/PACHYDERM   DGYZ89b
GERMAN
    GERMAN SONG/GRIMM/MARCH   r
    FELLOW CREATURES; THE NEIGHBORS/FRENCH/GERMAN/JAPANESE/SCANDINAVIA/ABYSSINIA   Z4
GERMS
    WINTER COMPLAINT/COLDS/GERMS   DW8
GERONTOCRAT
    YOU CAN BE A REPUBLICAN, I'M A GERONTOCRAT/FRIENDS/AGE   WZ5
GERTRUDE
    THEY DON'T SPEAK ENGLISH IN PARIS/GERTRUDE STEIN   D
GESUNDHEIT
    FAHRENHEIT GESUNDHEIT/COLD/SUMMER   WZ2
GET
    HOW TO GET ALONG WITH YOURSELF OR I RECOMMEND SOFTENING OF THE OUGHTERIES/FAULTS/TOLERANCE   Z5
    RING OUT THE OLD, RING IN THE NEW, BUT DON'T GET CAUGHT IN BETWEEN; FIRST CHIME; SECOND CHIME   Z6
    I'LL WRITE THEIR NUMBER DOWN WHEN WE GET HOME/WORDS/SOCIAL-LIFE   Z2
    EVERYBODY WANTS TO GET INTO THE BAEDEKER/TRAVELING/GEOGRAPHY   Z5

45

GET

TWO GOES INTO TWO ONCE, IF YOU CAN GET IT THERE/SQUARE PEG/ROUND HOLE   5
I'LL GET ONE TOMORROW/BARBER/HAIRCUT   Y49
LET'S NOT GO TO THE THEATER TONIGHT, OR WE COULDN'T GET SEATS ANYHOW/MANHATTAN D8
OH, DID YOU GET THE TICKETS? BECAUSE I DON'T THINK I'LL GO, AFTER ALL/WOMEN/DECISIONS 4
OH, PLEASE DON'T GET UP!/ETIQUETTE/WOMEN   Z4
GET UP, FELLOWS, IT'S TIME TO GO TO BED/FISH/ANCESTORS   2
CAN I GET YOU A GLASS OF WATER? OR PLEASE CLOSE THE GLOTTIS AFTER YOU/COUGHING Z6

GETS

CAESAR KNIFED AGAIN OR CULTURE BIZ GETS HEP, BOFFS PROFS/COLLEGE TEACHING   Z6
THE MAN IS FATHER OF THE CHILD OR, BUT HE NEVER QUITE GETS USED TO IT   9

GIANT

ADVENTURES OF ISABEL/BEAR/WITCH/GIANT/DOCTOR   G89a

GIANTS

THERE WERE GIANTS IN THOSE DAYS OR MAYBE THERE WEREN'T/ANECDOTES   Z3

GIBLETS

TELL ME NO FIBLETS, WHERE ARE THE GIBLETS/GRAVY/TURKEY DINNER   A

GIDEONS

GOD BLESS THE GIDEONS OR THERE'S ALWAYS THE KING JAMES VERSION/HOTEL/BOOKS   A

GIFTS

REMEMBER THE OLD FOLKS AT HOME/GIFTS/HOLIDAYS   C8

GIN

SING A SONG OF TASTE BUDS/WINE SNOB/GIN SNOB   7

GIRAFFE

THE GIRAFFE   D

GIRDLE

THE PERFECT HUSBAND/LIPSTICK/GIRDLE   BZ39

GIRL

BIOLOGICAL REFLECTION/GIRL/CHEEKS/PAINT   EYZ18
BENJAMIN/GIRL/CONNECTICUT   8
THE STRANGE CASE OF THE GIRL O' MR. SPONSOON'S DREAMS/RUN-OVER   Z4
THERE WAS A YOUNG GIRL OF MILWAUKEE   A
THE STRANGE CASE OF THE SOCIETY GIRL'S NECK/TANTRUMS   D
ALWAYS MARRY AN APRIL GIRL   BZ3
A BOY'S WILL IS THE WIND'S WILL/GIRL   Z6
THE HAT'S GOT MY TONGUE/SPRING/GIRL   Y2

GIRLS

OH, SHUCKS, MA'AM, I MEAN EXCUSE ME/GIRLS/PROFANITY   Z3
THE RETURN/SUMMER/GIRLS   DG9

GIVE

SURE, COME ON AND GIVE THANKS   D

GLAD

I'M GLAD YOU ASKED THAT QUESTION, BECAUSE IT SHOWS YOU IN YOUR TRUE COLORS/REMEMBERING 7

GLADIOLUS

NOT EVEN FOR BRUNCH/COINED WORDS/GLADIOLUS/CUCUMBER/CHRYSANTHEMUM/CANTALOUPE   Z3

GLADLY

I'LL GLADLY PULL OVER TO THE CURB/FIRES   3

GLASS

CAN I GET YOU A GLASS OF WATER? OR PLEASE CLOSE THE GLOTTIS AFTER YOU/COUGHING Z6

GLASSES

AND HOW KEEN WAS THE VISION OF SIR LAUNFAL?/MYOPIA/GLASSES   WZ6
LINES WRITTEN TO CONSOLE THOSE LADIES DISTRISSED BY THE LINES "MEN SELDOM MAKE PASSES"/GLASSES EG
PEEKABOO, I ALMOST SEE YOU/MIDDLE-AGE/GLASSES   WZ5

GLOSSINA

GLOSSINA MORSITANS, OR, THE TSETSE/WILL   YZ29

GLOTTIS

CAN I GET YOU A GLASS OF WATER? OR PLEASE CLOSE THE GLOTTIS AFTER YOU/COUGHING Z6

GLOWING

WE'RE FINE, JUST FINE/HEALTH/ILLNESS/GLOWING COMPLEXION   AW

GLUTTON

QUICK, HAMMACHER, MY STOMACHER/GLUTTON   WZ3

GO

LATHER AS YOU GO/BILLBOARDS/ACCIDENTS/ADVERTISING   Z29
SANTA GO HOME: A CASE HISTORY FOR PARENTS   #
ONE WESTERN TO GO/BLANCH/RANCH   A
IF HE SCHOLARS, LET HIM GO/HIPPOLYTE ADOLPHE TAINE   Z3
GO AHEAD, IT WILL DO YOU GOOD OR HER EYES ARE MUCH BIGGER THAN HIS STOMACH/WIFE/HUSBAND/EAT WZ6
GO AHEAD, LOOK, AND LISTEN/TRAINS   2
FATHER, DEAR FATHER, GO JUMP IN THE LAKE OR, YOU'RE COSTLIER THAN YOU THINK/PARENTS/SUPPORT Z5
I WILL ARISE AND GO NOW/TIBET/LAMA   WZ39m

GO
    HERE WE GO QUIETLY NUTS IN MAY   Z2
    GET UP, FELLOWS, IT'S TIME TO GO TO BED/FISH/ANCESTORS   2
    ALL GOOD AMERICANS GO TO LAROUSSE OR, I DON'T PRETEND TO BE MOLIERE THAN THOU/FRENCH   A
    LET'S NOT GO TO THE THEATER TONIGHT, OR WE COULDN'T GET SEATS ANYHOW/MANHATTAN   D8
    JUST HOW LOW CAN A HIGHBROW GO WHEN A HIGHBROW LOWERS HIS BROW   7
    OH, DID YOU GET THE TICKETS? BECAUSE I DON'T THINK I'LL GO, AFTER ALL/WOMEN/DECISIONS   4
GOD
    GOD BLESS THE GIDEONS OR THERE'S ALWAYS THE KING JAMES VERSION/HOTEL/BOOKS   A
    OUR CHILD DOESN'T KNOW ANYTHING OR THANK GOD!   DGZ8
    OH, STOP BEING THANKFUL ALL OVER THE PLACE/GRACE OF GOD   DYZ18
GODMOTHER
    CITRONELLA AND THE FAIRY GODMOTHER/MOTHER NATURE   D
    DEAR GODMOTHER, I HOPE SHE BRUISES EASY!/FAIRY/APRIL FOOL   4
GODS
    BEASTS, MEN AND GODS   D
GOES
    TWO GOES INTO TWO ONCE, IF YOU CAN GET IT THERE/SQUARE PEG/ROUND HOLE   5
    WHAT TO DO UNTIL THE DOCTOR GOES OR IT'S TOMORROW THAN YOU THINK/LIVING   WZ3
GOETH
    PRIDE GOETH BEFORE A RAISE, OR AH, THERE, MRS. CADWALLADER-SMITH/SOCIALITES/POISE   FZ8
GOING
    WHO'S GOING MR. PLATT'S WAY?/NEIGHBORS/CAR-SHARING   2
    HOW LONG HAS THIS BEEN GOING ON? OH, QUITE LONG/BETTING/HORSE-RACING   Z18
    THIS IS GOING TO HURT JUST A LITTLE BIT/DENTISTS   W4
GOLD
    OUR CITY, OUR CITIZENS/VILLAGE/GOLD COAST/PRESS CAFE/THEATER   7
    HEARTS OF GOLD OR A GOOD EXCUSE IS WORSE THAN NONE/APOLOGIES/REMORSE   FYZ8
GOLF
    LOW-PRESSURE ARIA/RAIN/GOLF/TENNIS   DG89
    BRAKEMAN, HAND ME MY NIBLICK/GOLF/TRAINS/TIMETABLES   2
    SLOW DOWN, MR. GANDERDONK, YOU'RE LATE/GOLF   Z2
    THE STRANGE CASE OF THE AMBITIOUS CADDY/GOLF   Z4
GOLFER
    WHO TAUGHT CADDIES TO COUNT? OR A BURNT GOLFER FEARS THE CHILD   Z3
    THE ARMCHAIR GOLFER OR, WHIMPERS OF A SHORTCHANGED VIEWER/TV   A
GOLFERS
    A WARNING TO FIANCEES/GOLFERS   D
GOLLY
    GOLLY, HOW THE TRUTH WILL OUT!/LIAR   Z18
GONE
    ALL, ALL ARE GONE, THE OLD FAMILIAR QUOTATIONS   Z5
    WHY THE POSTMAN HAS TO RING TWICE OR, YELLOW ENVELOPE, WHERE HAVE YOU GONE?/TELEGRAMS
GOOD
    ALL GOOD AMERICANS GO TO LAROUSSE OR, I DON'T PRETEND TO BE MOLIERE THAN THOU/FRENCH   A
    I HAVE IT ON GOOD AUTHORITY/GOSSIP   Z4
    HAVE YOU READ ANY GOOD BOOKS TOMORROW?   7
    FOR A GOOD DOG   Z3
    HEARTS OF GOLD OR A GOOD EXCUSE IS WORSE THAN NONE/APOLOGIES/REMORSE   FYZ8
    CAT NAPS ARE TOO GOOD FOR CATS   Z49
    DARKEST HALF HOUR; TOO EARLY IS THE TIME FOR ALL GOOD GUESTS TO COME TO THE AID OF A PARTY   A
    ONE GOOD HOARDER DESERVES ANOTHER/TIRES   2
    THE ONLY GOOD INDIAN IS A DEAD PUBLIC RELATIONS COUNSELLOR/INTERVIEWS   V
    TIN PAN ALLEY; GOOD NIGHT, SWEET MIND/WINTER WONDERLAND/SONGS   6
    WHAT'LL WE DO NOW, OR, I'M AFRAID I KNOW OR, GOOD OLD JUST PLAIN CHARADES, FAREWELL/GAMES   2
    GO AHEAD, IT WILL DO YOU GOOD OR HER EYES ARE MUCH BIGGER THAN HIS STOMACH/WIFE/HUSBAND/EAT   WZ6
    A GOOD PARENT'S GARDEN OF VISION; THE DREAM; THE NIGHTMARE; THE AWAKENING/DAUGHTER   FGZ89
    GOOD RIDDANCE, BUT NOW WHAT?/NEW YEAR'S EVE   WZ3
    I ALWAYS SAY A GOOD SAINT IS NO WORSE THAN A BAD COLD/VALENTINE   F8
    JACK DO-GOOD-FOR-NOTHING, A CURSORY NURSERY TALE FOR TOT-BAITERS/BEFRIENDING   7
    OAFISHNESS SELLS GOOD, LIKE AN ADVERTISEMENT SHOULD/GRAMMAR/ENGLISH   Z6
GOODBODY
    THE STRANGE CASE OF MR. GOODBODY OR A TEAM THAT WON'T BE BEATEN, CAN'T BE BEATEN/CLICHES   D1
GOODBYE
    GOODBYE NOW OR PARDON MY GAUNTLET/REFINED/JANET   6
    GOODBYE BUGS   Z2
    GOODBYE, OLD YEAR, YOU OAF, OR WHY DON'T THEY PAY THE BONUS?/NEW YEAR'S EVE   DYZ8
GOODY
    GOODY FOR OUR SIDE AND YOUR SIDE TOO/FOREIGNERS/NATIVES   DZ18
GOOSE
    THE GANDER/GOOSE   Z29

GRAVEL
    THE INDIVIDUALIST/JARVIS GRAVEL/SPRING   YZ8
GRAVY
    THE ABSENTEES/TURKEY DINNER/GRAVY/CRANBERRIES   Z29
    TELL ME NO FIBLETS, WHERE ARE THE GIBLETS/GRAVY/TURKEY DINNER   A
GREAT
    EVERYBODY'S MIND TO ME A KINGDOM IS OR, A GREAT BIG WONDERFUL WORLD IT'S/PUNS   Z5
    THE STRANGE CASE OF THE BLIGHT THAT FAILED/GREAT-AUNT/WRATH   6
GREBE
    WHO CALLED THAT PIED-BILLED GREBE A PODILYMBUS PODICEPS PODICEPS?/BIRD   A
GREECE
    CHLOE AND THE ROU'/GREECE/NYMPH/ZEUS   Z5
GREEK
    MEDUSA AND THE MOT JUSTE/GREEK MYTHOLOGY/GORGONS   Z5
GREEKS
    I SUPPOSE THE GREEKS HAD A COMMERCIAL FOR IT OR, HAIL, SOLON. HOW'S THY COLON/TV   7
    THE GREEKS HAD A WORD FOR IT, SO WHY SPEAK ENGLISH/DIALECTS/SOUTHERN/BROOKLYNESE   6
GREEN
    MAX SCHLING, MAX SCHLING, LEND ME YOUR GREEN THUMB; A CATALOG OF FLOWERY CATALOGUES   Z5
GREENHORNS
    DON'T LOOK NOW, BUT THERE'S SOMETHING BEHIND THE CURTAIN/ADVENTURE/GREENHORNS/AGING   7
GREETS
    JOHN PEEL, SHAKE HANDS WITH 37 MAMAS; BISHOP DE WOLFE GREETS 37 DEBUTANTES ON LONG ISLAND   A
GRIMM
    GERMAN SONG/GRIMM/MARCH   r
GRIN
    GRIN AND BEAR LEFT/DIRECTIONS   Z3
    DON'T GRIN OR YOU'LL HAVE TO BEAR IT/HUMOR/POINT-OF-VIEW   Z14
GRINDER
    NO BUSKIN, ALL SOCK, MAKES LAUGHINGSTOCK/MOUSETRAP/MEAT-GRINDER/HUSBAND   A
GRIPPE
    SONG FOR A TEMPERATURE OF A HUNDRED AND ONE/GRIPPE/INFLUENZA   FWYZ89
GROCERY
    THE MARKETEERS/GROCERY SHOPPING   D
GROOM
    EVERYBODY LOVES A BRIDE, EVEN THE GROOM/WEDDING   5
    FATHER-IN-LAW OF THE GROOM/WOMEN   6
GROOMING
    HAVE A SEAT BEHIND THE POTTED PALM, SIR/TRAVEL/ARRIVAL/GROOMING   Z5
GROUP
    BOOP-BOOP-ADIEUP, LITTLE GROUP!/AMATEUR THEATER   Z4
GROW
    ABSENCE MAKES THE HEART GROW HEART TROUBLE   BYZ
GROWN
    IT IS INDEED SPINACH/CHILD/GROWN-UP   4
GRYNCH
    THE GRYNCH/BORES   5
GUAM
    LIMERICK TWO/LADY/GUAM/CHARM/MAUGHAM   5
GUESS
    DON'T GUESS, LET ME TELL YOU/DETECTIVE STORIES   YZ18
GUEST
    LINES TO A WORLD-FAMOUS POET WHO FAILED TO COMPLETE A WORLD-FAMOUS POEM/MR. GUEST   FY189
    ON WAKING TO THE THIRD RAINY MORNING OF A LONG WEEK END/HOUSE GUEST   Z3
GUESTS
    I KNOW YOU'LL LIKE THEM/OUT-OF-TOWN GUESTS/FRIENDS   YZ18
    POLTERQUEST, MY POLTERGUEST/GUESTS/HOPPER   Z39
    DARKEST HALF HOUR; TOO EARLY IS THE TIME FOR ALL GOOD GUESTS TO COME TO THE AID OF A PARTY   A
    A VISIT FROM DOCTOR FELL/GUESTS   Z2
    SUPPOSE I DARKEN YOUR DOOR/VISITING/GUESTS   DYZ8
    THE DAY OF THE LOCUST OR, WHOSE WEDDING IS THIS ANYWAY?/GUESTS   A
    THERE'S A HOST BORN EVERY MINUTE/WEEKENDS/GUESTS   D1
GUIDE
    A BRIEF GUIDE TO NEW YORK   YZ8
    A CHILD'S GUIDE TO PARENTS   GZ89
    A BRIEF GUIDE TO RHYMING OR, HOW BE THE LITTLE BUSY DOTH?/ENGLISH/PLURAL   Z6
    A BEGINNER'S GUIDE TO THE OCEAN   YZ29
GULL
    THE SEA-GULL AND THE EA-GULL/SEX   3
    THE SEA-GULL   YZ189

GUPPY
    THE GUPPY   Z39g
HA
    YOU'RE THE DOCTOR, OR HA HA!   D
    HOW DO YOU SAY HA-HA IN FRENCH?/BARTENDER   Z3
    HA! ORIGINAL SIN/VANITY   CYZ8
HABITS
    THE RABBITS/HABITS   CYZ8
HACKS
    THE EDUCATION OF ATHELNY JONES OR, ARE THERE MORE RADIOS IN HACKS THAN HACKS IN RADIO/FRENCH/
        TAXIS   6
HAD
    I SUPPOSE THE GREEKS HAD A COMMERCIAL FOR IT OR, HAIL, SOLON. HOW'S THY COLON/TV   7
    THE GREEKS HAD A WORD FOR IT, SO WHY SPEAK ENGLISH/DIALECTS/SOUTHERN/BROOKLYNESE   6
    I HAD NO IDEA IT WAS SO LATE/WATCHES/WOMEN/MEN   YZ18
    WE WOULD REFER YOU TO OUR SERVICE DEPARTMENT, IF WE HAD ONE/APPLIANCES   Z3
    IF I HAD THE WINGS OF A HELICOPTER OR HALL'S MILLS THAT ENDS MILLS/QUESTIONS/ANSWERS   6
HAE
    EVERYTHING'S HAGGIS IN HOBOKEN OR, SCOTS WHA HAE HAE/ROBERT BURNS   Z5
HAGGIS
    EVERYTHING'S HAGGIS IN HOBOKEN OR, SCOTS WHA HAE HAE/ROBERT BURNS   Z5
HAGUE
    AMSTERDAM, ROTTERDAM, AND THE HAGUE/CANALS   7
HAIL
    I SUPPOSE THE GREEKS HAD A COMMERCIAL FOR IT OR, HAIL, SOLON. HOW'S THY COLON/TV   7
HAIR
    RAPUNZEL, RAPUNZEL, LET'S LET DOWN OUR HAIR/WITS   Z6
    MY MY; MY DREAM/HAIR; MY CONSCIENCE   Z6
    ELECTRA BECOMES MORBID/HAIR   FYZ8
HAIRCUT
    I'LL GET ONE TOMORROW/BARBER/HAIRCUT   Y49
HAIRY
    THE PULPITEERS HAVE HAIRY EARS/CLERICS/OPINIONS   E
HALCYON
    PRETTY HALCYON DAYS/BEACH/OCEAN   DYZ8
HALF
    DARKEST HALF HOUR; TOO EARLY IS THE TIME FOR ALL GOOD GUESTS TO COME TO THE AID OF A PARTY   A
HALL
    MUSEUM OF NATURAL HISTORY: TYRANNOSAURUS REX; PYTHON; ROCK ROOM; WHALE; HALL OF PRIMATES   N
    IF I HAD THE WINGS OF A HELICOPTER OR HALL'S MILLS THAT ENDS MILLS/QUESTIONS/ANSWERS   6
HALLOWEEN
    PERMISSIVE PICTURES PRESENTS 'HAPPY HALLOWEEN, EVERYBODY' AN ALFRED HITCHCOCK PRODUCTION   A
    TRICK OR TREK/HALLOWEEN   39
HAM
    M. C. LOVES TV OR A PERSONALITY IS BORN/HAM/EGO   5
HAMBURGER
    THE BEEFBURGER/HAMBURGER   7
HAMLET
    POLONIUS, YES, POLONIUS, NO/HAMLET/BORROWING/LOANING   5
HAMMACHER
    QUICK, HAMMACHER, MY STOMACHER/GLUTTON   WZ3
HAMMERSTEIN
    HARK, HARK, THE LARKS DO BARK/SHELLEY/HAMMERSTEIN   A
HAMSTER
    THE HAMSTER   Z5
HAND
    HAND ME DOWN MY OLD SCHOOL SLIDING PADS OR THERE'S HINT OF STRAWBERRY LEAVES IN THE AIR   5
    BRAKEMAN, HAND ME MY NIBLICK/GOLF/TRAINS/TIMETABLES   2
    DON'T BITE THE HAND THAT PUTS ITS FOOT IN YOUR MOUTH/TAMMANY/OCTOPUS   7
    THE BACK OF MINE HAND TO MINE HOST/HOTEL   7
HANDBAGS
    HOW TO HARRY A HUSBAND OR IS THAT ACCESSORY REALLY NECESSARY?/HANDBAGS/BOY/POCKETS   BZ6
HANDS
    JOHN PEEL, SHAKE HANDS WITH 37 MAMAS; BISHOP DE WOLFE GREETS 37 DEBUTANTES ON LONG ISLAND   A
HANDSOME
    A HANDSOME YOUNG RODENT NAMED GRATIAN   A
HANGOVER
    THEY WON'T BELIEVE, ON NEW YEAR'S EVE, THAT NEW YEAR'S DAY WILL COME WHAT MAY/HANGOVER   BZ5
HANNIBAL
    SHOO, SHOO, SHOEMAKER/HANNIBAL/CANNIBAL   5

HAVE
YOU HAVE MORE FREEDOM IN A HOUSE/MURRAYS   BGZ89
I'M NO SAINT, AND I HAVE MY DOUBTS ABOUT VALENTINE, TOO/VALENTINES   A
DON'T GRIN OR YOU'LL HAVE TO BEAR IT/HUMOR/POINT-OF-VIEW   Z14
I HAVE USED IT FOR YEARS/ADVERTISING/ENDORSEMENTS   F8
HOW TO BE MARRIED WITHOUT A SPOUSE; KIPLING OR WHAT HAVE YOU DONE WITH MR. HAUKSBEE/INDIA   BZ5
WHY THE POSTMAN HAS TO RING TWICE OR, YELLOW ENVELOPE, WHERE HAVE YOU GONE?/TELEGRAMS   Z5
HAVE YOU READ ANY GOOD BOOKS TOMORROW?   7
HAVE YOU TRIED STAYING AWAKE? OR THEY'LL FIND A WAY TO STOP THAT, TOO/BED-BOARD   WZ3
WILL YOU HAVE YOUR TEDIUM RARE OR MEDIUM?/BORES   Z3
HAVEN
THERE WAS A YOUNG MAN FROM NEW HAVEN   A
HAVEN'T
ELEPHANTS HAVEN'T GOT ANYTHING TO FORGET/MANKIND   D
VISITORS LAUGH AT LOCKSMITHS, OR, HOSPITAL DOORS HAVEN'T GOT LOCKS ANYHOW   WZ2
WHAT'S THE MATTER, HAVEN'T YOU GOT ANY SENSE OF HUMOR?/PRACTICAL JOKES   YZ18
HAYFEVER
ALLERGY IN A COUNTRY CHURCHYARD/HAYFEVER   2
HE
HE DIGS, HE DUG, HE HAS DUG/GARDEN   Z3
THE MAN IS FATHER OF THE CHILD OR, BUT HE NEVER QUITE GETS USED TO IT   9
WHEN THE DIVIL WAS SICK COULD HE PROVE IT?/SYMPTOMS   WZ18
IF HE SCHOLARS, LET HIM GO/HIPPOLYTE ADOLPHE TAINE   Z3
SUPPOSE HE THREW IT IN YOUR FACE/TIPPING/DECISIONS   YZ29
IF HE WERE ALIVE TODAY, MAYHAP, MR. MORGAN WOULD SIT ON THE MIDGET'S LAP/BANKER   A
ASK DADDY, HE WON'T KNOW/HOMEWORK/CHILDREN   GYZ29
A MAN CAN COMPLAIN, CAN'T HE? (A LAMENT FOR THOSE WHO THINK OLD)   AW
HEADED
WRONG-HEADED/DISHONORABLE   E
THE BUSSES HEADED FOR SCRANTON   Z6
HEAL
COUSIN EUPHEMIA KNOWS BEST OR PHYSICIAN, HEAL SOMEBODY ELSE/CURES   WZ3
HEALTH
TELL IT TO THE ESKIMOS OR TELL IT TO THE ESQUIMAUX/HEALTH/COLDBATH   DWZ18
WE'RE FINE, JUST FINE/HEALTH/ILLNESS/GLOWING COMPLEXION   AW
HEAR
HOW CAN ECHO ANSWER WHAT ECHO CANNOT HEAR?/VOICE/WIFE   B7
HEARING
I DIDN'T SAY A WORD OR WHO CALLED THAT PICCOLO PLAYER A FATHER?/HEARING/VOICE/LOUDNESS   Z5
HEART
THE STRANGE CASE OF THE ENTOMOLOGIST'S HEART/BUGS   Z3
STICKS AND STONES MAY BREAK MY BONES, BUT NAMES WILL BREAK MY HEART/INDIVIDUAL DIGNITY   7
ABSENCE MAKES THE HEART GROW HEART TROUBLE   BYZ
HEARTS
HEARTS AND FLOWERS OR WHAT I KNOW ABOUT BOLIVAR BLACK/GENEROSITY/LOANS   DZ8
HEARTS OF GOLD OR A GOOD EXCUSE IS WORSE THAN NONE/APOLOGIES/REMORSE   FYZ8
HEAT
LINES FOR A SUMMER'S END/HEAT/MANHATTAN   F8
HEAVEN
OUR CHILD DOESN'T KNOW ANYTHING OR THANK HEAVEN   9
HECUBA
WHAT'S HECUBA TO HIM? A ONE-MINUTE CLOSE-UP/TV REPORTING DISASTERS   A
HEIL
HEIL, HEILIGE NACHT/CHRISTMAS/WAR   2
HEILIGE
HEIL, HEILIGE NACHT/CHRISTMAS/WAR   2
HELICOPTER
IF I HAD THE WINGS OF A HELICOPTER OR HALL'S MILLS THAT ENDS MILLS/QUESTIONS/ANSWERS   6
HELP
ALLOW ME, MADAM, BUT IT WON'T HELP/WOMEN/COATS   YZ2
I'M TERRIBLY SORRY FOR YOU, BUT I CAN'T HELP LAUGHING/DISEASES   WZ4
HELPFUL
HELPFUL REFLECTION/SORROWS   E
HEMINGWAY
ROLL ON, THOU DEEP AND DARK BLUE COPY WRITER-ROLL/HEMINGWAY/MOVIES   Z3
A THOUGHT ON THE MANNER OF THOSE WHO STRIVE TO ACHIEVE THE MANNER CALLED HEMINGWAY/WRITERS   C
AN ENTHUSIAST IS A DEVOTEE IS A ROOTER OR, MR. HEMINGWAY, MEET MR. STENGEL   Z6
HENBANE
BOTANIST, AROINT THEE! OR, HENBANE BY ANY OTHER NAME   A
HENCE
A KNIGHT OF THE GARTER LONG HENCE   A
HENDERSON
MR. HENDERSON/NEON/APPOINTMENT   2

52

HIS
A DOG'S BEST FRIEND IS HIS ILLITERACY/CLICHES   Z5
OLD DOCTOR VALENTINE TO HIS ONLY MILLIONAIRE/BILLS   5
MR. JUDD AND HIS SNAIL, A SORRY TALE/AMOEBA/RACING   A
OLD DOCTOR VALENTINE TO HIS SON/LIVE/DIE   5
GO AHEAD, IT WILL DO YOU GOOD OR HER EYES ARE MUCH BIGGER THAN HIS STOMACH/WIFE/HUSBAND/EAT   WZ6
HISTORY
SANTA GO HOME: A CASE HISTORY FOR PARENTS   #
NEXT!/MUSEUM OF NATURAL HISTORY/BRONTOSAURUSES/FOSSIL/POLKA/MOZURKAS   WZ5
IT OUGHT TO BE HISTORY, OR DON'T SAY IT ISN'T SO/DEBUNKING   D
MUSEUM OF NATURAL HISTORY: TYRANNOSAURUS REX; PYTHON; ROCK ROOM; WHALE; HALL OF PRIMATES   N
CLEANLINESS IS NEXT TO CATASTROPHE/BATHING/HISTORY   D
HIT
DON'T WAIT, HIT ME NOW!/CRITICISM   BZ2
YOU CAN'T TELL THE HIT PARADE WITHOUT A DRUM MAJORETTE/DISKJOCKEY   5
HITCHCOCK
PERMISSIVE PICTURES PRESENTS 'HAPPY HALLOWEEN, EVERYBODY' AN ALFRED HITCHCOCK PRODUCTION   A
HITLER
ADOLF HITLER   D
HO
FEE FI HO HUM, NO WONDER BABY SUCKS HER THUMB/JUVENILE LITERATURE   Z6
HI-HO THE AMBULANCE-O/STREETS/WHEELS/FEET   Z5
HO, VARLET! MY TWO CENTS' WORTH OF PENNY POSTCARD!/POST OFFICE/MAIL   Z6
HOARDER
ONE GOOD HOARDER DESERVES ANOTHER/TIRES   2
HOBBIES
MR. TWOMBLEY'S ULTIMATE TRIUMPH/HOBBIES   A
HOBBY
HOBBY HORSE   r
HOBOKEN
EVERYTHING'S HAGGIS IN HOBOKEN OR, SCOTS WHA HAE HAE/ROBERT BURNS   Z5
HOLE
DEATH ON THE NINETEENTH HOLE/MADEMOISELLE FROM ARMENTIERES/AFFAIRS   F8
JUST PRESS THE BUTTON, THE BUTTON-HOLE IS REALLY A DEEPFREEZE/APPLIANCES   5
TWO GOES INTO TWO ONCE, IF YOU CAN GET IT THERE/ SQUARE PEG/ROUND HOLE   5
HOLIDAY
ELECTION DAY IS A HOLIDAY/VOTING   FZ8
HOLIDAYS
REMEMBER THE OLD FOLKS AT HOME/GIFTS/HOLIDAYS   C8
HOLLANDAISE
HOLLANDAISE/ASPERAGUS/EGGS BENEDICT   7
HOLMES
JUST HOLMES AND ME, AND MNEMOSYNE, MAKES THREE/MEMORY   A
HOLS
TRY IT SUNS. AND HOLS. IT'S CLOSED THEN/RESTAURANT   Z6
HOME
SANTA GO HOME: A CASE HISTORY FOR PARENTS   #
REMEMBER THE OLD FOLKS AT HOME/GIFTS/HOLIDAYS   C8
MS. FOUND UNDER A SERVIETTE IN A LOVELY HOME/NANCY MITFORD/DOLLARS   Z6
HOME, 99 44/100 PERCENT SWEET HOME/ORGIES   D
I'LL WRITE THEIR NUMBER DOWN WHEN WE GET HOME/WORDS/SOCIAL-LIFE   Z2
LET'S STAY HOME AND MAKE FRIENDS/THEATER   C
HOME THOUGHTS FROM LITTLE MOOSE/ADIRONDACKS/MOUNTAINS   F
GOSSIP THAT NEVER SHOULD BE UNLOOSED IS GOSSIP THAT CAN'T COME HOME TO ROOST   U
UNANSWERED BY REQUEST/LIFE'S RIDDLES/HOME-COOKING   Z4
MAY I DRIVE YOU HOME, MRS. MURGATROYD/AUTOMOBILES/CHAUFFEURS   DY1
DADDY'S HOME, SEE YOU TOMORROW/BOYFRIEND/DAUGHTER   Z6
THE ABSENTEES/CHILDREN/HOME   Z6
HOMER
WHILE HOMER NODDED: A FOOTNOTE TO THE ILIAD/ZEUS/ANTISCRUPULOS   A
HOMEWARD
HOMEWARD BUND/MOTH   Y29
HOMEWORK
ASK DADDY, HE WON'T KNOW/HOMEWORK/CHILDREN   GYZ29
HONESTY
REFLECTION ON HONESTY   E
HONEYMOON
THE STRANGE CASE OF MRS. MOODUS'S SECOND HONEYMOON/LYSISTRATAGEMS   A
HONORE'S
AND LO! HONORE'S NAME LED ALL THE REST/BALZAC/LITERATURE   Q

HOW
JUST HOW LOW CAN A HIGHBROW GO WHEN A HIGHBROW LOWERS HIS BROW   7
HOW MANY MILES TO THE DEAD LETTER OFFICE/POSTAGE STAMPS   A
HOW NOW, SIRRAH? OH, ANYHOW/ADVENTURE/COWARDICE   Z4
HOW PLEASANT TO APE MR. LEAR/LIMRICKS   A
HOW THE RHINOCEROS GOT ITS HIDE OR THE CONFESSIONS OF COUNT MOWGLI DE SADE/CHILD/READING   3
GOLLY, HOW THE TRUTH WILL OUT!/LIAR   Z18
HOW TO BE MARRIED WITHOUT A SPOUSE; KIPLING OR WHAT HAVE YOU DONE WITH MR. HAUKSBEE/INDIA   BZ5
TO THE CHILD WHO'S FARTHER FROM THE MANNERS OR, HOW TO BE YOUNG GRACEFULLY   7
HOW TO GET ALONG WITH YOURSELF OR I RECOMMEND SOFTENING OF THE OUGHTERIES/FAULTS/TOLERANCE   Z5
HOW TO HARRY A HUSBAND OR IS THAT ACCESSORY REALLY NECESSARY?/HANDBAGS/BOY/POCKETS   BZ6
HOW TO TELL A KITCHEN FROM A CUISINE: TAKE A QUICK LOOK AT OURS/COOKBOOKS   6
HOW TO TELL A QUAIL FROM A PARTRIDGE/BOB WHITE   D
I SUPPOSE THE GREEKS HAD A COMMERCIAL FOR IT OR, HAIL, SOLON. HOW'S THY COLON/TV   7
HUEY
HUEY LONG   D
HUH
PAJAMAS, HUH? OR DRESSES WERE SO NICE/PANTS   C
HUM
TALLYHO-HUM/RIDING/HORSES   C
FEE FI HO HUM, NO WONDER BABY SUCKS HER THUMB/JUVENILE LITERATURE   Z6
HUMAN
TO EE IS HUMAN/DICTIONARIES/MR. WEBSTER/MR. MERRIAM   Z6
NOTE ON HUMAN NATURE/WRITERS   E
PERIOD PERIOD; PERIOD I/INNOCENT/ACCUSED; PERIOD II/ALIEN/HUMAN   Z6
HUMANITY
A NECESSARY DIRGE/PERVERSITY/HUMANITY   Z4
HUMILIATION
REMEMBRANCE OF THINGS TO COME/FATHER/DAUGHTER/ADMIRATION/HUMILIATION   G89
HUMMED
LINES TO BE HUMMED FROM A SUPINE POSITION TO THE HUMMER'S OSTEOPATHIC PHYSICIAN/NECK   2
HUMMER
LINES TO BE HUMMED FROM A SUPINE POSITION TO THE HUMMER'S OSTEOPATHIC PHYSICIAN/NECK   2
HUMOR
KING LEER/HUMOR/OFF-COLOR   FZ8
DON'T GRIN OR YOU'LL HAVE TO BEAR IT/HUMOR/POINT-OF-VIEW   Z14
WHAT'S THE MATTER, HAVEN'T YOU GOT ANY SENSE OF HUMOR?/PRACTICAL JOKES   YZ18
THAT'S FUNNY, WASN'T IT? NO, IT WON'T BE/COMIC ARTISTS/HUMOR   Z6
THE LIFE OF THE PARTY/ARTIE/BEARD/HUMOR   FYZ8
VERY FUNNY, VERY FUNNY/SENSE OF HUMOR   Z3
HUMORISTS
IF FUN IS FUN, ISN'T THAT ENOUGH/HUMORISTS   Z6
HUNCH
HAS ANYBODY SEEN MY NOUMENON?/INTUITION/HUNCH   Z2
HUNDRED
SONG FOR A TEMPERATURE OF A HUNDRED AND ONE/GRIPPE/INFLUENZA   FWZ89
AND THREE HUNDRED AND SIXTY-SIX IN LEAP YEAR/SHAVING/BATHING   Z2
HUNTER
THE HUNTER/DUCK   Z39j
HUNTERS
THE SOUVENIR HUNTERS   F
HUNTSMAN
THE SOLITARY HUNTSMAN/FOX   A
HURDY-GURDY
THE ORGAN-GRINDER/HURDY/GURDY/WALTZ   r
HURT
THIS IS GOING TO HURT JUST A LITTLE BIT/DENTISTS   W4
HUSBAND
THE UNSELFISH HUSBAND/COLDS   BZ49
THE PERFECT HUSBAND/LIPSTICK/GIRDLE   BZ39
GO AHEAD, IT WILL DO YOU GOOD OR HER EYES ARE MUCH BIGGER THAN HIS STOMACH/WIFE/HUSBAND/EAT WZ6
HOW TO HARRY A HUSBAND OR IS THAT ACCESSORY REALLY NECESSARY?/HANDBAGS/BOY/POCKETS   BZ6
NO BUSKIN, ALL SOCK, MAKES LAUGHINSTOCK/MOUSETRAP/MEAT-GRINDER/HUSBAND   A
HUSBANDS
THE BOOK OF PROVERBS: A WORD TO HUSBANDS/MARRIAGE/ARGUMENTS   7
ASIDE TO HUSBANDS/WIVES/APPEARANCE   BGZ8
THERE'LL ALWAYS BE A WAR BETWEEN THE SEXES/HUSBANDS/WIVES   Z6
A WORD TO HUSBANDS   B
THE JOYOUS MALINGERER/HUSBANDS   A
THE TROUBLE WITH WOMEN IS MEN/MARRIAGE/HUSBANDS   BZ29
THE VOICE OF EXPERIENCE/LECTURES/HUSBANDS   BYZ29

HUSBANDS
     WHAT ALMOST EVERY WOMAN KNOWS SOONER OR LATER/HUSBANDS   BDYZ89
     WHAT EVERY WOMAN KNOWS SOONER OR LATER/HUSBANDS   1
     WHO SAYS IT'S SO NICE TO HAVE A MAN AROUND THE HOUSE?/HUSBANDS   A
HUSH
     I'LL HUSH IF YOU'LL HUSH/VOICES   D
     HUSH, HERE THEY COME/BACKBITERS/GOSSIP/FRANKNESS   Z18
     MA, WHAT'S A BANKER? OR HUSH, MY CHILD   DZ18
HUSHMOUTH
     CHAMPIONS AND CHIMPIONS/FOOTBALL/HUSHMOUTH MCGUNN/APES   7
HYMN
     HYMN TO THE SUN AND MYSELF/BIRTHDAY   E
HYPOCHONDRIACS
     OH, TO BE ODD/HYPOCHONDRIACS/NORMAL   CZ8
ICE
     REFLECTION ON ICE-BREAKING/CANDY/LIQUOR   EYZ8
     TABLEAU AT TWILIGHT/ICE-CREAM CONES   Z39
ICEBERG
     ICEBERG LETTUCE   7
IDE
     BEWARE OF THE IDES OF MARCH, OR BROTHER, CAN YOU SPARE AN IDE?   D
IDEA
     I HAD NO IDEA IT WAS SO LATE/WATCHES/WOMEN/MEN   YZ18
IDENTITY
     THE CASE OF IDENTITY/MEMORY/NAMES   D1
IDES
     SONG FOR THE SADDEST IDES/INCOME TAX   D1
     BEWARE THE IDES OF MARCH, OR BROTHER, CAN YOU SPARE AN IDE?   D
IF
     IF A BODER MEET A BODER, NEED A BODER CRY? YES/FORBODINGS/AFTBODINGS   A
     IF ANYTHING SHOULD ARISE, IT ISN'T I/INFLUENZA   B3
     IF FUN IS FUN, ISN'T THAT ENOUGH/HUMORISTS   Z6
     IF HE SCHOLARS, LET HIM GO/HIPPOLYTE ADOLPHE TAINE   Z3
     IF HE WERE ALIVE TODAY, MAYHAP, MR. MORGAN WOULD SIT ON THE MIDGET'S LAP/BANKER   A
     IF I HAD THE WINGS OF A HELICOPTER OR HALL'S MILLS THAT ENDS MILLS/QUESTIONS/ANSWERS   6
     IF THERE WERE NO ENGLAND, 'COUNTRY LIFE' WOULD INVENT IT/HOUSES   A
     WE WOULD REFER YOU TO OUR SERVICE DEPARTMENT, IF WE HAD ONE/APPLIANCES   Z3
     LET GEORGE DO IT, IF YOU CAN FIND HIM   D8
     TWO GOES INTO TWO ONCE, IF YOU CAN GET IT THERE/SQUARE PEG/ROUND HOLE   5
     YOU'VE GOT TO BE MR. PICKWICK IF YOU WANT TO ENJOY A PICNIC/PAPER   7
     I'LL HUSH IF YOU'LL HUSH/VOICES   D
     I'LL STAY OUT OF YOUR DIET IF YOU'LL STAY OUT OF MINE   2
IGNORE
     THE PARENT/CHILDREN/IGNORE   FGZ89
ILIAD
     WHILE HOMER NODDED: A FOOTNOTE TO THE ILIAD/ZEUS/ANTISCRUPULOS   A
ILL
     ILL-MET BY FLOURESCENCE/HOUSES/BOTTLENECK GAVOTTE   A
     TUNE FOR AN ILL-TEMPERED CLAVICHORD/YANKAKEE   Z5
ILLITERACY
     A DOG'S BEST FRIEND IS HIS ILLITERACY/CLICHES   Z5
ILLNESS
     ONE THIRD OF A CALENDAR/WINTER/ILLNESS/CHILDREN   WYZ189
     WE'RE FINE, JUST FINE/HEALTH/ILLNESS/GLOWING COMPLEXION   A
     PLATITUDINOUS REFLECTION/ILLNESS/INFIRMITY   EWYZ8
IMAGINATION
     THE CHEF HAS IMAGINATION OR, IT'S TOO HARD TO DO IT EASY/LETTUCE/SALAD DRESSING   5
IMMATERIAL
     INCOMPETENT AND IMMATERIAL/MEN/WOMEN   CY
IMMATURITY
     SONGLAND REVISITED OR, THERE'S NO PURITY LIKE IMMATURITY/POPULAR SONGS/AGE/YOUTH   A
IMMORTALS
     LINE-UP FOR YESTERDAY; AN ABC OF BASEBALL IMMORTALS   3
IMPERFECT
     EVERYBODY'S FULL OF CARBONACEOUS MATERIAL OBTAINED BY THE IMPERFECT COMBUSTION OF WOOD   A
IMPOSSIBLE
     A PENNY SAVED IS IMPOSSIBLE/THRIFT/SPENDTHRIFT   2
IMPRESSIONS
     IMPRESSIONS OF SUBURBIA BY ONE WHO HAS NEVER BEEN THERE OR, ALL I KNOW IS WHAT I SEE IN ADS   7
IMPROBABLE
     FOR ANY IMPROBABLE SHE/COURTSHIP   E
     FOR THE MOST IMPROBABLE SHE/COURTSHIP   Y18

IMPROPER
        INVOCATION (SMOOT PLANS TARIFF BAN ON IMPROPER BOOKS-NEWS ITEM)/PORNOGRAPHY   EYZ18
IN
        IS THIS SEAT TAKEN? YES OR, MY NECK IS STICKING IN/CONVERSATION   Z3
        A BULLETIN HAS JUST COME IN/DISEASE/ANIMALS   Z2
        ELEGY IN A CITY SHAMBLES/BICARBONATE/SLEEP   D
        ALLERGY IN A COUNTRY CHURCHYARD/HAYFEVER   2
        YOU HAVE MORE FREEDOM IN A HOUSE/MURRAYS   BGZ89
        MS. FOUND UNDER A SERVIETTE IN A LOVELY HOME/NANCY MITFORD/DOLLARS   Z6
        I'LL BE UP IN A MINUTE/BED   4
        WHAT'S IN A NAME? HERE'S WHAT'S IN A NAME OR I WONDER WHAT BECAME OF JOHN AND MARY   Z6
        WHAT'S IN A NAME? SOME LETTER I ALWAYS FORGET/SPELLING   Z5
        LIKE A RAT IN A TRAP/SPRING/SEASONS   2
        TURNS IN A WORM'S LANE/BETTING/SPORTS   FYZ18
        THE ETERNAL VERNAL OR IN ALL MY DREAMS MY FAIR FACE BEAMS/SPRING   Z3
        LECTURER IN BOOKSTORE/AUTOGRAPHING   Z5
        SOLILOQUY IN CIRCLES/FATHERS/CHILDREN   Z39
        THIS WAS TOLD ME IN CONFIDENCE/GOSSIP   Z4
        LINES IN DISPRAISE OF DISPRAISE/ANALYZING   E
        IN DULUTH THERE'S A HOSTESS, FORSOOTH   A
        SIC SEMPER MR. SHERMAN'S TEMPER OR KINDLY PLACE YOUR ORDER IN ENGLISH/COCKTAILS   6
        A FRIEND IN NEED WILL BE AROUND IN FIVE MINUTES   2
        HOW DO YOU SAY HA-HA IN FRENCH?/BARTENDER   Z3
        IT LOOKS LIKE SNOW OR MY LIFE IN GALOSHES   3
        PAVANE FOR A DEAD DOLL OR, THE PAIN IN GRANDFATHER'S NECK/PAPER DOLLS   7
        EVERYTHING'S HAGGIS IN HOBOKEN OR, SCOTS WHA HAE HAE/ROBERT BURNS   Z5
        A DRINK WITH SOMETHING IN IT/COCKTAILS   DYZ8
        IT'S ALWAYS JUNE IN JANUARY, ALSO VICE VERSA/SUMMER   A
        AND THREE HUNDRED AND SIXTY-SIX IN LEAP YEAR/SHAVING/BATHING   Z2
        A CAUTION TO HILLBILLY SINGERS, HARPISTS, HARPOONISTS, CHANNEL-SWIMMERS, PEOPLE FIRST IN LINE
                FOR WORLD SERIES TICKETS/FAME   5
        HERE WE GO QUIETLY NUTS IN MAY   Z2
        IN MEMORIAM - HERMAN MELVILLE   C
        I KNOW EXACTLY WHO DROPPED THE OVERALLS IN MRS. MURPHY'S CHOWDER/BORES   Z6
        THE DUST STORM OR I'VE GOT TEXAS IN MY LUNGS   5
        WHO PUT THAT SPOKESMAN IN MY WHEEL?/VAGUENESS/NEWS SOURCES   A
        BRIEF LIVES IN NOT SO BRIEF/GOSSIP/BIOGRAPHY/JOHN AUBREY   7
        ONE NIGHT IN OZ/DINNER PARTY/ENEMIES   YZ2
        THEY DON'T SPEAK ENGLISH IN PARIS/GERTRUDE STEIN   D
        THOUGHTS THOUGHT WHILE RESTING COMFORTABLY IN PHILLIPS HOUSE, MASSACHUSETTS GENERAL HOSPITAL A
        THEY DON'T READ DE QUINCEY IN PHILLY OR CINCY/MURDER   A
        LINES IN PRAISE OF A DATE MADE PRAISEWORTHY SOLELY BY SOMETHING VERY NICE THAT HAPPENED TO IT C
        MS. FOUND IN QUAGMINE/PHYSICIAN   YZ2
        THE EDUCATION OF ATHELNY JONES OR, ARE THERE MORE RADIOS IN HACKS THAN HACKS IN RADIO/
                FRENCH/TAXIS   6
        WHAT IS BIBBIDI-BOBBIDI-BOO IN SANSCRIT?/FRENCH   Z5
        NOTES FOR A DOCUMENTARY IN SEARCH OF A SPONSOR/TV   A
        IMPRESSIONS OF SUBURBIA BY ONE WHO HAS NEVER BEEN THERE OR, ALL I KNOW IS WHAT I SEE IN ADS   7
        HAND ME DOWN MY OLD SCHOOL SLIDING PADS OR THERE'S HINT OF STRAWBERRY LEAVES IN THE AIR   5
        OUR NUMBER'S IN THE BOOK/TELEPHONE SOLICITATION   D
        I'LL EAT MY SPLIT-LEVEL TURKEY IN THE BREEZEWAY/CHRISTMAS/LARGE HOUSES   Z6
        OTHERS IN THE CAST INCLUDE/ACTORS   3
        LINES TO BE MUTTERED THROUGH CLENCHED TEETH AND QUITE A LOT OF LATHER IN THE COUNTRY   C8
        IS THERE AN OCULIST IN THE HOUSE/WAR   7
        IS THERE A DOCTOR JOHNSON IN THE HOUSE?/MEMORY   K
        FATHER, DEAR FATHER, GO JUMP IN THE LAKE OR, YOU'RE COSTLIER THAN YOU THINK/PARENTS/SUPPORT   Z5
        RING OUT THE OLD, RING IN THE NEW, BUT DON'T GET CAUGHT IN BETWEEN; FIRST CHIME; SECOND CHIME Z6
        THE QUEEN IS IN THE PARLOR/GAMES/CHARADES   Z4
        I ALWAYS SAY THERE'S NO PLACE LIKE NEW YORK IN THE SUMMER/COTTAGES   Z6
        TARKINGTON, THOU SHOULD'ST BE LIVING IN THIS HOUR/ADOLESCENCE   Z39
        THERE WERE GIANTS IN THOSE DAYS OR MAYBE THERE WEREN'T/ANECDOTES   Z3
        BACKWARD, TURN BACKWARD, O COMMENTATOR, IN THY FLIGHTS/BASEBALL   A
        ALL'S BRILLIG IN TIN PAN ALLEY/POPULAR SONGS   Z6
        UNFORTUNATELY, IT'S THE ONLY GAME IN TOWN/ODDS   7
        IN WHICH THE POET IS ASHAMED BUT PLEASED/DAUGHTER/FATHER   DGYZ89
        SUPPOSE HE THREW IT IN YOUR FACE/TIPPING/DECISIONS   YZ29
        DON'T BITE THE HAND THAT PUTS IT'S FOOT IN YOUR MOUTH/TAMMANY/OCTOPUS   7
        I'M GLAD YOU ASKED THAT QUESTION, BECAUSE IT SHOWS YOU IN YOUR TRUE COLORS/REMEMBERING   7
        NOTES FOR THE CHART IN 306/HOSPITAL   A
        FATHER-IN-LAW OF THE GROOM/WOMEN   5
        COME ON IN, THE SENILITY IS FINE/GRANDPARENTS   BZ6

60

LAMB
BARNYARD COGITATIONS/DUCK/CHICKEN/LAMB/TURKEY/PIGEON   G
THE LAMB   19
LAMENT
A MAN CAN COMPLAIN, CAN'T HE? (A LAMENT FOR THOSE WHO THINK OLD)   AW
LAMENT ON THE EVE OF PARTING/ABEL/SERVANT   YZ2
LAMENTS
LAMENTS FOR A DYING LANGUAGE/ENGLISH/COINED WORDS   7
LANE
TURNS IN A WORM'S LANE/BETTING/SPORTS   FYZ18
SAVONAROLA OF MAZDA LANE/WALTER WINCHELL   C
LANGUAGE
LAMENTS FOR A DYING LANGUAGE/ENGLISH/COINED WORDS   7
PHILOLOGY, ETYMOLOGY, YOU OWE ME AN APOLOGY/ENGLISH LANGUAGE   7
LAP
IF HE WERE ALIVE TODAY, MAYHAP, MR. MORGAN WOULD SIT ON THE MIDGET'S LAP/BANKER   A
LARGE
I'LL EAT MY SPLIT-LEVEL TURKEY IN THE BREEZEWAY/CHRISTMAS/LARGE HOUSES   Z6
LARKS
HARK, HARK, THE LARKS DO BARK/SHELLEY/HAMMERSTEIN   A
LAROUSSE
ALL GOOD AMERICANS GO TO LAROUSSE OR, I DON'T PRETEND TO BE MOLIERE THAN THOU/FRENCH   A
LAST
HIGH, LOW THE COMEDY: A LAST WINTER'S TALE/BIRD/CAT $
LATE
SLOW DOWN, MR. GANDERDONK, YOU'RE LATE/GOLF   Z2
I HAD NO IDEA IT WAS SO LATE/WATCHES/WOMEN/MEN   YZ18
A STITCH TOO LATE IS MY FATE/PROMPTNESS/REMEMBERING   Z14
SEPTEMBER IS SUMMER, TOO OR IT'S NEVER TOO LATE TO BE UNCOMFORTABLE/HOT WEATHER   Z3
THE EVENING OUT/WOMEN/LATE   YZ4
LATER
WHAT EVERY WOMAN KNOWS SOONER OR LATER/HUSBANDS   1
WHAT ALMOST EVERY WOMAN KNOWS SOONER OR LATER/HUSBANDS   BDWZ89
JUST WRAP IT UP, AND I'LL THROW IT AWAY LATER/SHOPPING   BZ2
I'LL CALL YOU BACK LATER/WRITERS   C
LATHER
LATHER AS YOU GO/BILLBOARDS/ACCIDENTS/ADVERTISING   Z29
LINES TO BE MUTTERED THROUGH CLENCHED TEETH AND QUITE A LOT OF LATHER IN THE COUNTRY   C8
LATINS
THESE LATINS/DUENNA   Y8
LATOUR
LONG TIME NO SEE, 'BY NOW'/MR. LATOUR/BORES   5
LAUGH
BIRDIES, DON'T MAKE ME LAUGH/CHILDREN/QUARRELING   GYZ89
MACBETH HATH MURDERED SLEEP? OR DON'T MAKE ME LAUGH/DETECTIVES   F8
VISITORS LAUGH AT LOCKSMITHS, OR, HOSPITAL DOORS HAVEN'T GOT LOCKS ANYHOW   WZ2
LAUGHED
THE BOY WHO LAUGHED AT SANTA CLAUS/JABEZ DAWES   29c
LAUGHING
I'M TERRIBLY SORRY FOR YOU, BUT I CAN'T HELP LAUGHING/DISEASES   WZ4
LAUGHINGSTOCK
NO BUSKIN, ALL SOCK, MAKES LAUGHINSTOCK/MOUSETRAP/MEAT-GRINDER/HUSBAND   A
LAUNFAL
AND HOW KEEN WAS THE VISION OF SIR LAUNFAL?/MYOPIA/GLASSES   WZ6
LAVENDAR
THE PRIVATE DINING ROOM/DATING/LAVENDAR/TAFFETA   Z5
LAVISH
GENEALOGICAL REFLECTION/MCTAVISH/LAVISH   EYZ18
LAW
FATHER-IN-LAW OF THE GROOM/WOMEN   5
THERE'S A LAW, ISN'T THERE? OR I CAN CALL YOU NAMES BUT DON'T CALL ME NAMES/LIBEL   5
LAWYER
I YIELD TO MY LEARNED BROTHER/PROFESSIONALS/LAWYER/DOCTOR/MORTITIAN   DWZ18
LAY
PROGNOSTICATIONS ARE FOR THE BIRDS: LAY OFF ME, PLEASE, WHILE I EAT MY WORDS/FOOTBALL/COLTS   V
LAY THAT PUMPKIN DOWN/AUTUMN   3
LAZY
THE SPRING SITTING/SPRINGFEVER/LAZY   D
LEAD
YOUR LEAD, PARTNER, I HOPE WE'VE READ THE SAME BOOK/BRIDGE/CARDS   Z6

LEAGUE
    A PLEA FOR A LEAGUE OF SLEEP   Z49
LEAGUER
    THE ANTI-SALOON LEAGUER   C
LEAP
    AND THREE HUNDRED AND SIXTY-SIX IN LEAP YEAR/SHAVING/BATHING   Z2
LEAR
    HOW PLEASANT TO APE MR. LEAR/LIMRICKS   A
    THE INDIGNANT OWL/PUSSYCAT/LEAR   A
LEARNED
    I YIELD TO MY LEARNED BROTHER/PROFESSIONALS/LAWYER/DOCTOR/MORTITIAN   DWZ18
LEASES
    NATURE ABHORS A VACANCY/LEASES/RESIDENCE   3
LEAST
    AT LEAST I'M NOT THE KIND OF FOOL WHO SOBS; WHAT KIND OF FOOL AM I?   X
LEAVE
    PLEASE LEAVE FATHER ALONE/FATHER'S DAY/MOTHER'S DAY   DGZ8
    MAYBE YOU CAN'T TAKE IT WITH YOU, BUT LOOK WHAT HAPPENS WHEN YOU LEAVE IT BEHIND/MONEY Z5
    LEAVE ME ALONE, AND THE WORLD IS MINE/AUTOMOBILES/RADIOS   D
    LOVE ME BUT LEAVE MY DOG ALONE/MR. BEAMINGTON/POPULARITY   Z5
LEAVE
    WE DON'T NEED TO LEAVE YET, DO WE? OR, YES WE DO/MARRIAGE   29
LEAVES
    ALL OF THE PLEASURE AND NONE OF THE RESPONSIBILITY? LEAVES FROM GRANDFATHER'S SUMMER JOURNAL A
    HAND ME DOWN MY OLD SCHOOL SLIDING PADS OR THERE'S HINT OF STRAWBERRY LEAVES IN THE AIR 5
    ONE FROM ONE LEAVES TWO/FARMING/SUBSIDIES   D1
LECTURER
    LECTURER IN BOOKSTORE/AUTOGRAPHING   Z5
LECTURERS
    WITH MY OWN EYES/LECTURERS/UNITED STATES   5
LECTURES
    THE VOICE OF EXPERIENCE/LECTURES/HUSBANDS   BYZ29
LED
    AND LO! HONORE'S NAME LED ALL THE REST/BALZAC/LITERATURE   Q
LEDA
    FIFTH LIMICK/CEYLON/LEDA/SWAN   3
    LEDA'S FORTUNATE GAFFE/ZEUS/PATER   Z5
LEER
    KING LEER/HUMOR/OFF-COLOR   FZ8
LEFT
    GRIN AND BEAR LEFT/DIRECTIONS   Z3
    TO A LADY PASSING TIME BETTER LEFT UNPASSED/CARDS/SOLITAIRE   BZ4
LEGAL
    LEGAL REFLECTION/POSTOFFICE/PORNOGRAPHY   EZ8
LEISURE
    MORE ABOUT PEOPLE/WORKING/LEISURE   EYZ8
LEMMINGS
    THE LEMMINGS/TRAVEL   F
LEMON
    JUST A PIECE OF LETTUCE AND SOME LEMON JUICE, THANK YOU/DIETS   FY
LEND
    MEL ALLEN, MEL ALLEN, LEND ME YOUR CLICHE/BASEBALL/PITCHERS/MACTIVITY   6
    MAX SCHLING, MAX SCHLING, LEND ME YOUR GREEN THUMB; A CATALOG OF FLOWERY CATALOGUES Z5
LEPIDOPTERIST
    THE LEPIDOPTERIST/BUTTERFLIES   5
LEPRECHAUN
    THE MYSTERIOUS OUPHE/TWINS/LEPRECHAUN/MISCHIEF   t
LESS
    A PLEA FOR LESS MALICE TOWARD NONE/LOVE/HATE   FY8
LET
    RAPUNZEL, RAPUNZEL, LET'S LET DOWN OUR HAIR/WITS   Z6
    LET GEORGE DO IT, IF YOU CAN FIND HIM   D8
    IF HE SCHOLARS, LET HIM GO/HIPPOLYTE ADOLPHE TAINE   Z3
    LET ME BUY THIS ONE/RICH/MONEY   4
    DON'T GUESS, LET ME TELL YOU/DETECTIVE STORIES   YZ18
    EXPERIENCE TO LET   Z4
LET'S
    RAPUNZEL, RAPUNZEL, LET'S LET DOWN OUR HAIR/WITS   Z6
    LET'S NOT PLAY LOTTO, LET'S JUST TALK/CONVERSATION   Z5
    LET'S NOT CLIMB THE WASHINGTON MONUMENT TONIGHT/MIDDLE AGE   WZ3
    LET'S NOT GO TO THE THEATER TONIGHT, OR WE COULDN'T GET SEATS ANYHOW/MANHATTAN   D8

LINCOLN

A BIRTHDAY THAT NEVER WAS: A FEBRUARY FANTASY/JOHN WILKES BOOTH/LINCOLN/WASHINGTON   6
NOT GEORGE WASHINGTON'S, NOT ABRAHAM LINCOLN'S, BUT MINE/BIRTHDAY/THIRTY-EIGHT/CAREER   Z2

LINDBERGH

CHARLES AND ANNE LINDBERGH   D

LINE

THERE IS NO DANGER LINE/SCIENTIST/EXPERIMENT   D
HOOK, LINE AND ENNUI/FISHERMAN   A
LINE-UP FOR YESTERDAY; AN ABC OF BASEBALL IMMORTALS   3
A CAUTION TO HILLBILLY SINGERS, HARPISTS, HARPOONISTS, CHANNEL-SWIMMERS, PEOPLE FIRST IN
     LINE FOR WORLD SERIES TICKETS/FAME   5

LINES

LINES WRITTEN TO CONSOLE THOSE LADIES DISTRESSED BY THE LINES "MEN SELDOM MAKE PASSES"/
     GLASSES   EG
MEMORANDUM TO AMERICAN WOMANHOOD, OR LINES FOR A FASHION PAGE   F
LINES FOR A SUMMER'S END/HEAT/MANHATTAN   F8
ADMONITORY LINES FOR THE BIRTHDAY OF AN OVER-ENERGETIC CONTEMPORARY   A
LINES FRAUGHT WITH NAUGHT BUT THOUGHT   7
LINES IN DISPRAISE OF DISPRAISE/ANALYZING   E
LINES IN PRAISE OF A DATE MADE PRAISEWORTHY SOLELY BY SOMETHING VERY NICE THAT HAPPENED TO IT C
LINES INDITED WITH ALL THE DEPRAVITY OF POVERTY/RICH   EYZ8
LINES ON FACING FORTY/MATURING/AGE   Z2
LINES TO A THREE-NAME LADY/THINK   FYZ8
LINES TO A WORLD-FAMOUS POET WHO FAILED TO COMPLETE A WORLD-FAMOUS POEM/MR. GUEST   FY189
LINES TO BE EMBROIDERED ON A BIB OR, THE CHILD IS FATHER OF THE MAN, BUT NOT FOR QUITE A
     WHILE   Z39
LINES TO BE HUMMED FOR A SUPINE POSITION TO THE HUMMER'S OSTEOPATHIC PHYSICIAN/NECK   2
LINES TO BE MUMBLED AT THE OVINGTON'S/MARRIAGE CEREMONY   EYZ18
LINES TO BE MUTTERED THROUGH CLENCHED TEETH AND QUITE A LOT OF LATHER IN THE COUNTRY   C8
LINES TO BE SCRIBBLED ON SOMEBODY ELSE'S THIRTIETH MILESTONE/BIRTHDAY   Z4

LINGUAL

WHO'LL BUY MY LINGUAL? OR YOU PRONOUNCE PLUIE, LOUIE/FRENCH   6

LINING

DON'T LOOK FOR THE SILVER LINING, JUST WAIT FOR IT/SERENDIPITY   Z5
LOOK FOR THE SILVER LINING   FYZ8

LINOTYPE

LISTEN TO THE LINOTYPE/NEWSPAPERS/MOCKINGBIRD   Z3

LINTHICUM

SONGS FOR A BOSS NAMED MR. LINTHICUM   E

LION

SCRAM, LION/BRITISH/SLANG/ANGLOPHILS   CYZ8
THE LION   Z39

LIONS

SHORT SHORT STORY/LIONS/LIBRARY   E

LIP

NEVER MIND THE OVERCOAT, BUTTON UP THAT LIP/GOSSIP   Z6
THE CUP AND THE LIP/WOMEN/LIPSTICK   3

LIPSTICK

THE PERFECT HUSBAND/LIPSTICK/GIRDLE   BZ39
VIVA VAMP, VALE VAMP/BUSTS/LIPSTICK/MASCARA   7
THE CUP AND THE LIP/WOMEN/LIPSTICK   3

LIQUOR

ALMA MATTER 67, MIND AGGIES 3/BOOKSELLERS/LIQUOR-DEALERS/MONEY   C
REFLECTION ON ICE-BREAKING/CANDY/LIQUOR   EYZ8

LISTEN

LISTEN/LONELY/SKULL   Z8
GO AHEAD, LOOK, AND LISTEN/TRAINS   2
LISTEN TO THE LINOTYPE/NEWSPAPERS/MOCKINGBIRD   Z3

LITERARY

THE NON BIOGRAPHY OF A NOBODY/MINOR LITERARY FIGURE   A
LITERARY REFLECTION/VANCE/PANCE   EZ18
THE LITERARY SCENE/DE SADE/SPILLANE/SITWELL   Z6

LITERATURE

VERY LIKE A WHALE/LITERATURE/METAPHOR/SIMILE   DZ18
AND LO! HONORE'S NAME LED ALL THE REST/BALZAC/LITERATURE   Q
FEE FI HO HUM, NO WONDER BABY SUCKS HER THUMB/JUVENILE LITERATURE   Z6

LITTLE

THIS IS GOING TO HURT JUST A LITTLE BIT/DENTISTS   W4
HERE'S TO YOU, LITTLE BOY BLUE/SLEEP/DREAMS   2
A BRIEF GUIDE TO RHYMING OR, HOW BE THE LITTLE BUSY DOTH?/ENGLISH/PLURAL   Z6

LITTLE
    THE THREE LITTLE CHRISTMAS CAROLS/SCROOGE   D
    LITTLE FEET/CHILDREN/GENIUS/FAMILIES   GZ89
    BOOP-BOOP-ADIEUP, LITTLE GROUP!/AMATEUR THEATER   Z4
    AND HOW IS MY LITTLE MAN TODAY?/CONVALESCENCE   4
    LITTLE MISS MUFFET SAT ON A PROPHET - AND QUITE RIGHT, TOO!/TROUBLE   Z4
    HOME THOUGHTS FROM LITTLE MOOSE/ADIRONDACKS/MOUNTAINS   F
    VERY NICE, REMBRANDT, BUT HOW ABOUT A LITTLE MORE COLOR?/SONGS   A
    LITTLE PRETTY PENNY, LET'S SQUANDER THEE/MILLIONAIRES/WEALTH   A
LIVE
    OLD DOCTOR VALENTINE TO HIS SON/LIVE/DIE   5
    LONG LIVE DELAYS OF ANCIENT ROME/PROCRASTINATION   D
LIVED
    A PRINCESS WHO LIVED NEAR A BOG/FROG   A
LIVELIHOOD
    INTROSPECTIVE REFLECTION/WORKING/LIVELIHOOD   EYZ8
LIVES
    BRIEF LIVES IN NOT SO BRIEF/GOSSIP/BIOGRAPHY/JOHN AUBREY   7
    THE BARGAIN/SAINT IVES/SEVEN LIVES   6
LIVING
    TARKINGTON, THOUS SHOULD'ST BE LIVING IN THIS HOUR/ADOLESCENCE   Z39
    WHAT TO DO UNTIL THE DOCTOR GOES OR IT'S TOMORROW THAN YOU THINK/LIVING   WZ3
LIZARD
    THE SKINK/LIZARD   Z29
LLAMA
    THE LAMA/LLAMA   CGZ89a
LO
    AND LO! HONORE'S NAME LED ALL THE REST/BALZAC/LITERATURE   Q
LOANING
    POLONIUS, YES, POLONIUS, NO/HAMLET/BORROWING/LOANING   5
LOANS
    HEARTS AND FLOWERS OR WHAT I KNOW ABOUT BOLIVAR BLACK/GENEROSITY/LOANS   DZ8
LOCAL
    A RIDE ON THE BRONXIAL LOCAL/BRONCHITIS   14
LOCKS
    VISITORS LAUGH AT LOCKSMITHS, OR, HOSPITAL DOORS HAVEN'T GOT LOCKS ANYHOW   WZ2
LOCKSMITHS
    VISITORS LAUGH AT LOCKSMITHS, OR, HOSPITAL DOORS HAVEN'T GOT LOCKS ANYHOW   WZ2
LOCUST
    LOCUST LOVERS, ATTENTION!   Z4
    THE DAY OF THE LOCUST OR, WHOSE WEDDING IS THIS ANYWAY?/GUESTS   A
    I HAPPEN TO KNOW/BUFFALO/SEAL/LOCUST   Z29
LOG
    EPSTEIN SPARE THAT YULE LOG!/CHRISTMAS CARDS   DZ89
LOGGERHEAD
    NO TROUBLE AT ALL, IT'S AS EASY AS FALLING OFF A LOGGERHEAD/HOSTS/COCKTAILS   S
LONDON
    TRANSATLANTIC TRANSPORTS/LONDON/PARIS/SWITZERLAND/MALAGA/VENICE/MOSCOW/TAXIS   7
LONE
    NO, YOU BE A LONE EAGLE/AIRPLANES/FLYING   E
LONELY
    LISTEN/LONELY/SKULL   Z8
LONG
    THE PANDIT, OR PERHAPS WE WERE WRONG ABOUT THAT, BUT AS LONG AS WE'RE BEING FRANK   7
    HOW LONG HAS THIS BEEN GOING ON? OH, QUITE LONG/BETTING/HORSE-RACING   Z18
    A KNIGHT OF THE GARTER LONG HENCE   A
    LONG LIVE DELAYS OF ANCIENT ROME/PROCRASTINATION   D
    LONG TIME NO SEE, 'BY NOW'/MR. LATOUR/BORES   5
    ON WAKING TO THE THIRD RAINY MORNING OF A LONG WEEK END/HOUSE GUEST   Z3
    HUEY LONG   D
LONGEST
    MIDSUMMER'S DAYMARE/JUNE/LONGEST DAY   Z14
LONGWELL
    TWO SONGS FOR A BOSS NAMED MR. LONGWELL   Z8
LOOK
    HOW TO TELL A KITCHEN FROM A CUISINE: TAKE A QUICK LOOK AT OURS/COOKBOOKS   6
    DON'T LOOK FOR THE SILVER LINING, JUST WAIT FOR IT/SERENDIPITY   Z5
    LOOK FOR THE SILVER LINING   FYZ8
    DON'T LOOK NOW/BATHING SUITS/FIGURES   YZ18
    DON'T LOOK NOW, BUT THERE'S SOMETHING BEHIND THE CURTAIN/ADVENTURE/GREENHORNS/AGING   7
    DON'T LOOK NOW, BUT YOUR NOBLESSE OBLIGE IS SHOWING   3
    MAYBE YOU CAN'T TAKE IT WITH YOU, BUT LOOK WHAT HAPPENS WHEN YOU LEAVE IT BEHIND/MONEY Z5

LOOK
  LOOK WHAT YOU DID, CHRISTOPHER/COLUMBUS/AMERICA   FZ8
  GO AHEAD, LOOK, AND LISTEN/TRAINS   2
  WHAT THE WELL-READ PATIENT IS TALKING ABOUT OR LOOK, MA, WHAT I GOT!/MEDICAL TERMINOLOGY WZ6
LOOKED
  THE SNAKE, WITHOUT WHOM ADAM WOULD NEVER HAVE LOOKED AT THE LADY ONCE/KISSED   5
LOOKS
  IT LOOKS LIKE SNOW OR MY LIFE IN GALOSHES   3
LORD
  THANK YOU, LORD   &
LOS ANGELES
  DON'T SHOOT LOS ANGELES   2
LOSE
  STICKS AND STONES MAY BREAK THEIR BONES, BUT NAMES WILL LOSE A SPONSOR/BASEBALL   A
LOST
  THE LOST CAUSE/SLOGAN/CROWDS/SIT DOWN   4
LOT
  WHO WANTS TO TRAVEL ALL OVER EUROPE AND SEE NOTHING BUT A LOT OF AMERICAN TOURISTS? I DO 6
  EHEU! FUGACES OR, WHAT A DIFFERENCE A LOT OF DAYS MAKE/YOUTH/MIDDLE-AGE   WZ5
  LINES TO BE MUTTERED THROUGH CLENCHED TEETH AND QUITE A LOT OF LATHER IN THE COUNTRY   C8
LOTTO
  LET'S NOT PLAY LOTTO, LET'S JUST TALK/CONVERSATION   Z5
LOUDNESS
  I DIDN'T SAY A WORD OR WHO CALLED THAT PICCOLO PLAYER A FATHER?/HEARING/VOICE/LOUDNESS Z5
LOUIE
  WHO'LL BUY MY LINGUAL? OR YOU PRONOUNCE PLUIE, LOUIE/FRENCH   6
LOUSE
  THE LOUSE/ROBERT BURNS   2
LOUVRE
  POLITICAL REFLECTION/HERBERT HOOVER/LOUVRE   EZ8
LOVE
  A PLEA FOR LESS MALICE TOWARD NONE/LOVE/HATE   FY8
  SEDATIVE REFLECTION/LOVE/INSOMNIA   EWZ8
  TIN WEDDING WHISTLE/LOVE/MARRIAGE   BYZ29
  REPRISE/LOVE/MEMORABLE PHRASES   3
  THAT REMINDS ME/LOVE/ROMANCE   BYZ18
  QUARTET FOR PROSPEROUS LOVE CHILDREN   F
  LOVE FOR SALE/POETS/WRITING   D8
  LOVE ME BUT LEAVE MY DOG ALONE/MR. BEAMINGTON/POPULARITY   Z5
  LOVE UNDER THE REPUBLICANS (OR DEMOCRATS)/MARRIAGE/ECONOMY   BEZ8
  FELLOW CITIZENS, I LOVE YOU/POLITICIAN/VOTING   D
  ONCE MORE, TO MY VALENTINE/LOVE   B
  THE SECRET TOWN/LOVE   D18
  THE WINNER/POETS/LOVE   B
  TO MY VALENTINE/LOVE   BY2
  THE STRANGE CASE OF THE LOVELORN LETTER WRITER/MISS DIX/DALLIANCE/LOVE   Z5
LOVELORN
  THE STRANGE CASE OF THE LOVELORN LETTER WRITER/MISS DIX/DALLIANCE/LOVE   Z5
LOVELY
  MS. FOUND UNDER A SERVIETTE IN A LOVELY HOME/NANCY MITFORD/DOLLARS   Z6
LOVERS
  LOCUST LOVERS, ATTENTION!   Z4
LOVES
  EVERYBODY LOVES A BRIDE, EVEN THE GROOM/WEDDING   5
  M.C. LOVES TV OR A PERSONALITY IS BORN/HAM/EGO   5
LOW
  HIGH, LOW THE COMEDY: A LAST WINTER'S TALE/BIRD/CAT $
  JUST HOW LOW CAN A HIGHBROW GO WHEN A HIGHBROW LOWERS HIS BROW   7
  LOW-PRESSURE ARIA/RAIN/GOLF/TENNIS   DG89
LOWERS
  JUST HOW LOW CAN A HIGHBROW GO WHEN A HIGHBROW LOWERS HIS BROW   7
LOYAL
  SAID A COMMISSAR LOYAL BUT VAGUE   A
LUCK
  THE OUTCOME OF MR. BUCK'S SUPERSTITION/LUCK   Z3
LUCKY
  MIRIAM'S LUCKY DAY/DELIRIUM   Z4
LUCRATIVE
  THE STRANGE CASE OF THE LUCRATIVE COMPROMISE   WZ6
LUCY
  LUCY LAKE   FZ8

MALE
    ODE TO C.B.E., PRACTICALLY THE ONLY NEW MALE CHILD I KNOW OF   G9
    A MALE ENTOMOLOGIST AUTHOR   A
MALICE
    MALICE DOMESTIC/COOK   Z89
    A PLEA FOR LESS MALICE TOWARD NONE/LOVE/HATE   FY8
MALINGERER
    THE JOYOUS MALINGERER/HUSBANDS   A
MAMAS
    JOHN PEEL, SHAKE HANDS WITH 37 MAMAS; BISHOP DE WOLFE GREETS 37 DEBUTANTES ON LONG ISLAND   A
MAN
    ONE MAN'S OPIATE/SATRE/ENNUI   ?
    THE VERY UNCLUBBABLE MAN/CLUBS   DZ8
    A CAUTION TO EVERYBODY/AUK/MAN/FLY/WALK/THINK   Z5
    PORTRAIT OF THE ARTIST AS A PREMATURELY OLD MAN/SIN   DYZ8
    WHO SAYS IT'S SO NICE TO HAVE A MAN AROUND THE HOUSE?/HUSBANDS   A
    MAN BITES DOG DAYS/SUMMER/ITCH   WZ14
    A MAN CAN COMPLAIN, CAN'T HE? (A LAMENT FOR THOSE WHO THINK OLD)   AW
    DRIVE SLOW, MAN CHORTLING, OR, APRIL, 1941/NEW CAR   2
    THERE WAS A YOUNG MAN FROM NEW HAVEN   A
    THE MAN IS FATHER OF THE CHILD OR, BUT HE NEVER QUITE GETS USED TO IT   9
    THE MAN ON THE SHELF/CHILDREN'S BOOKS/DESERT ISLAND   6
    AND HOW IS MY LITTLE MAN TODAY?/CONVALESCENCE   4
    THE MAN WHO FRUSTRATED MADISON AVENUE/TV/COMMERCIALS   A
    THE MAN WITH TWO NEW SUITS   Z4
    LINES TO BE EMBROIDERED ON A BIB OR, THE CHILD IS FATHER OF THE MAN, BUT NOT FOR QUITE A
        WHILE   Z39
    THE CHILD IS FATHER TO THE MAN, BUT WITH MORE AUTHORITY/CHORES/PARENTS   Z5
    ONE MAN'S MEED IS ANOTHER MAN'S OVEREMPHASIS/COLLEGE FOOTBALL   Z4
    A BAS BEN ADHERN/REPRODUCTION/FELLOW MAN   EYZ8
MANATEE
    THE MANATEE   Z6
MANHATTAN
    AND SO MANHATTAN BECAME AN ISLE OF JOY/INDIANS   A
    MANHATTAN MONKEY   C
    FROM A MANHATTAN TOMB/BROODING/LACKADAISICLE   CWYZ8
    REFLECTION ON THE SKYLINE/MANHATTAN   C
    SPRING COMES TO MURRAY HILL/MANHATTAN   EZ8
    LET'S NOT GO TO THE THEATER TONIGHT, OR WE COULDN'T GET SEATS ANYHOW/MANHATTAN   D8
    LINES FOR A SUMMER'S END/HEAT/MANHATTAN   F8
MANKIND
    ELEPHANTS HAVEN'T GOT ANYTHING TO FORGET/MANKIND   D
MANNER
    A THOUGHT ON THE MANNER OF THOSE WHO STRIVE TO ACHIEVE THE MANNER CALLED HEMINGWAY/WRITERS   C
MANNERS
    TO THE CHILD WHO'S FARTHER FROM THE MANNERS OR, HOW TO BE YOUNG GRACEFULLY   7
MANTIS
    THE PRAYING MANTIS   Z6
MANY
    HOW MANY MILES TO THE DEAD LETTER OFFICE/POSTAGE STAMPS   A
MARCH
    GERMAN SONG/GRIMM/MARCH   r
    THAR SHE BLOWS/WIND/MARCH/TAXES   3
    BEWARE THE IDES OF MARCH, OR BROTHER, CAN YOU SPARE AN IDE?   D
    SPRING SONG/MARCH   Z14
MARCHES
    TIME MARCHES ON   Z4
MARCHING
    SO I RESIGNED FROM THE CHU CHIN CHOWDER AND MARCHING CLUB/ORIENT   Z6
MARCO
    MARCO POLO NOTWITHSTANDING/TRAVELERS   E
MARKET
    DON'T SELL AMERICA SHORT/STOCK MARKET   F
MARKETEERS
    THE MARKETEERS/GROCERY SHOPPING   D
MARMADUKE
    THE SEVEN SPIRITUAL AGES OF MRS. MARMADUKE MOORE/LIFETIME   FYZ8
MARRAKECH
    MOROCCO/MARRAKECH/CAMEL   7
MARRIAGE
    DOWN THE MOUSEHOLD, AND WHAT SCIENCE MISSED THERE/MARRIAGE/APOLOGY   WZ2

MARRIAGE
    THE BOOK OF PROVERBS: A WORD TO HUSBANDS/MARRIAGE/ARGUMENTS   7
    LOVE UNDER THE REPUBLICANS (OR DEMOCRATS)/MARRIAGE/ECONOMY   BEZ8
    THE TROUBLE WITH WOMEN IS MEN/MARRIAGE/HUSBANDS   BZ29
    THE STILLY NIGHT: A SOPORIFIC REFLECTION/MARRIAGE/INSOMNIA/SNORING   AW
    THE STRANGE CASE OF MR. ORMANTUDE'S BRIDE/MARRIAGE/UNDERSTANDING   BYZ29
    THE BLISSFUL DREAM OF MR. FARR/MARRIAGE/WIFE   3
    FRAILTY, THY NAME IS MISNOMER/MARRAIGE/WOMEN   BZ2
    LINES TO BE MUMBLED AT THE OVINGTON'S/MARRIAGE CEREMONY   EYZ18
    I DO, I WILL, I HAVE/MARRIAGE   BZ3
    THE ANNIVERSARY/MARRIAGE   BZ5
    TIN WEDDING WHISTLE/LOVE/MARRIAGE   BYZ29
    ADVICE OUTSIDE A CHURCH/BACHELORHOOD/MARRIAGE   GZ8
    I NEVER EVEN SUGGESTED IT/QUARRELS/MARRIAGE   BYZ18
    MR. MINIKIN'S WAKING NIGHTMARE/TRAVEL/MARRIAGE   A
    SONG TO BE SUNG BY THE FATHER OF SIX-MONTHS-OLD FEMALE CHILDREN/BOYS/MARRIAGE   FG
    SONG TO BE SUNG BY THE FATHER OF INFANT FEMALE CHILDREN/BOYS/MARRIAGE   YZ189
    WE DON'T NEED TO LEAVE YET, DO WE? YES WE DO/MARRIAGE   29
MARRIED
    MACHINERY DOESN'T ANSWER, EITHER, BUT YOU AREN'T MARRIED TO IT/WIVES/KNITTING   GZ89
    HOW TO BE MARRIED WITHOUT A SPOUSE; KIPLING OR WHAT HAVE YOU DONE WITH MR. HAUKSBEE/INDIA   BZ5
MARRY
    ALWAYS MARRY AN APRIL GIRL   BZ3
MARTHA
    MARTHA'S VINEYARD   Z3
MARTINI
    I CAN'T HAVE A MARTINI, DEAR, BUT YOU TAKE ONE/DIETING   WZ6
MARY
    WHAT'S IN A NAME? HERE'S WHAT'S IN A NAME OR I WONDER WHAT BECAME OF JOHN AND MARRY   Z6
MASCARA
    VIVA VAMP, VALE VAMP/BUSTS/LIPSTICK/MASCARA   7
MASSACHUSETTS
    THOUGHT THOUGHT WHILE RESTING COMFORTABLY IN PHILLIPS HOUSE, MASSACHUSETTS GENERAL HOSPITAL   A
MATCHMAKING
    THERE'S ALWAYS AN UBBLEBUB/MATCHMAKING/PARTIES   Z2
MATERIAL
    EVERYBODY'S FULL OF CARBONACEOUS MATERIAL OBTAINED BY THE IMPERFECT COMBUSTION OF WOOD   A
MATINEE
    WEDNESDAY MATINEE/THEATER/WOMEN   Z4
MATRIMONY
    NUPTIAL REFLECTION/MATRIMONY/PATRIMONY   8
    WOODPILE-RAKING/MATRIMONY/PATRIMONY   E
MATRONIZED
    NOW TELL ME ABOUT YOURSELF/PATRONIZED/MATRONIZED   Z2
MATTER
    ALMA MATTER 67, MIND AGGIES 3/BOOKSELLERS/LIQUOR-DEALERS/MONEY   C
    WHAT'S THE MATTER, HAVEN'T YOU GOT ANY SENSE OF HUMOR?/PRACTICAL JOKES   YZ18
MATURING
    LINES ON FACING FORTY/MATURING/AGE   Z2
MAUGHAM
    LIMERICK TWO/LADY/GUAM/CHARM/MAUGHAM   5
MAX
    MAX SCHLING, MAX SCHLING, LEND ME YOUR GREEN THUMB/A CATALOG OF FLOWERY CATALOGUES   Z5
MAY
    THEY WON'T BELIEVE, ON NEW YEAR'S EVE, THAT NEW YEAR'S DAY WILL COME WHAT MAY/HANGOVER   BZ5
    I AMY BE WRONG/BENDER   E
    STICKS AND STONES MAY BREAK MY BONES, BUT NAMES WILL BREAK MY HEART/INDIVIDUAL DIGNITY   7
    STICKS AND STONES MAY BREAK THEIR BONES, BUT NAMES WILL LOSE A SPONSOR/BASEBALL   A
    MAY I DRIVE YOU HOME, MRS. MURGATROYD/AUTOMOBILES/CHAUFFEURS   DY1
    HERE WE GO QUIETLY NUTS IN MAY   Z2
MAYBE
    A POTTED WATCH NEVER BOILS OR, MAYBE THAT'S WHAT THEY'VE BEEN TRYING PROVE/WRISTWATCH   7
    THERE WERE GIANTS IN THOSE DAYS OR MAYBE THERE WEREN'T/ANECDOTES   Z3
    MAYBE YOU CAN'T TAKE IT WITH YOU, BUT LOOK WHAT HAPPENS WHEN YOU LEAVE IT BEHIND/MONEY   Z5
MAYFLOWER
    PILGRIM'S PROGRESS/THANKSGIVING/MAYFLOWER/DESCENDANTS   D
MAYHAP
    IF HE WERE ALIVE TODAY, MAYHAP, MR. MORGAN WOULD SIT ON THE MIDGET'S LAP/BANKER   A
MAZDA
    SAVONAROLA OF MAZDA LANE/WALTER WINCHELL   C
MCGUNN
    CHAMPIONS AND CHIMPIONS/FOOTBALL/HUSHMOUTH MCGUNN/APES   7

MCKUEN
     WE HAVE MET THE SASSENACHS AND THEY ARE OURS; EVEN THE YEAR IS NOW MCMLXIV/MCLUHAN/MCKUEN   P
MCLUHAN
     WE HAVE MET THE SASSENACHS AND THEY ARE OURS; EVEN THE YEAR IS NOW MCMLXIV/MCLUHAN/MCKUEN   P
MCMLXIV
     WE HAVE MET THE SASSENACHS AND THEY ARE OURS; EVEN THE YEAR IS NOW MCMLXIV/MCLUHAN/MCKUEN   P
MCMURRAY
     SECOND LIMICK/COOK/MCMURRAY/CURRY   Z3
MCPHERSON
     AIMEE MCPHERSON   D
MCTAVISH
     GENEALOGICAL REFLECTION/MCTAVISH/LAVISH   EYZ18
ME
     WHO, SIR? ME, SIR? NO SIR, THE TIMES SIR!   --
     OH SHUCKS, MA'AM, I MEAN EXCUSE ME/GIRLS/PROFANITY   Z3
     THAT REMINDS ME/LOVE/ROMANCE   BYZ18
     EVERYBODY'S MIND TO ME A KINGDOM IS OR, A GREAT BIG WONDERFUL WORLD IT'S/PUNS   Z5
     NOW TELL ME ABOUT YOURSELF/PATRONIZED/MATRONIZED   Z2
     LEAVE ME ALONE, AND THE WORLD IS MINE/AUTOMOBILES/RADIOS   D
     PHILOLOGY, ETYMOLOGY, YOU OWE ME AN APOLOGY/ENGLISH LANGUAGE   7
     YOU AND ME AND P.B. SHELLEY/LIFE/FRUSTRATION   Z2
     PLEASE REMIND ME BEFORE I FORGET/MEMORY   R
     LOVE ME BUT LEAVE MY DOG ALONE/MR. BEAMINGTON/POPULARITY   Z5
     LET ME BUY THIS ONE/RICH/MONEY   4
     HAND ME DOWN MY OLD SCHOOL SLIDING PADS OR THERE'S HINT OF STRAWBERRY LEAVES IN THE AIR   5
     EVERYBODY TELLS ME EVERYTHING/NEWS   Z18
     THIS WAS TOLD ME IN CONFIDENCE/GOSSIP   Z4
     BIRDIES, DON'T MAKE ME LAUGH/CHILDREN/QUARRELING   GYZ89
     MACBETH HATH MURDERED SLEEP? OR DON'T MAKE ME LAUGH/DETECTIVES   F8
     BRAKEMAN, HAND ME MY NIBLICK/GOLF/TRAINS/TIMETABLES   2
     THERE'S A LAW, ISN'T THERE? OR I CAN CALL YOU NAMES BUT DON'T CALL ME NAMES/LIBEL   5
     TELL ME NO FIBLETS, WHERE ARE THE GIBLETS/GRAVY/TURKEY DINNER   A
     ASK ME NOW QUESTIONS/MOTHER/FATHER/WATCHES   D
     DON'T WAIT, HIT ME NOW!/CRITICISM   BZ2
     SO THAT'S WHO I REMIND ME OF/RESEMBLANCE TO THE TALENTED   Z2
     ALIAS AND MELISANDE OR, GAMMON ME ONCE, GAMMON ME TWICE,/PUBLISHING   7
     DON'T GUESS, LET ME TELL YOU/DETECTIVE STORIES   YZ18
     PIANO TUNER, UNTUNE ME THAT TUNE/CHOPSTICKS   Z39e
     IT WOULD HAVE BEEN QUICKER TO WALK OR DON'T TELL ME WE'RE THERE ALREADY/TAXI/PAYING   Z6
     ARCHER, ARCH ME YON CARRIER PIGEON/CUMMUNICATION   D
     MEL ALLEN, MEL ALLEN, LEND ME YOUR CLICHE/BASEBALL/PITCHERS/MACTIVITY   6
     MAX SCHLING, MAX SCHLING, LEND ME YOUR GREEN THUMB; A CATALOG OF FLOWERY CATALOGUES   Z5
     JUST HOLMES AND ME, AND MNEMOSYNE, MAKES THREE/MEMORY   A
     ME, I PLAY THE HARP, IT'S JUST ONE SYLLABLE/PRONUNCIATION/PIANIST   6
     ALLOW ME, MADAM, BUT IT WON'T HELP/WOMEN/COATS   YZ2
     PROGNOSTICATIONS ARE FOR THE BIRDS; LAY OFF ME PLEASE, WHILE I EAT MY WORDS/FOOTBALL/COLTS   B
     COMPLIMENTS OF A FRIEND/ME   Z3
MEAL
     COFFEE WITH THE MEAL   Z4
     THE EEL/MEAL   YZ29f
MEAN
     OH SHUCKS, MA'AM, I MEAN EXCUSE ME/GIRLS/PROFANITY   Z3
     I DON'T MEAN US, EXCEPT OCCASIONALLY/LIFE/PESSIMISM   Y2
MEAT
     EXPERIMENT DEGUSTATORY/RATTLESNAKE MEAT/CHICKEN   A
     NO BUSKIN, ALL SOCK, MAKES LAUGHINGSTOCK/MOUSETRAP/MEAT-GRINDER/HUSBAND   A
MEDICAL
     WHAT THE WELL-READ PATIENT IS TALKING ABOUT OR LOOK, MA, WHAT I GOT!/MEDICAL TERMINOLOGY   WZ6
MEDICINE
     OLD DOCTOR VALENTINE TO A COLLEAGUE/CURES/MEDICINE   5
MEDITATIONS
     MODEST MEDITATIONS ON THE HERE, THE HERETOFORE AND THE HEREAFTER   A
MEDIUM
     WILL YOU HAVE YOUR TEDIUM RARE OR MEDIUM?/BORES   Z3
MEDUSA
     MEDUSA AND THE MOT JUSTE/GREEK MYTHOLOGY/GORGONS   Z5
MEED
     ONE MAN'S MEED IS ANOTHER MAN'S OVEREMPHASIS/COLLEGE FOOTBALL   Z4

MIDGET
     IF HE WERE ALIVE TODAY, MAYHAP, MR. MORGAN WOULD SIT ON THE MIDGET'S LAP/BANKER   A
MIDSUMMER
     MIDSUMMER WARNING/SUNBURN/MOONLIGHT   Y2
     MIDSUMMER'S DAYMARE/JUNE/LONGEST DAY   Z14
MILES
     HOW MANY MILES TO THE DEAD LETTER OFFICE/POSTAGE STAMPS   A
     NINE MILES TO THE RAILROAD/COUNTRYSIDE   Z4
MILESTONE
     LINES TO BE SCRIBBLED ON SOMEBODY ELSE'S THIRTIETH MILESTONE/BIRTHDAY   Z4
MILK
     IT MUST BE THE MILK/INFANTS/DRUNKS   GZ189
MILLENNIUMS
     ANY MILLENNIUMS TODAY, LADY?/PILLOWS   Z3
MILLIONAIRE
     OLD DOCTOR VALENTINE TO HIS ONLY MILLIONAIRE/BILLS   5
     I BURN MONEY/MILLIONAIRE   Z2
MILLIONAIRES
     LITTLE PRETTY PENNY, LET'S SQUANDER THEE/MILLIONAIRES/WEALTH   A
MILLS
     IF I HAD THE WINGS OF A HELICOPTER OR HALL'S MILLS THAT ENDS MILLS/QUESTIONS/ANSWERS   6
MILTON
     ROLL ON, THOU DEEP AND DARK BLUE SYLLABLES, ROLL ON/METROPOLITAN OPERA/MILTON CROSS   A
MILWAUKEE
     THERE WAS A YOUNG GIRL OF MILWAUKEE   A
MIND
     TIN PAN ALLEY; GOOD NIGHT, SWEET MIND/WINTER WONDERLAND/SONGS   6
     MR. BETTS'S MIND A KINGDOM IS/FORGET/MEMORY   Z5
     ALMA MATTER 67, MIND AGGIES 3/BOOKSELLERS/LIQUOR-DEALERS/MONEY   C
     THE MIND OF PROFESSOR PRIMROSE/ABSENTMINDED/HARVARD   YZ18
     NEVER MIND THE OVERCOAT, BUTTON UP THAT LIP/GOSSIP   Z6
     EVERYBODY'S MIND TO ME A KINGDOM IS OR, A GREAT BIG WONDERFUL WORLD IT'S/PUNS   Z5
     THE STRANGE CASE OF MR. PAUNCEFOOT'S BROAD MIND   Z2
MINE
     LEAVE ME ALONE, AND THE WORLD IS MINE/AUTOMOBILES/RADIOS   D
     NOT GEORGE WASHINGTON'S, NOT ABRAHAM LINCOLN'S, BUT MINE/BIRTHDAY/THIRTY-EIGHT/CAREER   Z2
     THE BACK OF MINE HAND TO MINE HOST/HOTEL   7
     I'LL STAY OUT OF YOUR DIET IF YOU'LL STAY OUT OF MINE   2
MINIKIN
     MR. MINIKIN'S WAKING NIGHTMARE/TRAVEL/MARRIAGE   A
MINOR
     THE NON BIOGRAPHY OF A NOBODY/MINOR LITERARY FIGURE   A
MINT
     THE STRANGE CASE OF THE DEAD DIVORCEE/MINT JULEP   Z4
     A MINT OF PHRASES OR, A TEAM IS AS STRONG AS ITS BENCH/ORATORS/ELOQUENCE   7
MINUTE
     I'LL BE UP IN A MINUTE/BED   4
     THERE'S A HOST BORN EVERY MINUTE/WEEKENDS/GUESTS   D1
     WHAT'S HECUBA TO HIM? A ONE-MINUTE CLOSE-UP/TV REPORTING DISASTERS   A
MINUTES
     A FRIEND IN NEED WILL BE AROUND IN FIVE MINUTES   2
MIRACULOUS
     THE MIRACULOUS COUNTDOWN/DOCTOR FAUSTUS FOSTER/SCIENTIST/PEACE   7
MIRANDA
     A LADY THINKS SHE IS THIRTY/MIRANDA   BGYZ18
MIRIAM
     MIRIAM'S LUCKY DAY/DELIRIUM   Z4
MISAPPREHENSION
     REFLECTION ON A COMMON MISAPPREHENSION/LADIES/HARD-BOILED/FREUD   C1
MISCHIEF
     THE MYSTERIOUS OUPHE/TWINS/LEPRECHAUN/MISCHIEF   t
MISER
     FRAGONARD/MISER/SIMONIZE   Z89
MISNOMER
     FRAILTY, THY NAME IS MISNOMER/MARRIAGE/WOMEN   BZ2
MISS
     THE STRANGE CASE OF THE LOVELORN LETTER WRITER/MISS DIX/DALLIANCE/LOVE   Z5
     LITTLE MISS MUFFET SAT ON A PROPHET - AND QUITE RIGHT, TOO!/TROUBLE   Z4
MISSED
     DOWN THE MOUSEHOLE, AND WHAT SCIENCE MISSED THERE/MARRIAGE/APOLOGY   WZ2
MISTRESS
     THE VISIT/DALLIANCE/MISTRESS/YACHT   Z5

MITFORD
     MS. FOUND UNDER A SERVIETTE IN A LOVELY HOME/NANCY MITFORD/DOLLARS   Z6

MMMC
     CALLING SPRING VII-MMMC/MYSTERIES/ROMAN-NUMERALS/PUBLISHERS   Z5

MNEMOSYNE
     JUST HOLMES AND ME, AND MNEMOSYNE, MAKES THREE/MEMORY   A

MOBILES
     BABY, IT'S CALDER INSIDE/MOBILES/ART   5

MOCKINGBIRD
     LISTEN TO THE LINOTYPE/NEWSPAPERS/MOCKINGBIRD   Z3

MODERN
     IT'S A GRAND PARADE IT WILL BE, MODERN DESIGN/SAINT PATRICK   YZ2

MODEST
     MODEST MEDITATIONS ON THE HERE, THE HERETOFORE AND THE HEREAFTER   A
     A MODEST PROPOSAL TO ABOLISH THE SALIVA TEST/POSTMASTER/POSTAGE STAMPS   A

MOEURS
     AUTRES BETES, AUTRES MOEURS/FISH/TURTLE   E

MOI
     WHAT'S SAUCE POUR L'OIE IS SAUCE POUR L'ETAT C'EST MOI/FRENCH   M

MOLIERE
     ALL GOOD AMERICANS GO TO LAROUSSE OR, I DON'T PRETEND TO BE MOLIERE THAN THOU/FRENCH   7

MONASTERY
     AWAY FROM IT ALL/MONASTERY   Z4

MONDAY
     EVERY DAY IS MONDAY/WEEKDAYS   Z4
     WE'LL ALL FEEL BETTER BY WEDNESDAY/MONDAY/WEEKENDS   3

MONEY
     I BURN MONEY/MILLIONAIRE   Z2
     MONEY IS EVERYTHING   C8
     ANYBODY FOR MONEY? OR JUST BRING YOUR OWN BASKET/BANKER   Z6
     LET ME BUY THIS ONE/RICH/MONEY   4
     THE TERRIBLE PEOPLE/WEALTH/MONEY   FYZ18
     ALMA MATTER 67, MIND AGGIES 3/BOOKSELLERS/LIQUOR-DEALERS/MONEY   C
     BANKERS ARE JUST LIKE ANYBODY ELSE, EXCEPT RICHER/MONEY   Z4
     MAYBE YOU CAN'T TAKE IT WITH YOU, BUT LOOK WHAT HAPPENS WHEN YOU LEAVE IT BEHIND/MONEY   Z5
     TO BARGAIN, TOBOGGAN, TO-WHOO!/SAVING MONEY   4

MONGOLIA
     A LAMA OF OUTER MONGOLIA   A

MONKEY
     MANHATTAN MONKEY   C

MONSTERS
     DRAGONS ARE TOO SELDOM/MONSTERS/MYTHOLOGY/SEA-SERPENTS   DYZ8

MONTH
     THE MIDDLE OF THE MONTH/BILLS   Z49
     THE SECOND MONTH IT'S NOT ITEMIZED/BILLS/DESK   Z3

MONTHS
     SONG TO BE SUNG BY THE FATHER OF SIX-MONTHS-OLD FEMALE CHILDREN/BOYS/MARRIAGE   FG

MONUMENT
     LET'S NOT CLIMB THE WASHINGTON MONUMENT TONIGHT/MIDDLE AGE   WZ3

MOODUS
     THE STRANGE CASE OF MRS. MOODUS'S SECOND HONEYMOON/LYSISTRATAGEMS   A

MOON
     WHEN THE MOON SHINES OVER AND OVER/RADIO   F

MOONLIGHT
     MIDSUMMER WARNING/SUNBURN/MOONLIGHT   Y2

MOORE
     THE SEVEN SPIRITUAL AGES OF MRS. MARMADUKE MOORE/LIFETIME   FYZ8

MOOSE
     HOME THOUGHTS FROM LITTLE MOOSE/ADIRONDACKS/MOUNTAINS   F
     THE MOOSE ON THE BEACH/GEESE   A

MOPE
     SO PENSEROSO/MELANCHOLY/MOPE   WYZ49

MORBID
     ELECTRA BECOMES MORBID/HAIR   FYZ8

MORE
     MORE ABOUT PEOPLE/WORKING/LEISURE   EYZ8
     THE CHILD IS FATHER TO THE MAN, BUT WITH MORE AUTHORITY/CHORES/PARENTS   Z5
     WHAT THIS COUNTRY NEEDS IS MORE BROADMINDED BABIES   G
     VERY NICE, REMBRANDT, BUT HOW ABOUT A LITTLE MORE COLOR?/SONGS   A
     YOU HAVE MORE FREEDOM IN A HOUSE/MURRAYS   BGZ89
     IS TOMORROW REALLY ANOTHER DAY? OR NO MORE OF THE SAME, PLEASE   3
     JUST ONE MORE PLEA TO THE SULTAN OF THE METROPULTAN/BALLET/METROPOLITAN   C

MORE
>
SPRING COMES TO BALTIMORE OR CHRISTMAS COMES MORE PROMPTLY 3
THE EDUCATION OF ATHELNY JONES OR, ARE THERE MORE RADIOS IN HACKS THAN HACKS IN RADIO/FRENCH/
TAXIS 6
THERE'S MORE TIME AT THE TOP, OR I WANT TO SEE MR. MURGATROYD/EXECUTIVES/ASSISTANTS D
THERE ARE MORE WAYS TO ROAST A PIG THAN BURNING THE HOUSE DOWN/CIGARETTE LIGHTERS Z3
ONCE MORE, TO MY VALENTINE/LOVE B

MORGAN
IF HE WERE ALIVE TODAY, MAYHAP, MR. MORGAN WOULD SIT ON THE MIDGET'S LAP/BANKER A

MORN
SEPTEMBER MORN/VACATION/TRAINS GZ89

MORNING
MORNING PRAYER/SULKING/FIGHTING r
NATURE KNOWS BEST/MORNING/RISING Z4
ON WAKING TO THE THIRD RAINY MORNING OF A LONG WEEK END/HOUSE GUEST Z3
WINTER MORNING/SNOW r

MOROCCO
MOROCCO/MARRAKECH/CAMEL 7

MORSITANS
GLOSSINA MORSITANS, OR, THE TSETSE/WILL YZ29

MORTITIAN
I YIELD TO MY LEARNED BROTHER/PROFESSIONALS/LAWYER/DOCTOR/MORTITIAN DWZ18

MOSCOW
TRANSATLANTIC TRANSPORTS/LONDON/PARIS/SWITZERLAND/MALAGA/VENICE/MOSCOW/TAXIS 7

MOSQUITO
BOO/MOSQUITO 2

MOST
FOR THE MOST IMPROBABLE SHE/COURTSHIP Y18

MOT
MEDUSA AND THE MOT JUSTE/GREEK MYTHOLOGY/GORGONS Z5
MR. PEACHEY'S PREDICAMENT OR NO MOT PARADES/SOCIAL LIFE/HARP/EPIGRAMS YZ18

MOTH
HOMEWARD BUND/MOTH Y29

MOTHER
ASK ME NO QUESTIONS/MOTHER/FATHER/WATCHES D
MOTHER ISN'T WELL/ENGLISH PRONOUNCIATION 7
CITRONELLA AND THE FAIRY GODMOTHER/MOTHER NATURE D
THE MOTHER TONGUE 7
EPILOGUE TO MOTHER'S DAY, WHICH IS TO BE PUBLISHED ON ANY DAY BUT MOTHER'S DAY Z4
PLEASE LEAVE FATHER ALONE/FATHER'S DAY/MOTHER'S DAY DGZ8
BIRTH COMES TO THE ARCHBISHOP/UNMARRIED MOTHER EYZ8

MOTORIST
THE STRANGE CASE OF MR. NIOBOB'S TRANSMOGRIFICATION/MOTORIST/FOURLANED-HIGHWAYS/TRUCKS Z2
THE STRANGE CASE OF THE CAUTIOUS MOTORIST/SCHWELLENBACH Z5

MOULTING
THE CANARY/MOULTING YZ189

MOUNTAINS
HOME THOUGHTS FROM LITTLE MOOSE/ADIRONDACKS/MOUNTAINS F

MOUSE
THE CAT/MOUSE/HOUSE F8

MOUSEHOLE
DOWN THE MOUSEHOLE, AND WHAT SCIENCE MISSED THERE/MARRIAGE/APOLOGY WZ2

MOUSETRAP
NO BUSKIN, ALL SOCK, MAKES LAUGHINGSTOCK/MOUSETRAP/MEAT-GRINDER/HUSBAND A

MOUTH
DON'T BITE THE HAND THAT PUTS ITS FOOT IN YOUR MOUTH/TAMMANY/OCTOPUS 7

MOVE
FIRST FAMILIES, MOVE OVER!/VIRGINIA/SOUTHERN Z4

MOVIES
ROLL ON, THOU DEEP AND DARK BLUE COPY WRITER-ROLL/HEMINGWAY/MOVIES Z3
THE SCREEN WITH THE FACE WITH THE VOICE/MOVIES Z2

MOWGLI
HOW THE RHINOCEROS GOT ITS HIDE OR THE CONFESSIONS OF COUNT MOWGLI DE SADE/CHILD/READING 3

MOZART
EINE KLEINE NASHMUSIK/MOZART L

MOZURKAS
NEXT!/MUSEUM OF NATURAL HISTORY/BRONTOSAURUSES/FOSSIL/POLKA/MOZURKAS WZ5

MR
MR. ARTESIAN'S CONSCIENTIOUSNESS/TIME SAVING YZ18
THE STRANGE CASE OF MR. BALLENTINE'S VALENTINE Z4

MR

MR. BARCALOW'S BREAKDOWN/TACT/VISITING	Z4
MR. BURGESS, MEET MR. BARMECIDE/NATURE STORIES/YOWLER THE BOBCAT	Z6
LOVE ME BUT LEAVE MY DOG ALONE/MR. BEAMINGTON/POPULARITY	Z5
NO WOE IS GOSSAMER TO MR. BESSEMER/PESSIMISTS	Z6
MR. BETTS'S MIND A KINGDOM IS/FORGET/MEMORY	Z5
THE OUTCOME OF MR. BUCK'S SUPERSTITION/LUCK	Z3
THE STRANGE CASE OF MR. DONNYBROOK'S BOREDOM	BWZ4
THE BLISSFUL DREAM OF MR. FARR/MARRIAGE/WIFE	3
THE STRANGE CASE OF MR. FORTAGUE'S DISAPPOINTMENT/INNISFREE	Z4
SLOW DOWN, MR. GANDERDONK, YOU'RE LATE/GOLF	Z2
THE STRANGE CASE OF MR. GOODBODY OR A TEAM THAT WON'T BE BEATEN, CAN'T BE BEATEN/CLICHES	D1
LINES TO A WORLD-FAMOUS POET WHO FAILED TO COMPLETE A WORLD-FAMOUS POEM/MR. GUEST	FY189
HOW TO BE MARRIED WITHOUT A SPOUSE; KIPLING OR WHAT HAVE YOU DONE WITH MR. HAUKSBEE/INDIA	BZ5
AN ENTHUSIAST IS A DEVOTEE IS A ROOTER OR, MR. HEMINGWAY, MEET MR. STENGEL	Z6
MR. HENDERSON/NEON/APPOINTMENT	2
MR. JUDD AND HIS SNAIL, A SORRY TALE/AMOEBA/RACING	A
LONG TIME NO SEE, 'BY NOW'/MR. LATOUR/BORES	5
HOW PLEASANT TO APE MR. LEAR/LIMRICKS	A
SONGS FOR A BOSS NAMED MR. LINTHICUM	E
TWO SONGS FOR A BOSS NAMED MR. LONGWELL	Z8
THE OUTCOME OF MR. MACLEOD'S GRATITUDE/OPTIMISM	3
MR. MINIKIN'S WAKING NIGHTMARE/TRAVEL/MARRIAGE	A
IF HE WERE ALIVE TODAY, MAYHAP, MR. MORGAN WOULD SIT ON THE MIDGET'S LAP/BANKER	A
THERE'S MORE TIME AT THE TOP, I WANT TO SEE MR. MURGATROYD/EXECUTIVES/ASSISTANTS	D
THE STRANGE CASE OF MR. NIOBOB'S TRANSMOGRIFICATION/MOTORIST/FOURLANED-HIGHWAYS/TRUCKS	Z2
THE STRANGE CASE OF MR. O'BANION'S COME-UPPANCE/CLINICAL/SKEPTIC	Z5
THE UNIQUENESS OF MR. ONATIVIA/TRIVIA	A
THE STRANGE CASE OF MR. ORMANTUDE'S BRIDE/MARRIAGE/UNDERSTANDING	BYZ29
THE STRANGE CASE OF MR. PALLISER'S PALATE/GOURMET COOKING	BZ3
THE STRANGE CASE OF MR. PAUNCEFOOT'S BROAD MIND	Z2
MR. PEACHEY'S PREDICAMENT OR NO MOT PARADES/SOCIAL LIFE/HARP/EPIGRAMS	YZ18
YOU'VE GOT TO BE MR. PICKWICK IF YOU WANT TO ENJOY A PICNIC/PAPER	7
WHO'S GOING MR. PLATT'S WAY?/NEIGHBORS/CAR-SHARING	2
THE EMANCIPATION OF MR. POPLIN OR SKOAL TO THE SKIMMERLESS/ALLERGY/HAT-CHECK	Z6
THE SOLITUDE OF MR. POWERS/FLOWERS/ARRANGING	BZ6
MRS. PURVIS DREADS ROOM SERVICE OR, MR. PURVIS DREADS IT, TOO/HOTEL	Z3
THE HAPPY ENDING OF MR. TRAIN/MR. SLOAN/MR. RHODES	Z5
SIC SEMPER MR. SHERMAN'S TEMPER OR KINDLY PLACE YOUR ORDER IN ENGLISH/COCKTAILS	6
THE STRANGE CASE OF THE GIRL O' MR. SPONSOON'S DREAMS/RUN-OVER	Z4
POOR MR. STRAWBRIDGE/DRAWBRIDGE	Z14
MR. TICKLEFEATHER/TREE	G
MR. TWOMBLEY'S ULTIMATE TRIUMPH/HOBBIES	A
TO EE IS HUMAN/DICTIONARIES/MR. WEBSTER/MR. MERRIAM	Z6
THE STRANGE CASE OF MR. WOOD'S FRUSTRATION/BEING FIRST	Z6

MRS

PRIDE GOETH BEFORE A RAISE, OR AH, THERE, MRS. CADWALLADER-SMITH!/SOCIALITES/POISE	FZ8
WATCHMAN, WHAT OF THE FIRST FIRST LADY?/MRS. GEORGE WASHINGTON	CYZ8
THE SEVEN SPIRITUAL AGES OF MRS. MARMADUKE MOORE/LIFETIME	FYZ8
THE STRANGE CASE OF MRS. MOODUS'S SECOND HONEYMOON/LYSISTRATAGEMS	A
MAY I DRIVE YOU HOME, MRS. MURGATROYD/AUTOMOBILES/CHAUFFEURS	DY1
I KNOW EXACTLY WHO DROPPED THE OVERALLS IN MRS. MURPHY'S CHOWDER/BORES	Z6
MRS. PURVIS DREADS ROOM SERVICE OR, MR. PURVIS DREADS IT, TOO/HOTEL	Z3

MS

MS. FOUND IN QUAGMINE/PHYSICIAN	YZ2
MS. FOUND UNDER A SERVIETTE IN A LOVELY HOME/NANCY MITFORD/DOLLARS	Z6

MUCH

SO DOES EVERYBODY ELSE, ONLY NOT SO MUCH/ANECDOTES/REPEATING	Z2
EVERYBODY EATS TOO MUCH ANYHOW/AUTOMOBILES/TRAVEL/LUNCH	YZ149
GO AHEAD, IT WILL DO YOU GOOD OR HER EYES ARE MUCH BIGGER THAN HIS STOMACH/WIFE/HUSBAND/EAT	WZ6
DO POETS KNOW TOO MUCH?	4

MUFFET

LITTLE MISS MUFFET SAT ON A PROPHET - AND QUITE RIGHT, TOO!/TROUBLE	Z4

MULES

THE MULES	Z5

MUMBLED

LINES TO BE MUMBLED AT THE OVINGTON'S/MARRIAGE CEREMONY	EYZ18

MURDER

A WARNING TO WIVES/INSURANCE/MURDER	BDZ8
THEY DON'T READ DE QUINCEY IN PHILLY OR CINCY/MURDER	A

MURDERED
    MACBETH HATH MURDERED SLEEP? OR DON'T MAKE ME LAUGH/DETECTIVES   F8
MURDERS
    WHY CAN'T MURDERS BE MYSTERIOUS   D
MURGATROYD
    MAY I DRIVE YOU HOME, MRS. MURGATROYD/AUTOMOBILES/CHAUFFEURS   DY1
    THERE'S MORE TIME AT THE TOP, OR I WANT TO SEE MR. MURGATROYD/EXECUTIVES/ASSISTANTS   D
MURPHY
    I KNOW EXACTLY WHO DROPPED THE OVERALLS IN MRS. MURPHY'S CHOWDER/BORES   Z6
MURRAY
    SPRING COMES TO MURRAY HILL/MANHATTAN   EZ8
MURRAYS
    APARTMENT TO SUBLET-UNFURNISHED/HOUSE/MURRAYS   BFG89
    YOU HAVE MORE FREEDOM IN A HOUSE/MURRAYS   BGZ89
MUSEUM
    NEXT!/MUSEUM OF NATURAL HISTORY/BRONTOSAURUSES/FOSSIL/POLKA/MOZURKAS   WZ5
    MUSEUM OF NATURAL HISTORY: TYRANNOSAURUS REX; PYTHON; ROCK ROOM; WHALE; HALL OF PRIMATES   N
MUSIC
    INVIDIOUS REFLECTION/RAVEL/MUSIC   E
MUST
    STAMP TOO BIG FOR LETTER, MUST BE FOR ALBUM/POSTMASTER   A
    IT MUST BE THE MILK/INFANTS/DRUNKS   GZ189
    I MUST TELL YOU ABOUT MY NOVEL/RELATIVES/GRANDPA   Z3
MUSTARD
    MUSTARD/CUSTARD   7
MUTTERED
    LINES TO BE MUTTERED THROUGH CLENCHED TEETH AND QUITE A LOT OF LATHER IN THE COUNTRY   C8
MUTUELS
    HARK! HARK! THE PARI-MUTUELS BARK/HORSE RACING/BETTING   4
MY
    SOME OF MY BEST FRIENDS ARE CHILDREN   FGYZ89
    STICKS AND STONES MAY BREAK MY BONES, BUT NAMES WILL BREAK MY HEART/INDIVIDUAL DIGNITY   7
    'MY CHILD IS PHLEGMATIC,,,' - ANXIOUS PARENT   CGYZ89
    MA, WHAT'S A BANKER? OR HUSH, MY CHILD   DZ18
    MY MY; MY DREAM/HAIR; MY CONSCIENCE   Z6
    MY DADDY/BABY/VERSE   FGZ8
    MY DEAR, HOW DID YOU EVER THINK UP THIS DELICIOUS SALAD?   DYZ18
    LOVE ME BUT LEAVE MY DOG ALONE/MR. BEAMINGTON/POPULARITY   Z5
    RAVEN, DON'T STAY AWAY FROM MY DOOR - A CHANT FOR APRIL FIRST   FZ8
    I'M NO SAINT, AND I HAVE MY DOUBTS ABOUT VALENTINE, TOO/VALENTINES   A
    MY DREAM   B
    THE ETERNAL VERNAL OR IN ALL MY DREAMS MY FAIR FACE BEAMS/SPRING   Z3
    A STITCH TOO LATE IS MY FATE/PROMPTNESS/REMEMBERING   Z14
    FRIEND OF MY FRIEND   4
    GOODBYE NOW OR PARDON MY GAUNTLET/REFINED/JANET   6
    COME, COME, KEROUAC. MY GENERATION IS BEATER THAN YOURS/PROGRESS   7
    I YIELD TO MY LEARNED BROTHER/PROFESSIONALS/LAWYER/DOCTOR/MORTITIAN   DWZ18
    IT LOOKS LIKE SNOW OR MY LIFE IN GALOSHES   3
    WHO'LL BUY MY LINGUAL? OR YOU PRONOUNCE PLUIE, LOUIE/FRENCH   6
    AND HOW IS MY LITTLE MAN TODAY?/CONVALESCENCE   4
    THE DUST STORM OR I'VE GOT TEXAS IN MY LUNGS   5
    THIS IS MY OWN, MY NATIVE TONGUE/RADIO/ACCENTS   Z5
    IS THIS SEAT TAKEN? YES OR, MY NECK IS STICKING IN/CONVERSATION   Z3
    BRAKEMAN, HAND ME MY NIBLICK/GOLF/TRAINS/TIMETABLES   2
    HAS ANYBODY SEEN MY NOUMENON?/INTUITION/HUNCH   Z2
    I MUST TELL YOU ABOUT MY NOVEL/RELATIVES/GRANDPA   Z3
    HAND ME DOWN MY OLD SCHOOL SLIDING PADS OR THERE'S HINT OF STRAWBERRY LEAVES IN THE AIR   5
    WITH MY OWN EYES/LECTURES/UNITED STATES   5
    POLTERQUEST, MY POLTERGUEST/GUESTS/HOPPER   Z39
    ONE, TWO, BUCKLE MY SHOE/BIRTHDAY/DAUGHTER   DG89ℓ
    TO A SMALL BOY STANDING ON MY SHOES WHILE I AM WEARING THEM   CGY9
    I'LL EAT MY SPLIT-LEVEL TURKEY IN THE BREEZEWAY/CHRISTMAS/LARGE HOUSES   Z6
    QUICK, HAMMACHER, MY STOMACHER/GLUTTON   WZ3
    THE HAT'S GOT MY TONGUE/SPRING/GIRL   Y2
    MY TRIP DAORBA/EUROPE/TRAVELING/BACKWARD   Z5
    HO, VARLET! MY TWO CENTS' WORTH OF PENNY POSTCARD!/POST OFFICE/MAIL   Z6
    ONCE MORE, TO MY VALENTINE/LOVE   B
    TO MY VALENTINE/LOVE   BY2
    DADDY, I WANT A PET FOR MY VERY OWN, I PROMISE TO TAKE CARE OF IT   9
    CHANGE HERE FOR WICHITA FALLS OR, HAS ANYBODY SEEN MY WANDERLUST?/TRAVEL   Z5
    WHO PUT THAT SPOKESMAN IN MY WHEEL?/VAGUENESS/NEWS SOURCES   A
    PROGNOSTICATIONS ARE FOR THE BIRDS: LAY OFF ME, PLEASE, WHILE I EAT MY WORDS/FOOTBALL/COLTS   V

NEXT
    THE PARTY NEXT DOOR   Z4
    CLEANLINESS IS NEXT TO CATASTROPHE/BATHING/HISTORY   D
    I WANT TO SIT NEXT TO EMILY/CONVERSATION   D
    NEXT!/MUSEUM OF NATURAL HISTORY/BRONTOSAURUSES/FOSSIL/POLKA/MOZURKAS   WZ5

NIBLICK
    BRAKEMAN, HAND ME MY NIBLICK/GOLF/TRAINS/TIMETABLES   2

NICE
    PAJAMAS, HUH? OR DRESSES WERE SO NICE/PANTS   D
    LINES IN PRAISE OF A DATE MADE PRAISEWORTHY SOLELY BY SOMETHING VERY NICE THAT HAPPENED TO IT C
    WHO SAYS IT'S SO NICE TO HAVE A MAN AROUND THE HOUSE?/HUSBANDS   A
    VERY NICE, REMBRANDT, BUT HOW ABOUT A LITTLE MORE COLOR?/SONGS   A

NICHOLAS
    THE CHRISTMAS THAT ALMOST WASN'T/NICHOLAS/LULLAPAT/HEROES   V
    ODE TO SAINT NICHOLAS/SANTA/CHRISTMAS   D

NICKNAMES
    ANY FULL NAME IS A GRAND OLD NAME/NICKNAMES   A

NICKYNAMES
    ANYBODY ELSE HATE NICKYNAMES?   Z6

NIGHT
    A TALE OF THE THIRTEENTH FLOOR/WALPURGIS NIGHT/DOUBLE-DAMNED   6
    ONE NIGHT IN OZ/DINNER PARTY/ENEMIES   YZ2
    THE STILLY NIGHT: A SOPORIFIC REFLECTION/MARRIAGE/INSOMNIA/SNORING   AW
    STAG NIGHT, PALEOLITHIC/OYSTER/WOMAN   3
    TIN PAN ALLEY; GOOD NIGHT, SWEET MIND/WINTER WONDERLAND/SONGS   6

NIGHTINGALE
    FLOW GENTLY, SWEET ETYMOLOGY, ORNITHOLOGY, AND PENOLOGY/NIGHTINGALE/PERSION/BULBUL   5

NIGHTMARE
    MR. MINIKIN'S WAKING NIGHTMARE/TRAVEL/MARRIAGE   A
    A GOOD PARENT'S GARDEN OF VISION; THE DREAM; THE NIGHTMARE; THE AWAKENING/DUAGHTER   FGZ89

NINE
    NINE MILES TO THE RAILROAD/COUNTRYSIDE   Z4
    POSSESSIONS ARE NINE POINTS OF CONVERSATION   Z3

NINETEENTH
    DEATH ON THE NINETEENTH HOLE/MADEMOISELLE FROM ARMENTIERES/AFFAIRS   F8

NIOBOB
    THE STRANGE CASE OF MR. NIOBOB'S TRANSMOGRIFICATION/MOTORIST/FOURLANED-HIGHWAYS/TRUCKS   Z2

NO
    WHO, SIR? ME, SIR? NO SIR, THE TIMES SIR!   --
    POLONIUS, YES, POLINUS, NO/HAMLET/BORROWING/LOANING   5
    YES AND NO/TOLERANCE/SPINELESS   Z14
    THE WRONGS OF SPRING OR, NO ALL FOOLS' DAY LIKE AN ALL OLD FOOLS'DAY/BIRTHDAY   A
    NO BONDS TODAY   2
    NO BUSKIN, ALL SOCK, MAKES LAUGHINSTOCK/MOUSETRAP/MEAT-GRINDER/HUSBAND   A
    NO CONFORMITY TO ENORMITY, THE BIGGER THEY ARE THE HARDER I FALL/CARS/STAMPS/BANKS   7
    THERE IS NO DANGER LINE/SCIENTIST/EXPERIMENT   D
    NO DOCTORS TODAY, THANK YOU/EUPHORIA   WYZ29
    IF THERE WERE NO ENGLAND, 'COUNTRY LIFE' WOULD INVENT IT/HOUSES   A
    TELL ME NO FIBLETS, WHERE ARE THE GIBLETS/GRAVY/TURKEY DINNER   A
    I HAD NO IDEA IT WAS SO LATE/WATCHES/WOMEN/MEN   YZ18
    IS TOMORROW REALLY ANOTHER DAY? OR NO MORE OF THE SAME, PLEASE   3
    MR. PEACHEY'S PREDICAMENT OR NO MOT PARADES/SOCIAL LIFE/HARP/EPIGRAMS   YZ18
    WHAT, NO OYSTERS?   Z2
    I ALWAYS SAY THERE'S NO PLACE LIKE NEW YORK IN THE SUMMER/COTTAGES   Z6
    SONGLAND REVISITED OR, THERE'S NO PURITY LIKE IMMATURITY/POPULAR SONGS/AGE/YOUTH   A
    ASK ME NO QUESTIONS/MOTHER/FATHER/WATCHES   D
    I'M NO SAINT, AND I HAVE MY DOUBTS ABOUT VALENTINE, TOO/VALENTINES   A
    LONG TIME NO SEE, 'BY NOW'/MR. LATOUR/BORES   5
    WHAT, NO SHEEP?/SLEEP-INDUCERS   WZ6
    SO THIS IS WASHINGTON OR DEAD MEN RESENT NO TALES/PROHIBITION   D
    NO TROUBLE AT ALL, IT'S AS EASY AS FALLING OFF A LOGGERHEAD/HOSTS/COCKTAILS   S
    NO WOE IS GOSSAMER TO MR. BESSEMER/PESSIMISTS   Z6
    FEE FI HO HUM, NO WONDER BABY SUCKS HER THUMB/JUVENILE LITERATURE   Z6
    NO WONDER OUR FATHERS DIED/HOUSES/PLUMBING/FURNACES   YZ4
    I ALWAYS SAY A GOOD SAINT IS NO WORSE THAN A BAD COLD/VALENTINE   F8
    A VISITOR FROM PORTLOCK, BUT ALAS, NO XANADU/TRUISMS/THOUGHTS   A
    ISN'T THAT A DAINTY DISH? NO!/COCKTAILS/GADGETS   Z14
    THAT'S FUNNY, WASN'T IT? NO, IT WON'T BE/COMIC ARTISTS/HUMOR   Z6
    NO, NO, NOVEMBER   2
    NO, YOU BE A LONE EAGLE/AIRPLANES/FLYING   E

NOW
    NOW TELL ME ABOUT YOURSELF/PATRONIZED/MATRONIZED   Z2
    GOOD RIDDANCE, BUT NOW WHAT?/NEW YEAR'S EVE   WZ39
    DON'T WAIT, HIT ME NOW/CRITICISM   BZ2
    DON'T LOOK NOW, BUT THERE'S SOMETHING BEHIND THE CURTAIN/ADVENTURE/GREENHORNS/AGING   7
    DON'T LOOK NOW, BUT YOUR NOBLESSE OBLIGE IS SHOWING   3
    WHAT'LL WE DO NOW, OR, I'M AFRAID I KNOW OR, GOOD OLD JUST PLAIN CHARADES, FAREWELL/GAMES   2
    HOW NOW, SIRRAH? OH, ANYHOW/ADVENTURE/COWARDICE   Z4
    LONG TIME NO SEE, 'BY NOW'/MR. LATOUR/BORES   5
NUDISTS
    THIRD LIMICK/DOVER/COW/CLOVER/NUDISTS   Z3
NUMBER
    I'LL WRITE THEIR NUMBER DOWN WHEN WE GET HOME/WORDS/SOCIAL-LIFE   Z2
    OUR NUMBER'S IN THE BOOK/TELEPHONE SOLICITATION   D
NUMERALS
    CALLING SPRING VII-MMMC/MYSTERIES/ROMAN-NUMERALS/PUBLISHERS   Z5
NUPTIAL
    NUPTIAL REFLECTION/MATRIMONY/PATRIMONY   8
NURSERY
    THUNDER OVER THE NURSERY/BABY/DADDY   GYZ89
    JACK DO-GOOD-FOR-NOTHING, A CURSORY NURSERY TALE FOR TOT-BAITERS/BEFRIENDING   7
NUTCRACKER
    NUTCRACKER SUITE NARRATIVE/CHRISTMAS/TOYS   r
NUTHATCH
    UP FROM THE EGG: THE CONFESSIONS OF A NUTHATCH AVOIDER/BIRD WATCHERS   WZ6
NUTS
    HERE WE GO QUIETLY NUTS IN MAY   Z2
NYMPH
    CHLOE AND THE ROUE/GREECE/NYMPH/ZEUS   Z5
    THE NYMPH AND THE SHEPHERD OR SHE WENT THAT-AWAY/WIVES/WANDERING-OFF   BZ6
OAF
    GOODBYE, OLD YEAR, YOU OAF, OR WHY DON'T THEY PAY THE BONUS?/NEW YEAR'S EVE   DYZ8
OAFISHNESS
    OAFISHNESS SELLS GOOD, LIKE AN ADVERTISEMENT SHOULD/GRAMMAR/ENGLISH   Z6
OAKLAND
    AND THAT'S WHY I ALWAYS TAKE THE OAKLAND FERRY TO BEVERLY HILLS/TRAIN STATIONS   6
O'BANION'S
    THE STRANGE CASE OF MR. O'BANION'S COME-UPPANCE/CLINICAL/SKEPTIC   Z5
OBEISANCE
    WHICH CAME FIRST, OBEISANCE OR OBESITY/PLATE-WATCHERS/WEIGHT-WATCHERS   7
OBESITY
    WHICH CAME FIRST, OBEISANCE OR OBESITY/PLATE-WATCHERS/WEIGHT-WATCHERS   7
OBLIGE
    DON'T LOOK NOW, BUT YOUR NOBLESSE OBLIGE IS SHOWING   3
OBSCURITY
    REFLECTION ON VERACITY/PURITY/OBSCURITY   E
    REFLECTION ON A WICKED WORLD/PURITY/OBSCURITY   YZ8
OBSERVER
    THE UNSEEING EYE: THE TRAVEL DIARY OF A NON-OBSERVER   7
OBTAINED
    EVERYBODY'S FULL OF CARBONACEOUS MATERIAL OBTAINED BY THE IMPERFECT COMBUSTION OF WOOD   A
OCCASIONALLY
    I DON'T MEAN US, EXCEPT OCCASIONALLY/LIFE/PESSIMISM   Y2
OCEAN
    BARMAIDS ARE DIVINER THAN MERMAIDS/FISH/OCEAN/SWIMMING   Z4
    SEASIDE SERENADE/OCEAN BREEZE/BEACH   GYZ89
    OCEAN, KEEP RIGHT ON ROLLING/BEACH   D
    A BEGINNER'S GUIDE TO THE OCEAN   YZ29
    PRETTY HALCYON DAYS/BEACH/OCEAN   DYZ8
OCTOPUS
    THE OCTOPUS   Z29a
    DON'T BITE THE HAND THAT PUTS ITS FOOT IN YOUR MOUTH/TAMMANY/OCTOPUS   7
OCULIST
    IS THERE AN OCULIST IN THE HOUSE/WAR   7
ODD
    OH, TO BE ODD/HYPOCHONDRIACS/NORMAL   CZ8
ODDS
    UNFORTUNATELY, IT'S THE ONLY GAME IN TOWN/ODDS   7
ODE
    ODE TO C.B.E., PRACTICALLY THE ONLY NEW MALE CHILD I KNOW OF   G9
    KIND OF AN ODE TO DUTY   YZ4
    ODE TO SAINT NICHOLAS/SANTA/CHRISTMAS   D
    ODE TO THE N.W. BY W. WIND/AUTUMN   F

OFF

    NO TROUBLE AT ALL, IT'S AS EASY AS FALLING OFF A LOGGERHEAD/HOSTS/COCKTAILS   S

    PROGNOSTICATIONS ARE FOR THE BIRDS: LAY OFF ME, PLEASE, WHILE I EAT MY WORDS/FOOTBALL/COLTS   V

    KING LEER/HUMOR/OFF-COLOR   FZ8

    THE NYMPH AND THE SHEPHERD OR SHE WENT THAT-AWAY/WIVES/WANDERING-OFF   BZ6

OFFICE

    HO, VARLET! MY TWO CENTS' WORTH OF PENNY POSTCARD!/POST OFFICE/MAIL   Z6

    HOW MANY MILES TO THE DEAD LETTER OFFICE/POSTAGE STAMPS   A

    INTER-OFFICE MEMORANDUM/SIN/CONSCIENCE   Z4

OH

    OH, SHUCKS, MA'AM, I MEAN EXCUSE ME/GIRLS/PROFANITY   Z3

    OH, TO BE ODD/HYPOCHONDRIACS/NORMAL   CZ8

    O TEMPORA, OH-OH!/NEWSPAPERS/BOOK-REVIEWS/EROTICA   A

    HOW NOW, SIRRAH? OH, ANYHOW/ADVENTURE/COWARDICE   Z4

    OH, DID YOU GET THE TICKETS? BECAUSE I DON'T THINK I'LL GO, AFTER ALL/WOMEN/DECISIONS   4

    OH, PLEASE DON'T GET UP!/ETIQUETTE/WOMEN   Z4

    HOW LONG HAS THIS BEEN GOING ON? OH, QUITE LONG/BETTING/HORSE-RACING   Z18

    OH, STOP BEING THANKFUL ALL OVER THE PLACE/GRACE OF GOD   DYZ18

OLD

    AN OLD DANISH JESTER NAMED YORICK   A

    OLD DOCTOR VALENTINE FOR ONCE DREAMS OF WEALTH/BRA/PEPS-OO-LA-LA/BOUNCE   5

    OLD DOCTOR VALENTINE TO A COLLEAGUE/CURES/MEDICINE   5

    OLD DOCTOR VALENTINE TO HIS ONLY MILLIONAIRE/BILLS   5

    OLD DOCTOR VALENTINE TO HIS SON/LIVE/DIE   5

    OLD DOCTOR VALENTINE TO THAT KIND OF PATIENT/TELEPHONE   5

    ROLL OVER AND PLAY ALIVE, WHO SAYS YOU CAN'T TEACH AN OLD DOG TIRESOME TRICKS/KIPLING/JOKE   5

    ALL, ALL ARE GONE, THE OLD FAMILIAR QUOTATIONS   Z5

    SONG TO BE SUNG BY THE FATHER OF SIX-MONTHS-OLD FEMALE CHILDREN/BOYS/MARRIAGE   FG

    REMEMBER THE OLD FOLKS AT HOME/GIFTS/HOLIDAYS   C8

    THE WRONGS OF SPRING OR, NO ALL FOOLS' DAY LIKE AN ALL OLD FOOLS' DAY/BIRTHDAY   A

    OLD IS FOR BOOKS/AGING   Z6

    WHAT'LL WE DO NOW, OR, I'M AFRAID I KNOW, OR GOOD OLD JUST PLAIN CHARADES, FAREWELL/GAMES   2

    PORTRAIT OF THE ARTIST AS A PREMATURELY OLD MAN/SIN   DYZ8

    OLD MEN/DEATH   EYZ8j

    ANY FULL NAME IS A GRAND OLD NAME/NICKNAMES   A

    YOU'RE ONLY OLD ONCE/BABY-SITTING   6

    HAND ME DOWN MY OLD SCHOOL SLIDING PADS OR THERE'S HINT OF STRAWBERRY LEAVES IN THE AIR   5

    SUCH AN OLD THEME, BUT SUCH FRESH DISTRESS/CULTURE   C

    GOODBYE, OLD YEAR, YOU OAF, OR WHY DON'T THEY PAY THE BONUS?/NEW YEAR'S EVE   DYZ8

    A MAN CAN COMPLAIN, CAN'T HE? (A LAMENT FOR THOSE WHO THINK OLD)   AW

    YOU ARE OLD, FATHER BERTRAND/TRIALS/RUSSELL   A

    RING OUT THE OLD, RING IN THE NEW, BUT DON'T GET CAUGHT IN BETWEEN; FIRST CHIME; SECOND CHIME   Z6

OLIPHANT

    THE STRANGE CASE OF THE BAFFLED HERMIT/OLIPHANT   D1

OLYMPIANS

    EPISTLE TO THE OLYMPIANS/PARENTS/CHILD/SIZE   G89

ONATIVIA

    THE UNIQUENESS OF MR. ONATIVIA/TRIVIA   A

ONCE

    YOU'RE ONLY OLD ONCE/BABY-SITTING   6

    THE SNAKE, WITHOUT WHOM ADAM WOULD NEVER HAVE LOOKED AT THE LADY ONCE/KISSED   5

    OLD DOCTOR VALENTINE FOR ONCE DREAMS OF WEALTH/BRA/PEPS-OO-LA-LA/BOUNCE   5

    ONCE MORE, TO MY VALENTINE/LOVE   B

    THERE ONCE WAS AN UMPIRE WHOSE VISION   A

    ALIAS AND MELISANDE OR, GAMMON ME ONCE, GAMMON ME TWICE,/PUBLISHING   7

    TWO GOES INTO TWO ONCE, IF YOU CAN GET IT THERE/SQUARE PEG/ROUND HOLE   5

ONE

    WE WOULD REFER YOU TO OUR SERVICE DEPARTMENT, IF WE HAD ONE/APPLIANCES   Z3

    ONE MAN'S OPIATE/SATRE/ENNUI   ?

    THE ONE-L LAMA   k

    I CAN'T HAVE A MARTINI, DEAR, BUT YOU TAKE ONE/DIETING   WZ6

    SONG FOR A TEMPERATURE OF A HUNDRED AND ONE/GRIPPE/INFLUENZA   FWYZ89

    LIMERICK ONE/JERVIS/NERVIS/BRIDE/TOMB   5

    LET ME BUY THIS ONE/RICH/MONEY   4

    TWO AND ONE ARE A PROBLEM/BIRDS   YZ18

    THE SHORT ORDER COCKTAIL OR, ONE COOK TO TAKE OUT/DOMESTIC SERVANT   A

    ONE FROM ONE LEAVES TWO/FARMING/SUBSIDIES   D1

    ONE GOOD HOARDER DESERVES ANOTHER/TIRES   2

    ONE TIMES ONE IS EIGHT/GRANDFATHER'S JOURNAL   A

    ONE MAN'S MEED IS ANOTHER MAN'S OVEREMPHASIS/COLLEGE FOOTBALL   Z4

ONE
    JUST ONE MORE PLEA TO THE SULTAN OF THE METROPULTAN/BALLET/METROPOLITAN   C
    ONE NIGHT IN OZ/DINNER PARTY/ENEMIES   YZ2
    ME, I PLAY THE HARP, IT'S JUST ONE SYLLABLE/PRONUNCIATION/PIANIST   6
    ONE THIRD OF A CALENDAR/WINTER/ILLNESS/CHILDREN   WYZ189
    ONE TIMES ONE IS EIGHT/GRANDFATHER'S JOURNAL   A
    I'LL GET ONE TOMORROW/BARBER/HAIRCUT   Y49
    ONE WESTERN, TO GO/BLANCH/RANCH   A
    IMPRESSIONS OF SUBURBIA BY ONE WHO HAS NEVER BEEN THERE OR, ALL I KNOW IS WHAT I SEE IN ADS   7
    WHAT'S HECUBA TO HIM? A ONE-MINUTE CLOSE UP/TV REPORTING DISASTERS   8
    ONE, TWO, BUCKLE MY SHOE/BIRTHDAY/DAUGHTER   DG89ℓ

ONES
    THE UNWINGED ONES/TRAINS/PLANES   Z5

ONLY
    UNFORTUNATELY, IT'S THE ONLY GAME IN TOWN/ODDS   7
    THE ONLY GOOD INDIAN IS A DEAD PUBLIC RELATIONS COUNSELLOR/INTERVIEWS   D
    OLD DOCTOR VALENTINE TO HIS ONLY MILLIONAIRE/BILLS   5
    ODE TO C.B.E., PRACTICALLY THE ONLY NEW MALE CHILD I KNOW OF   G9
    SO DOES EVERYBODY ELSE, ONLY NOT SO MUCH/ANECDOTES/REPEATING   Z2
    YOU'RE ONLY OLD ONCE/BABY-SITTING   6

OO
    OLD DOCTOR VALENTINE FOR ONCE DREAMS OF WEALTH/BRA/PEPS-OO-LA-LA/BOUNCE   5

OOP
    PEACOCK ALLEY-OOP/WALDORF ASTORIA HOTEL   C

OPEN
    SONG OF THE OPEN ROAD/BILLBOARDS/TREE   FYZ189n

OPERA
    ROLL ON, THOU DEEP AND DARK BLUE SYLLABLES, ROLL ON/METROPOLITAN OPERA/MILTON CROSS   A

OPIATE
    ONE MAN'S OPIATE/SATRE/ENNUI   ?

OPINIONS
    THE PULPITEERS HAVE HAIRY EARS/CLERICS/OPINIONS   E

OPSIMATHY
    AS I WAS SAYING TO SAINT PAUL JUST THE OTHER DAY/OPSIMATHY/LIFE   7

OPTIMISM
    THE OUTCOME OF MR. MACLEOD'S GRATITUDE/OPTIMISM   3

ORANGE
    YOU'LL DRINK YOUR ORANGE JUICE AND LIKE IT, COMRADE/CYPRUS/SOVIET UNION   7

ORATORS
    A MINT OF PHRASES OR, A TEAM IS AS STRONG AS ITS BENCH/ORATORS/ELOQUENCE   7

ORDER
    THE SHORT ORDER COCKTAIL OR, ONE COOK TO TAKE OUT/DOMESTIC SERVANT   A
    SIC SEMPER MR. SHERMAN'S TEMPER OR KINDLY PLACE YOUR ORDER IN ENGLISH/COCKTAILS   6

ORGAN-GRINDER
    THE ORGAN-GRINDER/HURDY-GURDY/WALTZ   r

ORGIES
    DREAM OF INNOCENT ORGIES/STAGE-DOOR-JOHNNY   J
    HOME, 99 44/100 PERCENT SWEET HOME/ORGIES   D

ORIENT
    SO I RESIGNED FROM THE CHUN CHIN CHOWDER AND MARCHING CLUB/ORIENT   Z6

ORIGINAL
    HA! ORIGINAL SIN/VANITY   CYZ8

ORMANTUDE
    THE STRANGE CASE OF MR. ORMANTUDE'S BRIDE/MARRIAGE/UNDERSTANDING   BYZ29

ORNITHOLOGY
    FLOW GENTLY, SWEET ETYMOLOGY, ORNITHOLOGY, AND PENOLOGY/NIGHTINGALE/PERSION/BULBUL   5

OSSIPEE
    REFLECTION ON THE VERNACULAR/RECEIPTS/RECIPES/LAKE OSSIPEE   Z5

OSTEOPATHIC
    LINES TO BE HUMMED FROM A SUPINE POSITION TO THE HUMMER'S OSTEOPATHIC PHYSICIAN/NECK   2

OSTRICH
    THE OSTRICH   Z6

OTHER
    SONG FOR PIER SOMETHING OR OTHER/SHIPS   7
    AS I WAS SAYING TO SAINT PAUL JUST THE OTHER DAY/OPSIMATHY/LIFE   7
    BOTANIST, AROINT THEE! OR, HENBANE BY ANY OTHER NAME   BZ4

OTHERS
    OTHERS IN THE CAST INCLUDE/ACTORS   3

OTTO
    WITHOUT ALL DUE RESPECT/OTTO KAHN/PUBLICITY   C

OUGHT
    IT OUGHT TO BE HISTORY, OR DON'T SAY IT ISN'T SO/DEBUNKING   D

OUGHTERIES
    HOW TO GET ALONG WITH YOURSELF OR I RECOMMEND SOFTENING OF THE OUGHTERIES/FAULTS/TOLERANCE   Z5
OUPHE
    THE MYSTERIOUS OUPHE/TWINS/LEPRECHAUN/MISCHIEF   t
OUR
    OUR CHILD DOESN'T KNOW ANYTHING OR THANK GOD!   DGZ8
    OUR CHILD DOESN'T KNOW ANYTHING OR THANK HEAVEN   9
    OUR CITY, OUR CITIZENS/VILLAGE/GOLD COAST/PRESS CAFE/THEATER   7
    NO WONDER OUR FATHERS DIED/HOUSES/PLUMBING/FURNACES   YZ4
    RAPUNZEL, RAPUNZEL, LET'S LET DOWN OUR HAIR/WITS   Z6
    REFLECTION ON THE PHYSICAL TASTES OF OUR INTELLECTUAL BETTERS/UNIVERSITIES   C
    OUR NUMBER'S IN THE BOOK/TELEPHONE SOLICITATION   D
    WE WOULD REFER YOU TO OUR SERVICE DEPARTMENT, IF WE HAD ONE/APPLIANCES   Z3
    GOODY FOR OUR SIDE AND YOUR SIDE TOO/FOREIGNERS/NATIVES   DZ18
OURS
    HOW TO TELL A KITCHEN FROM A CUISINE: TAKE A QUICK LOOK AT OURS/COOKBOOKS   6
    WE HAVE MET THE SASSENACHS AND THEY ARE OURS; EVEN THE YEAR IS NOW MCMLXIV/MCLUHAN/MCKUEN   P
OUT
    OUT IS OUT/EATING OUTSIDE   Z149
    THE SHORT ORDER COCKTAIL OR, ONE COOK TO TAKE OUT/DOMESTIC SERVANT   A
    THE EVENING OUT/WOMEN/LATE   YZ4
    I'LL STAY OUT OF YOUR DIET IF YOU'LL STAY OUT OF MINE   2
    RING OUT THE OLD, RING IN THE NEW, BUT DON'T GET CAUGHT IN BETWEEN; FIRST CHIME: SECOND CHIME   Z6
    GOLLY, HOW THE TRUTH WILL OUT!/LIAR   Z18
    I KNOW YOU'LL LIKE THEM/OUT-OF-TOWN GUESTS/FRIENDS   YZ18
OUTCOME
    THE OUTCOME OF MR. BUCK'S SUPERSTITION/LUCK   Z3
    THE OUTCOME OF MR. MACLEOD'S GRATITUDE/OPTIMISM   3
OUTER
    A LAMA OF OUTER MONGOLIA   A
OUTLINE
    A SHORT OUTLINE OF THANKSGIVING   D
OUTSIDE
    ADVICE OUTSIDE A CHURCH/BACHELORHOOD/MARRIAGE   GZ8
    WHAT'S IT LIKE OUTSIDE? OR IT'S ALWAYS FAIR WEATHER UNLESS SOMEBODY SAYS IT ISN'T   O
    OUT IS OUT/EATING OUTSIDE   Z149
OVEN
    THE QUACK FROWN SOX LUMPS OVEN THE... OR, FAREWELL, PHI BETA KAFKA/SECRETARIES   A
OVER
    JUST SHUT YOUR EYES TILL IT'S OVER/CIRCUS   D
    WHEN THE MOON SHINES OVER AND OVER/RADIO   F
    ROLL OVER AND PLAY ALIVE, WHO SAYS YOU CAN'T TEACH AN OLD DOG TIRESOME TRICKS/KIPLING/JOKE   5
    WHO WANTS TO TRAVEL ALL OVER EUROPE AND SEE NOTHING BUT A LOT OF AMERICAN TOURISTS? I DO   6
    THUNDER OVER THE NURSERY/BABY/DADDY   GYZ89
    OH, STOP BEING THANKFUL ALL OVER THE PLACE/GRACE OF GOD   DYZ18
    I'LL GLADLY PULL OVER TO THE CURB/FIRES   3
    FIRST FAMILIES, MOVE OVER!/VIRGINIA/SOUTHERN   Z4
    ADMONITORY LINES FOR THE BIRTHDAY OF AN OVER-ENERGETIC CONTEMPORARY   A
    THE STRANGE CASE OF THE GIRL O' MR. SPONSOON'S DREAMS/RUN-OVER   Z4
OVERALLS
    I KNOW EXACTLY WHO DROPPED THE OVERALLS IN MRS. MURPHY'S CHOWDER/BORES   Z6
OVERCOAT
    NEVER MIND THE OVERCOAT, BUTTON UP THAT LIP/GOSSIP   Z6
OVEREMPHASIS
    ONE MAN'S MEED IS ANOTHER MAN'S OVEREMPHASIS/COLLEGE FOOTBALL   Z4
OVERTAKER
    TWEEDLEDEE AND TWEEDLEDOOM/UNDERTAKER/OVERTAKER   Z5
OVINGTON
    LINES TO BE MUMBLED AT THE OVINGTON'S/MARRIAGE CEREMONY   EYZ18
OWE
    PHILOLOGY, ETYMOLOGY, YOU OWE ME AN APOLOGY/ENGLISH LANGUAGE   7
OWL
    THE INDIGNANT OWL/PUSSYCAT/LEAR   A
OWN
    ANYBODY FOR MONEY? OR JUST BRING YOUR OWN BASKET/BANKER   Z6
    WITH MY OWN EYES/LECTURERS/UNITED STATES   5
    DADDY, I WANT A PET FOR MY VERY OWN, I PROMISE TO TAKE CARE OF IT   9
    THIS IS MY OWN, MY NATIVE TONGUE/RADIO/ACCENTS   Z5
OYSTER
    STAG NIGHT, PALEOLITHIC/OYSTER/WOMAN   3
    THE OYSTER   CZ8

PERMISSIVE
   PERMISSIVE PICTURES PRESENTS 'HAPPY HALLOWEEN, EVERYBODY' AN ALFRED HITCHCOCK PRODUCTION   A
PERSION
   FLOW GENTLY, SWEET ETYMOLOGY, ORNITHOLOGY, AND PENOLOGY/NIGHTINGALE/PERSION/BULBUL   5
PERSONALITY
   M.C. LOVES TV OR A PERSONALITY IS BORN/HAM/EGO   5
PERVERSITY
   A NECESSARY DIRGE/PERVERSITY/HUMANITY   Z4
PESSIMISM
   I DON'T MEAN US, EXCEPT OCCASIONALLY/LIFE/PESSIMISM   Y2
PESSIMISTS
   NO WOE IS GOSSAMER TO MR. BESSEMER/PESSIMISTS   Z6
PET
   DADDY, I WANT A PET FOR MY VERY OWN, I PROMISE TO TAKE CARE OF IT   9
PETS
   ANIMAL GARDEN/ABIDON/PETS/CHILDREN   w
PHI
   THE QUACK FROWN SOX LUMPS OVEN THE... OR, FAREWELL, PHI BETA KAFKA/SECRETARIES   A
PHILLIPS
   THOUGHTS THOUGHT WHILE RESTING COMFORTABLY IN PHILLIPS HOUSE, MASSACHUSETTS GENERAL HOSPITAL A
PHILLY
   THEY DON'T READ DE QUINCEY IN PHILLY OR CINCY/MURDER   A
PHILOLOGY
   PHILOLOGY, ETYMOLOGY, YOU OWE ME AN APOLOGY/ENGLISH LANGUAGE   7
PHILOPROGENTIVE
   AH, WHO?/PHILOPROGENTIVE   E
PHILOSOPHY
   IT WAS NOT I WHO POSED FOR RODIN OR WHY I FLUNKED PHILOSOPHY IV/THINKING/FRENCH   5
PHLEGMATIC
   'MY CHILD IS PHLEGMATIC,,,' - ANXIOUS PARENT   CGYZ89
PHOENIX
   THE PHOENIX/BIRD/EUGENICS   CZ89
PHOOIE
   WEATHER CLEAR, TRACK FAST, HORSES PHOOIE!/BETTING   D
PHOTOGRAPHERS
   WAITING FOR THE BIRDIE/PHOTOGRAPHERS   Y4
PHRASES
   A MINT OF PHRASES OR, A TEAM IS AS STRONG AS ITS BENCH/ORATORS/ELOQUENCE   7
   REPRISE/LOVE/MEMORABLE PHRASES   3
PHYSICAL
   REFLECTION ON THE PHYSICAL TASTES OF OUR INTELLECTUAL BETTERS/UNIVERSITIES   C
PHYSICIAN
   LINES TO BE HUMMED FROM A SUPINE POSITION TO THE HUMMER'S OSTEOPATHIC PHYSICIAN/NECK   2
   COUSIN EUPHEMIA KNOWS BEST OR PHYSICIAN, HEAL SOMEBODY ELSE/CURES   WZ3
   MS. FOUND IN QUAGMINE/PHYSICIAN   YZ2
PIANIST
   ME, I PLAY THE HARP, IT'S JUST ONE SYLLABLE/PRONUNCIATION/PIANIST   6
PIANO
   PIANO TUNER, UNTUNE ME THAT TUNE/CHOPSTICKS   Z39e
PICCOLO
   WHO CALLED THAT ROBIN A PICCOLO PLAYER/BIRDS   Z3
   I DIDN'T SAY A WORD OR WHO CALLED THAT PICCOLO PLAYER A FATHER?/HEARING/VOICE/LOUDNESS   Z5
PICKWICK
   YOU'VE GOT TO BE MR. PICKWICK IF YOU WANT TO ENJOY A PICNIC/PAPER   7
PICNIC
   YOU'VE GOT TO BE MR. PICKWICK IF YOU WANT TO ENJOY A PICNIC/PAPER   7
PICTURES
   THE CRUISE OF THE AARDVARK/ADVENTURES/PAINTING PICTURES   q
   PERMISSIVE PICTURES PRESENTS 'HAPPY HALLOWEEN, EVERYBODY' AN ALFRED HITCHCOCK PRODUCTION   A
PIDDLE
   PARADISE FOR SALE/FARMHOUSE/RIVER PIDDLE   7
PIECE
   JUST A PIECE OF LETTUCE AND SOME LEMON JUICE, THANK YOU/DIETS   FY
PIED
   WHO CALLED THAT PIED-BILLED GREBE A PODILYMBUS PODICEPS PODICEPS?/BIRD   A
PIER
   SONG FOR PIER SOMETHING OR OTHER/SHIPS   BZ4
PIG
   THERE ARE MORE WAYS TO ROAST A PIG THAN BURNING THE HOUSE DOWN/CIGARETTE LIGHTERS   Z3
   THE PIG   FGZ89

92

PIGEON
    ARCHER, ARCH ME YON CARRIER PIGEON/COMMUNICATION   D
    BARNYARD COGITATIONS/DUCK/CHICKEN/LAMB/TURKEY/PIGEON   G
PIGMY
    THE PIGMY   F
PILGRIM
    PILGRIM'S PROGRESS/THANKSGIVING/MAYFLOWER/DESCENDANTS   D
PILGRIMS
    THE PILGRIMS ATE QUAHAUGS AND CORN YET   A
    THE ENTRAPMENT OF JOHN ALDEN/PILGRIMS   A
PILLOWS
    ANY MILLENNIUMS TODAY, LADY?/PILLOWS   Z3
PINNED
    POEMS TO BE PINNED TO THE CALENDAR   D
PIONEER
    THE PIONEER/ARTICHOKE   A
PIPE
    PIPE DREAMS/PLUMBER/SUMMER COTTAGE   Z4
PITCHERS
    MEL ALLEN, MEL ALLEN, LEND ME YOUR CLICHE/BASEBALL/PITCHERS/MACTIVITY   6
PIZZA
    TABLE TALK; YORKSHIRE PUDDING; THE SWEETBREAD; THE PIZZA; THE SHAD   Z67
PLACE
    OH, STOP BEING THANKFUL ALL OVER THE PLACE/GRACE OF GOD   DYZ18
    I ALWAYS SAY THERE'S NO PLACE LIKE NEW YORK IN THE SUMMER/COTTAGES   Z6
    SIC SEMPER MR. SHERMAN'S TEMPER OR KINDLY PLACE YOUR ORDER IN ENGLISH/COCKTAILS   6
PLAIN
    WHAT'LL WE DO NOW, OR, I'M AFRAID I KNOW OR, GOOD OLD JUST PLAIN CHARADES, FAREWELL/GAMES   2
PLAN
    DO YOU PLAN TO SPEAK BANTU? OR ABGREVIATION IS THE THIEF OF SANITY   Z6
PLANES
    THE UNWINGED ONES/TRAINS/PLANES   Z5
PLANS
    INVOCATION (SMOOT PLANS TARIFF BAN ON IMPROPER BOOKS-NEWS ITEM)/PORNOGRAPHY   EYZ18
PLATE
    WHICH CAME FIRST, OBEISANCE OR OBESITY/PLATE-WATCHERS/WEIGHT-WATCHERS   7
PLATITUDES
    ARTHUR BRISBANE/WRITERS/PLATITUDES   E
PLATITUDINOUS
    PLATITUDINOUS REFLECTION/ILLNESS/INFIRMITY   EWYZ8
PLATONIC
    REFLECTION ON RELATIONSHIPS/PLATONIC   C
PLATT
    WHO'S GOING MR. PLATT'S WAY?/NEIGHBORS/CAR-SHARING   2
PLATTER
    THE CLEAN PLATTER/FOOD   DZ8
PLATYPUS
    THE PLATYPUS   Z5
PLAY
    ROLL OVER AND PLAY ALIVE, WHO SAYS YOU CAN'T TEACH AN OLD DOG TIRESOME TRICKS/KIPLING/JOKE   5
    LET'S NOT PLAY LOTTO, LET'S JUST TALK/CONVERSATION   Z5
    ME, I PLAY THE HARP, IT'S JUST ONE SYLLABLE/PRONUNCIATION/PIANIST   6
PLAYER
    WHO CALLED THAT ROBIN A PICCOLO PLAYER/BIRDS   Z3
    I DIDN'T SAY A WORD OR WHO CALLED THAT PICCOLO PLAYER A FATHER?/HEARING/VOICE/LOUDNESS   Z5
PLEA
    A PLEA FOR A LEAGUE OF SLEEP   Z49
    A PLEA FOR LESS MALICE TOWARD NONE/LOVE/HATE   FY8
    JUST ONE MORE PLEA TO THE SULTAN OF THE METROPULTAN/BALLET/METROPOLITAN   C
PLEASANT
    HOW PLEASANT TO APE MR. LEAR/LIMRICKS   A
PLEASE
    I'LL TAKE A BROMIDE, PLEASE/BEAUTY/TRUTH   D
    CAN I GET YOU A GLASS OF WATER? OR PLEASE CLOSE THE GLOTTIS AFTER YOU/COUGHING   Z6
    OH, PLEASE DON'T GET UP!/ETIQUETTE/WOMEN   Z4
    PLEASE KEEP ON FORWARDING/POSTAGE-DUE   Z2
    PLEASE LEAVE FATHER ALONE/FATHER'S DAY/MOTHER'S DAY   DGZ8
    PLEASE PASS THE BISCUIT/DOG/SPANGLE   YZ29
    PLEASE REMIND ME BEFORE I FORGET/MEMORY   R
    PROGNOSTICATIONS ARE FOR THE BIRDS: LAY OFF ME, PLEASE, WHILE I EAT MY WORDS/FOOTBALL/COLTS   V
    IS TOMORROW REALLY ANOTHER DAY? OR NO MORE OF THE SAME, PLEASE   3

PRACTICALLY
        ODE TO C.B.E., PRACTICALLY THE ONLY NEW MALE CHILD I KNOW OF   G9
PRAISE
        LINES IN PRAISE OF A DATE MADE PRAISEWORTHY SOLELY BY SOMETHING VERY NICE THAT HAPPENED TO IT C
PRAISEWORTHY
        LINES IN PRAISE OF A DATE MADE PRAISEWORTHY SOLELY BY SOMETHING VERY NICE THAT HAPPENED TO IT C
PRAWN
        THE SNARK WAS A BOOJUM WAS A PRAWN/SANTIAGO   Z6
PRAYER
        MORNING PRAYER/SULKING/FIGHTING   r
        PRAYER AT THE END OF A ROPE/JAMS/DISASTER   YZ14
PRAYING
        THE PRAYING MANTIS   Z6
PREDICAMENT
        MR. PEACHEY'S PREDICAMENT OR NO MOT PARADES/SOCIAL LIFE/HARP/EPIGRAMS   YZ18
PREFACE
        PREFACE TO THE PAST/AGING/BACHELOR/GRANDPA/CHILDREN   Z6
PREMATURELY
        PORTRAIT OF AN ARTIST AS A PREMATURELY OLD MAN/SIN   DYZ8
PRESENTING
        PRESENTING DOCTOR FELL/DRIVERS   2
PRESENTS
        I'M A PLEASURE TO SHOP FOR/PRESENTS/CHRISTMAS   Z5
        PERMISSIVE PICTURES PRESENTS 'HAPPY HALLOWEEN, EVERYBODY' AN ALFRED HITCHCOCK PRODUCTION   A
PRESIDENT
        SUMMERGREEN FOR PRESIDENT/WINTER   Z4
        PARSLEY FOR VICE-PRESIDENT   Z4
PRESS
        OUR CITY, OUR CITIZENS/VILLAGE/GOLD COAST/PRESS CAFE/THEATER   7
        JUST PRESS THE BUTTON, THE BUTTON-HOLE IS REALLY A DEEPFREEZE/APPLIANCES   5
PRESSURE
        LOW-PRESSURE ARIA/RAIN/GOLF/TENNIS   DG89
PRETEND
        ALL GOOD AMERICANS GO TO LAROUSSE OR, I DON'T PRETEND TO BE MOLIERE THAN THOU/FRENCH   A
PRETTY
        PRETTY HALCYON DAYS/BEACH/OCEAN   DYZ8
        LITTLE PRETTY PENNY, LET'S SQUANDER THEE/MILLIONAIRES/WEALTH   A
PREVIOUS
        I AM FULL OF PREVIOUS EXPERIENCE/NEWSPAPERMEN   Z3
PRIDE
        PRIDE GOETH BEFORE A RAISE, OR AH, THERE, MRS. CADWALLADER-SMITH!/SOCIALITES/POISE   FZ8
PRIMATES
        MUSEUM OF NATURAL HISTORY: TYRANNOSAURUS REX; PYTHON; ROCK ROOM; WHALE; HALL OF PRIMATES   N
PRIMROSE
        THE MIND OF PROFESSOR PRIMROSE/ABSENTMINDED/HARVARD   YZ18
        THE STRANGE CASE OF PROFESSOR PRIMROSE/ABSENTMINDED/HARVARD   D
        THE PRIMROSE PATH   D
PRINCESS
        A PRINCESS WHO LIVED NEAR A BOG/FROG   A
PRIVACY
        I SPY OR THE DEPRAVITY OF PRIVACY/PUBLICITY   Z6
PRIVATE
        THE PRIVATE DINING ROOM/DATING/LAVENDAR/TAFFETA   Z5
PROBLEM
        TWO AND ONE ARE A PROBLEM/BIRDS   YZ18
PROCRASTINATION
        PROCRASTINATION IS ALL THE TIME/TORPOR/SLOTH   Z189
        LONG LIVE DELAYS OF ANCIENT ROME/PROCRASTINATION   D
PRODUCTION
        PERMISSIVE PICTURES PRESENTS 'HAPPY HALLOWEEN, EVERYBODY' AN ALFRED HITCHCOCK PRODUCTION   A
PROFANITY
        OH, SHUCKS, MA'AM, I MEAN EXCUSE ME/GIRLS/PROFANITY   Z3
PROFESSIONALS
        I YIELD TO MY LEARNED BROTHER/PROFESSIONALS/LAWYER/DOCTOR/MORTITIAN   DWZ18
PROFESSOR
        THE MIND OF PROFESSOR PRIMROSE/ABSENTMINDED/HARVARD   YZ18
        THE STRANGE CASE OF PROFESSOR PRIMROSE/ABSENTMINDED/HARVARD   D
PROFS
        CAESAR KNIFED AGAIN OR CULTURE BIZ GETS HEP, BOFFS PROFS/COLLEGE TEACHING   Z6

PURIST
    THE PURIST/SCIENTIST/ALLIGATOR   YZ49a
PURITY
    REFLECTION ON A WICKED WORLD/PURITY/OBSCURITY   YZ8
    REFLECTION ON VERACITY/PURITY/OBSCURITY   E
    SONGLAND REVISITED OR, THERE'S NO PURITY LIKE IMMATURITY/POPULAR SONGS/AGE/YOUTH   A
PURSUED
    EXIST, PURSUED BY A BEAR   Z6
PURVIS
    MRS. PURVIS DREADS ROOM SERVICE OR, MR. PURVIS DREADS IT, TOO/HOTEL   Z3
PUSHOVER
    PUSHOVER/BABY-TALK   6
PUSSYCAT
    THE INDIGNANT OWL/PUSSYCAT/LEAR   A
PUT
    PUT BACK THOSE WHISKERS, I KNOW YOU/NEW YEAR   Z2
    WHO PUT THAT SPOKESMAN IN MY WHEEL?/VAGUENESS/NEWS SOURCES   A
PUTS
    DON'T BITE THE HAND THAT PUTS ITS FOOT IN YOUR MOUTH/TAMMANY/OCTOPUS   7
PYGMY
    THE THIRD JUNGLE BOOK/PYGMY/POLYGAMY   Y2
PYTHON
    MUSEUM OF NATURAL HISTORY: TYRANNOSAURUS REX; PYTHON; ROCK ROOM; WHALE; HALL OF PRIMATES   N
QUACK
    THE QUACK FROWN SOX LUMPS OVEN THE... OR, FAREWELL, PHI BETA KAFKA/SECRETARIES   A
QUAGMINE
    MS. FOUND IN QUAGMINE/PHYSICIAN   YZ2
QUAHAUGS
    THE PILGRIMS ATE QUAHAUGS AND CORN YET   A
QUAIL
    HOW TO TELL A QUAIL FROM A PARTRIDGE/BOB WHITE   D
QUARRELING
    BIRDIES, DON'T MAKE ME LAUGH/CHILDREN/QUARRELING   GYZ89
QUARRELS
    I NEVER EVEN SUGGESTED IT/QUARRELS/MARRIAGE   BYZ18
QUARRY
    DRUSILLA/QUARRY/SOIREE   Z8
QUARTET
    QUARTET FOR PROSPEROUS LOVE CHILDREN   F
QUEEN
    THE QUEEN IS IN THE PARLOR/GAMES/CHARADES   Z4
QUESTION
    I'M GLAD YOU ASKED THAT QUESTION, BECAUSE IT SHOWS YOU IN YOUR TRUE COLORS/REMEMBERING   7
QUESTIONS
    IF I HAD THE WINGS OF A HELICOPTER OR HALL'S MILLS THAT ENDS MILLS/QUESTIONS/ANSWERS   6
    ASK ME NO QUESTIONS/MOTHER/FATHER/WATCHES   D
QUICK
    HOW TO TELL A KITCHEN FROM A CUISINE: TAKE A QUICK LOOK AT OURS/COOKBOOKS   6
    QUICK, HAMMACHER, MY STOMACHER/GLUTTON   WZ3
QUICKER
    IT WOULD HAVE BEEN QUICKER TO WALK OR DON'T TELL ME WE'RE THERE ALREADY/TAXI/PAYING   Z6
QUICKLY
    FRIDAY COMES AROUND SO QUICKLY/FISH   4
QUIET
    ALL QUIET ALONG THE POTOMAC EXCEPT THE LETTER G/WASHINGTON/KISSINGER/KIPLINGER   7
    JUST KEEP QUIET AND NOBODY WILL NOTICE/APOLOGIES   Z4
QUIETLY
    HERE WE GO QUIETLY NUTS IN MAY   Z2
QUINCEY
    THEY DON'T READ DE QUINCEY IN PHILLY OR CINCY/MURDER   A
QUIRKS
    REFLECTION ON THE PASSAGE OF TIME, ITS INEVITABILITY AND ITS QUIRKS   CYZ18
QUITE
    LINES TO BE MUTTERED THROUGH CLENCHED TEETH AND QUITE A LOT OF LATHER IN THE COUNTRY   C8
    LINES TO BE EMBROIDERED ON A BIB OR, THE CHILD IS FATHER OF THE MAN, BUT NOT FOR QUITE A
           WHILE   Z39
    AIRY, AIRY, QUITE CONTRARY/GRANDFATHER'S JOURNAL   A
    THE MAN IS FATHER OF THE CHILD OR, BUT HE NEVER QUITE GETS USED TO IT   9
    HOW LONG HAS THIS BEEN GOING ON? OH, QUITE LONG/BETTING/HORSE-RACING   Z18
    LITTLE MISS MUFFET SAT ON A PROPHET - AND QUITE RIGHT, TOO!/TROUBLE   Z4

REX
    MUSEUM OF NATURAL HISTORY: TYRANNOSAURUS REX; PYTHON; ROCK ROOM; WHALE; HALL OF PRIMATES   N
RHINOCEROS
    HOW THE RHINOCEROS GOT ITS HIDE OR THE CONFESSIONS OF COUNT MOWGLI DE SADE/CHILD/READING   3
    THE RHINOCEROS   FGYZ189a
RHODES
    THE HAPPY ENDING OF MR. TRAIN/MR. SLOAN/MR. RHODES   Z5
RHYMING
    A BRIEF GUIDE TO RHYMING OR, HOW BE THE LITTLE BUSY DOTH?/ENGLISH/PLURAL   Z6
RIBALD
    THE CLUB CAR/RIBALD/HIGHBALLED   Z5
RICH
    LET ME BUY THIS ONE/RICH/MONEY   4
    LINES INDITED WITH ALL THE DEPRAVITY OF POVERTY/RICH   EYZ8
RICHER
    BANKERS ARE JUST LIKE ANYBODY ELSE, EXCEPT RICHER/MONEY   Z4
RIDDANCE
    GOOD RIDDANCE, BUT NOW WHAT? NEW YEAR'S EVE   WZ39
RIDDLES
    UNANSWERED BY REQUEST/LIFE'S RIDDLES/HOME-COOKING   Z4
RIDE
    A RIDE ON THE BRONXIAL LOCAL/BRONCHITIS   14
RIDING
    TALLYHO-HUM/RIDING/HORSES   C
    NOW YOU SEE IT, NOW I DON'T/TRAINS/RIDING FOREWARD/BACKWARD   YZ2
    RIDING ON A RAILROAD TRAIN   YZ4
RIGHT
    DON'T CRY, DARLING, IT'S BLOOD ALL RIGHT/CHILDREN/BLOODTHIRSTY   DGZ89
    NEVER WAS I BORN TO SET THEM RIGHT/VEXATION   A
    OCEAN, KEEP RIGHT ON ROLLING/BEACH   D
    WHEN YOU SAY THAT, SMILE! OR ALL RIGHT THEN, DON'T SMILE/UPHILL FIGHTS   FYZ18
    LITTLE MISS MUFFET SAT ON A PROPHET - AND QUITE RIGHT, TOO!/TROUBLE   Z4
RING
    RING OUT THE OLD, RING IN THE NEW, BUT DON'T GET CAUGHT IN BETWEEN; FIRST CHIME; SECOND CHIME   Z6
    WHY THE POSTMAN HAS TO RING TWICE OR, YELLOW ENVELOPE, WHERE HAVE YOU GONE?/TELEGRAMS   Z5
RISING
    LIMERICK THREE/RISING SUN/DREAM   5
    NATURE KNOWS BEST/MORNING/RISING   Z4
RIVER
    PARADISE FOR SALE/FARMHOUSE/RIVER PIDDLE   7
ROACH
    THE ROACH   C
ROAD
    SONG OF THE OPEN ROAD/BILLBOARDS/TREE   FYZ189n
    I'LL TAKE THE HIGH ROAD COMMISSION/SIGNS   Z39
ROAST
    THERE ARE MORE WAYS TO ROAST A PIG THAN BURNING THE HOUSE DOWN/CIGARETTE LIGHTERS   Z3
ROBERT
    THE LOUSE/ROBERT BURNS   2
    EVERYTHING'S HAGGIS IN HOBOKEN OR, SCOTS WHA HAE HAE/ROBERT BURNS   Z5
ROBIN
    WHO CALLED THAT ROBIN A PICCOLO PLAYER/BIRDS   Z3
ROCK
    MUSEUM OF NATURAL HISTORY: TYRANNOSAURUS REX; PYTHON; ROCK ROOM; WHALE; HALL OF PRIMATES   n
RODENT
    A HANDSOME YOUNG RODENT NAMED GRATIAN   A
RODIN
    IT WAS NOT I WHO POSED FOR RODIN OR WHY I FLUNKED PHILOSOPHY IV/THINKING/FRENCH   5
ROLL
    ROLL ON, THOU DEEP AND DARK BLUE SYLLABLES, ROLL ON/METROPOLITAN OPERA/MILTON CROSS   A
    ROLL ON, THOU DEEP AND DARK BLUE COPY WRITER-ROLL/HEMINGWAY/MOVIES   Z3
    ROLL OVER AND PLAY ALIVE, WHO SAYS YOU CAN'T TEACH AN OLD DOG TIRESOME TRICKS/KIPLING/JOKE   5
ROLLING
    OCEAN, KEEP RIGHT ON ROLLING/BEACH   D
ROMAN
    DECLINE AND FALL OF A ROMAN UMPIRE/BASEBALL   7
    CALLING SPRING VII-MMMC/MYSTERIES/ROMAN-NUMERALS/PUBLISHERS   Z5
ROMANCE
    THAT REMINDS ME/LOVE/ROMANCE   BYZ18

SHAKE
      JOHN PEEL, SHAKE HANDS WITH 37 MAMAS; BISHOP DE WOLFE GREETS 37 DEBUTANTES ON LONG ISLAND   A
SHAKESPEARE
      THE TROUBLE WITH SHAKESPEARE YOU REMEMBER HIM/BOOKS/DESERT ISLAND/AGATHA CHRISTIE   6
SHALL
      WHO SHALL I SAY IS CALLING?/NAMES/PSEUDONYMS   2
      SHALL WE DANCE? BEING THE CONFESSIONS OF A BALLETRAMUS   7
SHAMBLES
      ELEGY IN A CITY SHAMBLES/BICARBONATE/SLEEP   D
SHARING
      WHO'S GOING MR. PLATT'S WAY?/NEIGHBORS/CAR-SHARING   2
SHARK
      THE SHARK   Z29
SHAVING
      AND THREE HUNDRED AND SIXTY-SIX IN LEAP YEAR/SHAVING/BÁTHING   Z2
SHE
      FOR ANY IMPROBABLE SHE/COURTSHIP   E
      FOR THE MOST IMPROBABLE SHE/COURTSHIP   Y18
      THAR SHE BLOWS/WIND/MARCH/TAXES   3
      DEAR GODMOTHER, I HOPE SHE BRUISES EASY!/FAIRY/APRIL FOOL   4
      A LADY THINKS SHE IS THIRTY/MIRANDA   BGYZ18
      I'M SURE SHE SAID SIX-THIRTY/WAITING/WIVES   BZ2
      THE NYMPH AND THE SHEPHERD OR SHE WENT THAT-AWAY/WIVES/WANDERING-OFF   BZ6
SHEEP
      WHAT, NO SHEEP?/SLEEP-INDUCERS   WZ6
SHELDRAKES
      NATURE-WALKS OR NOT TO MENTION A DOPPING OF SHELDRAKES   Z6
SHELF
      THE MAN ON THE SHELF/CHILDREN'S BOOKS/DESERT ISLAND   6
SHELLEY
      HARK, HARK, THE LARKS DO BARK/SHELLEY/HAMMERSTEIN   A
      YOU AND ME AND P.B. SHELLEY/LIFE/FRUSTRATION   Z2
SHEPHERD
      THE NYMPH AND THE SHEPHERD OR SHE WENT THAT-AWAY/WIVES/WANDERING-OFF   BZ6
SHERMAN
      SIC SEMPER MR. SHERMAN'S TEMPER OR KINDLY PLACE YOUR ORDER IN ENGLISH/COCKTAILS   6
SHINES
      WHEN THE MOON SHINES OVER AND OVER/RADIO   F
SHIPS
      A DAY ON A CRUISE OR, WHAT A DAY. WHAT A CRUISE./SHIPS   7
      SONG FOR PIER SOMETHING OR OTHER/SHIPS   BZ4
SHOE
      ONE, TWO, BUCKLE MY SHOE/BIRTHDAY/DAUGHTER   DG89ℓ
SHOEMAKER
      SHOO, SHOO, SHOEMAKER/HANNIBAL/CANNIBAL   5
SHOES
      TO A SMALL BOY STANDING ON MY SHOES WHILE I AM WEARING THEM   CGY9
SHOO
      SHOO, SHOO, SHOEMAKER/HANNIBAL/CANNIBAL   5
SHOOT
      DON'T SHOOT LOS ANGELES   2
SHOP
      I'M A PLEASURE TO SHOP FOR/PRESENTS/CHRISTMAS   Z5
SHOPPING
      THE MARKETEERS/GROCERY SHOPPING   D
      ALL'S NOEL THAT ENDS NOEL OR, INCOMPATIBILITY IS THE SPICE OF CHRISTMAS/SHOPPING   7
      JUST WRAP IT UP, AND I'LL THROW IT AWAY LATER/SHOPPING   BZ2
SHORT
      DON'T SELL AMERICA SHORT/STOCK MARKET   F
      THE SHORT ORDER COCKTAIL OR, ONE COOK TO TAKE OUT/DOMESTIC SERVANT   A
      A SHORT OUTLINE OF THANKSGIVING   D
      SHORT SHORT STORY/LIONS/LIBRARY   E
SHORTCHANGED
      THE ARMCHAIR GOLFER OR, WHIMPERS OF A SHORTCHANGED VIEWER/TV   A
SHOTPUTTING
      AND DON'T FORGET WEIGHT-LIFTING, SHOTPUTTING, AND THE LADIES' JUNIOR BACKSTROKE CHAMPIONSHIP   7
SHOULD
      OAFISHNESS SELLS GOOD, LIKE AN ADVERTISEMENT SHOULD/GRAMMAR/ENGLISH   Z6
      IF ANYTHING SHOULD ARISE, IT ISN'T I/INFLUENZA   B3

SNAKE
        THE SNAKE, WITHOUT WHOM ADAM WOULD NEVER HAVE LOOKED AT THE LADY ONCE/KISSED   5
SNARK
        THE SNARK WAS A BOOJUM WAS A PRAWN/SANTIAGO   Z6
SNIFFLE
        THE SNIFFLE/COLD   WYZ29
SNOB
        SING A SONG OF TASTE BUDS/WINE SNOB/GIN SNOB   7
        WILL CONSIDER SITUATION/JOBS/SNOB   Z18
SNODGRASS
        ARE YOU A SNODGRASS?/SWOOZLER/CREAM/SUGAR   DYZ8
SNORING
        ARTHUR/CALCUTTA/SNORING   WZ18a
        THE STILLY NIGHT: A SOPORIFIC REFLECTION/MARRIAGE/INSOMNIA/SNORING   AW
SNOW
        WINTER MORNING/SNOW   r
        IT LOOKS LIKE SNOW OR MY LIFE IN GALOSHES   3
        JANGLE BELLS/SNOW   Z4
SNOWMAN
        THE ABOMINABLE SNOWMAN   Z6
SNUG
        IT'S SNUG TO BE SMUG/COURAGE/INNOCENT   Z4
SO
        DOCTOR FELL? I THOUGHT SO/ANECDOTES   Z2
        IT OUGHT TO BE HISTORY, OR DON'T SAY IT ISN'T SO/DEBUNKING   D
        BRIEF LIVES IN NOT SO BRIEF/GOSSIP/BIOGRAPHY/JOHN AUBREY   7
        SO DOES EVERYBODY ELSE, ONLY NOT SO MUCH/ANECDOTES/REPEATING   Z2
        SO I RESIGNED FROM THE CHU CHIN CHOWDER AND MARCHING CLUB/ORIENT   Z6
        I HAD NO IDEA IT WAS SO LATE/WATCHES/WOMEN/MEN   YZ18
        AND SO MANHATTAN BECAME AN ISLE OF JOY/INDIANS   A
        PAJAMAS, HUH? OR DRESSES WERE SO NICE/PANTS   C
        WHO SAYS IT'S SO NICE TO HAVE A MAN AROUND THE HOUSE?/HUSBANDS   A
        SO PENSEROSO/MELANCHOLY/MOPE   WYZ49
        FRIDAY COMES AROUND SO QUICKLY/FISH   4
        SO THAT'S WHO I REMIND ME OF/RESEMBLANCE TO THE TALENTED   Z2
        SO THIS IS WASHINGTON OR DEAD MEN RESENT NO TALES/PROHIBITION   D
        THE GREEKS HAD A WORD FOR IT, SO WHY SPEAK ENGLISH/DIALECTS/SOUTHERN/BROOKLYNESE   6
        THE CALENDAR-WATCHERS OR WHAT'S SO WONDERFUL ABOUT BEING A PATRIARCH?/AGE   Z5
SOBS
        AT LEAST I'M NOT THE KIND OF FOOL WHO SOBS; WHAT KIND OF FOOL AM I?   X
SOCIAL
        MR. PEACHEY'S PREDICAMENT OR NO MOT PARADES/SOCIAL LIFE/HARP/EPIGRAMS   YZ18
        I'LL WRITE THEIR NUMBER DOWN WHEN WE GET HOME/WORDS/SOCIAL-LIFE   Z2
SOCIALITES
        PRIDE GOETH BEFORE A RAISE, OR AH, THERE, MRS. CADWALLADER-SMITH!/SOCIALITES/POISE   FZ8
SOCIETY
        A PARABLE FOR SPORTS WRITERS, SOCIETY COLUMNISTS, BOND SALESMEN AND POETS/PUBLISHING BOOKS   FZ8
        THE STRANGE CASE OF THE SOCIETY GIRL'S NECK/TANTRUMS   D
SOCK
        NO BUSKIN, ALL SOCK, MAKES LAUGHINGSTOCK/MOUSETRAP/MEAT-GRINDER/HUSBAND   A
SOCKS
        SHRINKING SONG/WOOLEN SOCKS   YZ149
SOFTENING
        HOW TO GET ALONG WITH YOURSELF OR I RECOMMEND SOFTENING OF THE OUGHTERIES/FAULTS/TOLERANCE   Z5
SOIREE
        DRUSILLA/QUARRY/SOIREE   Z8
SOLELY
        LINES IN PRIASE OF A DATE MADE PRAISEWORTHY SOLELY BE SOMETHING VERY NICE THAT HAPPENED TO IT C
SOLICITATION
        OUR NUMBER'S IN THE BOOK/TELEPHONE SOLICITATION   D
SOLILOQUY
        SOLILOQUY IN CIRCLES/FATHERS/CHILDREN   Z39
SOLITAIRE
        TO A LADY PASSING TIME BETTER LEFT UNPASSED/CARDS/SOLITAIRE   BZ4
SOLITARY
        THE SOLITARY HUNTSMAN/FOX   A
SOLITUDE
        THE SOLITUDE OF MR. POWERS/FLOWERS/ARRANGING   BZ6
SOLON
        I SUPPOSE THE GREEKS HAD A COMMERCIAL FOR IT OR, HAIL, SOLON. HOW'S THY COLON/TV   7

SOME
JUST A PIECE OF LETTUCE AND SOME LEMON JUICE, THANK YOU/DIETS   FY
WHAT'S IN A NAME? SOME LETTER I ALWAYS FORGET/SPELLING   Z5
SOME OF MY BEST FRIENDS ARE CHILDREN   FGYZ89
SOMEBODY
COUSIN EUPHEMIA KNOWS BEST OR PHYSICIAN, HEAL SOMEBODY ELSE/CURES   WZ3
LINES TO BE SCRIBBLED ON SOMEBODY ELSE'S THIRTIETH MILESTONE/BIRTHDAY   Z4
WHAT'S IT LIKE OUTSIDE? OR ITS ALWAYS FAIR WEATHER UNLESS SOMEBODY SAYS IT ISN'T   O
SOMEONE
DID SOMEONE SAY 'BABIES'?   CG19
SOMETHING
DON'T LOOK NOW, BUT THERE'S SOMETHING BEHIND THE CURTAIN/ADVENTURE/GREENHORNS/AGING   7
A DRINK WITH SOMETHING IN IT/COCKTAILS   DYZ8
SONG FOR PIER SOMETHING OR OTHER/SHIPS   BZ4
FRANCO-SOMETHING REFLECTION/FRENCH   F
LINES IN PRAISE OF A DATE MADE PRAISEWORTHY SOLELY BY SOMETHING VERY NICE THAT HAPPENED TO IT C
SON
OLD DOCTOR VALENTINE TO HIS SON/LIVE/DIE   5
CHACUN A' SON BERLITZ/FRENCH   Z6
SONG
FRENCH SONG/FRERE JACQUES/DANCE   r
SPRING SONG/MARCH   Z14
SHRINKING SONG/WOOLEN SOCKS   YZ149
SONG BEFORE BREAKFAST/CHARACTER   Z4
SONG FOR A TEMPERATURE OF A HUNDRED AND ONE/GRIPPE/INFLUENZA   FWYZ89
SONG FOR DITHERERS   WZ4
SONG FOR PIER SOMETHING OR OTHER/SHIPS   BZ4
SONG FOR THE SADDEST IDES/INCOME TAX   D1
THE SONG OF SONGS/WEALTH/DISTRIBUTION   4
SING A SONG OF TASTE BUDS/WINE SNOB/GIN SNOB   7n
NEAPOLITAN SONG/SEA   r
SONG OF THE OPEN ROAD/BILLBOARDS/TREE   FYZ189
SONG TO BE SUNG BY THE FATHER OF SIX-MONTHS-OLD FEMALE CHILDREN/BOYS/MARRIAGE   FG
SONG TO BE SUNG BY THE FATHER OF INFANT FEMALE CHILDREN/BOYS/MARRIAGE   YZ189
GERMAN SONG/GRIMM/MARCH   r
SONGLAND
SONGLAND REVISITED OR, THERE'S NO PURITY LIKE IMMATURITY/POPULAR SONGS/AGE/YOUTH   A
SONGS
SONGLAND REVISITED OR, THERE'S NO PURITY LIKE IMMATURITY/POPULAR SONGS/AGE/YOUTH   A
THE SONG OF SONGS/WEALTH/DISTRIBUTION   4
SONGS FOR A BOSS NAMED MR. LINTHICUM   E
TWO SONGS FOR A BOSS NAMED MR. LONGWELL   Z8
SONGS OF EXPERIENCE   A
ALL'S BRILLIG IN TIN PAN ALLEY/POPULAR SONGS   Z6
CAPERCAILLIE, AVE ATQUE VAILLIE/BIRD SONGS   7
TIN PAN ALLEY; GOOD NIGHT, SWEET MIND/WINTER WONDERLAND/SONGS   6
VERY NICE, REMBRANDT, BUT HOW ABOUT A LITTLE MORE COLOR?/SONGS   A
SOONER
WHAT ALMOST EVERY WOMAN KNOWS SOONER OR LATER/HUSBANDS   BDYZ89
WHAT EVERY WOMAN KNOWS SOONER OR LATER/HUSBANDS   1
SOPORIFIC
THE STILLY NIGHT: A SOPORIFIC REFLECTION/MARRIAGE/INSOMNIA/SNORING   AW
SOPRANO
A THRIFTY SOPRANO OF HINGHAM   A
SORROWS
HELPFUL REFLECTION/SORROWS   E
SORRY
I'M TERRIBLY SORRY FOR YOU, BUT I CAN'T HELP LAUGHING/DISEASES   WZ4
MR. JUDD AND HIS SNAIL, A SORRY TALE/AMOEBA/RACING   A
SORT
HOW HIGH IS UP? A SORT OF CHANTEY/AIRPLANES/FLYING   5
SOURCES
WHO PUT THAT SPOKESMAN IN MY WHEEL?/VAGUENESS/NEWS SOURCES   A
SOUTHERN
THE GREEKS HAD A WORD FOR IT, SO WHY SPEAK ENGLISH/DIALECTS/SOUTHERN/BROOKLYNESE   6
FIRST FAMILIES, MOVE OVER!/VIRGINIA/SOUTHERN   Z4
SOUVENIE
THE SOUVENIR HUNTERS   F
SOVIET
YOU'LL DRINK YOUR ORANGE JUICE AND LIKE IT, COMRADE/CYPRUS/SOVIET UNION   7
SOX
THE QUACK FROWN SOX LUMPS OVEN...OR, FAREWELL, PHI BETA KAFKA/SECRETARIES   A

SPAN
        CORRECTION: EVE DELVED AND ADAM SPAN/GARDEN CLUB/LADIES   Z5
SPANIARDS
        THESE LADIES/SPANIARDS/DUENNA   E
SPANGLE
        PLEASE PASS THE BISCUIT/DOG/SPANGLE   YZ29
SPARE
        BEWARE THE IDES OF MARCH, OR BROTHER, CAN YOU SPARE AN IDE?   D
        WOODMAN, SPARE NOT THAT UNDERBRUSH/WHISKERS   D8
        DETROIT, SPARE THAT WHEEL!/AUTOMOBILES/HORSEPOWER   6
        EPSTEIN, SPARE THAT YULE LOG!/CHRISTMAS CARDS   DZ89
SPEAK
        DO YOU PLAN TO SPEAK BANTU? OR ABBREVIATION IS THE THIEF OF SANITY   Z6
        THE GREEKS HAD A WORD FOR IT, SO WHY SPEAK ENGLISH/DIALECTS/SOUTHERN/BROOKLYNESE   6
        THEY DON'T SPEAK ENGLISH IN PARIS/GERTRUDE STEIN   D
SPEAKING
        FABLES BULFINCH FORGOT: NARCISSUS AND THE TREACHEROUS VOWEL/SPEAKING   A5
SPECIAL
        THE BANKER'S SPECIAL/COMMUTERS   3
SPECTATOR
        CONFESSIONS OF A BORN SPECTATOR/ATHLETES   4
SPECULATIVE
        SPECULATIVE REFLECTION/TAMMANY   E
SPELLING
        WHAT'S IN A NAME? SOME LETTER I ALWAYS FORGET/SPELLING   Z5
SPENDTHRIFT
        A PENNY SAVED IS IMPOSSIBLE/THRIFT/SPENDTHRIFT   2
SPHINX
        THE THIRTEENTH LABOR OF HERCULES/SPHINX   Z5
SPHINXES
        DO SPHINXES THINK?/FINGERNAILS/ELEVATORS   Z4
SPICE
        ALL'S NOEL THAT ENDS NOEL OR, INCOMPATIBILITY IS THE SPICE OF CHRISTMAS/SHOPPING   7
SPILLANE
        THE LITERARY SCENE/DE SADE/SPILLANE/SITWELL   Z6
SPINACH
        IT IS INDEED SPINACH/CHILD/GROWN-UP   4
SPINELESS
        YES AND NO/TOLERANCE/SPINELESS   Z14
SPINSTER
        THE SPINSTER DETECTIVE   3
SPIRIT
        THE COMIC SPIRIT NEVER SAY DIE, SAY KICK THE BUCKET   6
SPIRITUAL
        THE SEVEN SPIRITUAL AGES OF MRS. MARMADUKE MOORE/LIFETIME   FYZ8
SPLASH
        SPLASH!/BATHTUBS/SHOWERS   Z4
SPLINTERS
        SPLINTERS FROM THE FESTIVE BOARD   A
SPLIT
        I'LL EAT MY SPLIT-LEVEL TURKEY IN THE BREEZEWAY/CHRISTMAS/LARGE HOUSES   Z6
SPOKESMAN
        WHO PUT THAT SPOKESMAN IN MY WHEEL?/VAGUENESS/NEWS SOURCES   A
SPONSOON
        THE STRANGE CASE OF THE GIRL O' MR. SPONSOON'S DREAMS/RUN-OVER   Z4
SPONSOR
        STICKS AND STONES MAY BREAK THEIR BONES, BUT NAMES WILL LOSE A SPONSOR/BASEBALL   A
        NOTES FOR A DOCUMENTARY IN SEARCH OF A SPONSOR/TV   A
SPOON
        THE STRANGE CASE OF THE SILVER SPOON/DOCTORS   D
        THE SPOON RAN AWAY WITH THE DISH?/TV COMMERCIALS/DISHWASHING   7
SPORTS
        A PARABLE FOR SPORTS WRITERS, SOCIETY COLUMNISTS, BOND SALESMEN AND POETS/PUBLISHING BOOKS FZ8
        TURNS IN A WORM'S LANE/BETTING/SPORTS   FYZ18
SPOUSE
        HOW TO BE MARRIED WITHOUT A SPOUSE; KIPLING OR WHAT HAVE YOU DONE WITH MR. HAUKSBEE/INDIA   BZ4
SPRING
        THE HAT'S GOT MY TONGUE/SPRING/GIRL   Y2
        LIKE A RAT IN A TRAP/SPRING/SEASONS   2

SPRING
SPRING COMES TO BALTIMORE OR CHRISTMAS COMES MORE PROMPTLY 3
SPRING COMES TO MURRAY HILL/MANHATTAN EZ8
THE WRONGS OF SPRING OR, NO ALL FOOLS' DAY LIKE AN ALL OLD FOOLS' DAY/BIRTHDAY A
THE SPRING SITTING/SPRINGFEVER/LAZY D
SPRING SONG/MARCH Z14
CALLING SPRING VII-MMMC/MYSTERIES/ROMAN-NUMERALS/PUBLISHERS Z5
THE ETERNAL VERNAL OR IN ALL MY DREAMS MY FAIR FACE BEAMS/SPRING Z3
THE INDIVIDUALIST/JARVIS/GRAVEL/SPRING YZ8
THE PASSIONATE PAGAN AND THE DISPASSIONATE PUBLIC, A TRAGEDY OF THE MACHINE AGE/SPRING FYZ8
SPRINGFEVER
THE SPRING SITTING/SPRINGFEVER/LAZY D
SPY
I SPY/TV 3
I SPY OR THE DEPRAVITY OF PRIVACY/PUBLICITY Z6
SQUAB
THE SQUAB Z6
SQUANDER
LITTLE PRETTY PENNY, LET'S SQUANDER THEE/MILLIONAIRES/WEALTH A
SQUARE
TWO GOES INTO TWO ONCE, IF YOU CAN GET IT THERE/SQUARE PEG/ROUND HOLE 5
SQUID
THE SQUID Z6
SQUIRREL
THE SQUIRREL Z189
STAG
STAG NIGHT, PALEOLITHIC/OYSTER/WOMAN 3
STAGE
DREAM OF INNOCENT ORGIES/STAGE-DOOR-JOHNNY J
STAMP
STAMP TOO BIG FOR LETTER, MUST BE FOR ALBUM/POSTMASTER A
STAMPS
NO CONFORMITY TO ENORMITY, THE BIGGER THEY ARE THE HARDER I FALL/CARS/STAMPS/BANKS 7
A MODEST PROPOSAL TO ABOLISH THE SALIVA TEST/POSTMASTER/POSTAGE STAMPS A
HOW MANY MILES TO THE DEAD LETTER OFFICE/POSTAGE STAMPS A
STAND
ON GRATITUDE WE STAND PATITUDE/THANKSGIVING 2
STANDING
TO A SMALL BOY STANDING ON MY SHOES WHILE I AM WEARING THEM CGY9
STAR
KINDLY UNHITCH THAT STAR, BUDDY/SUCCESS/FAILURE DYZ18
STATES
WITH MY OWN EYES/LECTURES/UNITED STATES 5
STATIONS
AND THAT'S WHY I ALWAYS TAKE THE OAKLAND FERRY TO BEVERLY HILLS/TRAIN STATIONS 6
STAY
RAVEN, DON'T STAY AWAY FROM MY DOOR - A CHANT FOR APRIL FIRST FZ8
LET'S STAY HOME AND MAKE FRIENDS/THEATER C
I'LL STAY OUT OF YOUR DIET IF YOU'LL STAY OUT OF MINE 2
STAYING
HAVE YOU TRIED STAYING AWAKE? OR THEY'LL FIND A WAY TO STOP THAT, TOO/BED-BOARD WZ3
STEIN
THEY DON'T SPEAK ENGLISH IN PARIS/GERTRUDE STEIN D
STENGEL
AN ENTHUSIAST IS A DEVOTEE IS A ROOTER OR, MR HEMINGWAY, MEET MR. STENGEL Z6
STEPS
REFLECTION ON STEPS TO BE TAKEN/PARTHENOGENESIS C
STICKING
IS THIS SEAT TAKEN? YES OR, MY NECK IS STICKING IN/CONVERSATION Z3
STICKS
STICKS AND STONES MAY BREAK MY BONES, BUT NAMES WILL BREAK MY HEART/INDIVIDUAL DIGNITY 7
STICKS AND STONES MAY BREAK THEIR BONES, BUT NAMES WILL LOSE A SPONSOR/BASEBALL A
STILLY
THE STILLY NIGHT: A SOPORIFIC REFLECTION/MARRIAGE/INSOMNIA/SNORING AW
STITCH
A STITCH TOO LATE IS MY FATE/PROMPTNESS/REMEMBERING Z14
STOCK
DON'T SELL AMERICA SHORT/STOCK MARKET F
STOMACH
GO AHEAD, IT WILL DO YOU GOOD OR HER EYES ARE MUCH BIGGER THAN HIS STOMACH/WIFE/HUSBAND/EAT WZ6
THEIR STOMACH IS BIGGER THAN YOUR EYES/GRANDFATHER'S JOURNAL A

113

STOMACHER
        QUICK, HAMMACHER, MY STOMACHER/GLUTTON   WZ3
STONES
        STICKS AND STONES MAY BREAK MY BONES, BUT NAMES WILL BREAK MY HEART/INDIVIDUAL DIGNITY   7
        STICKS AND STONES MAY BREAK THEIR BONES, BUT NAMES WILL LOSE A SPONSOR/BASEBALL   A
STOP
        I CAN'T STOP UNLESS YOU STOP/TIPPING/POLITENESS   5
        OH, STOP BEING THANKFUL ALL OVER THE PLACE/GRACE OF GOD   DYZ18
        HAVE YOU TRIED STAYING AWAKE? OR THEY'LL FIND A WAY TO STOP THAT, TOO/BED-BOARD   WZ3
STORIES
        MR. BURGESS, MEET MR. BARMECIDE/NATURE STORIES/YOWLER THE BOBCAT   Z6
        DON'T GUESS, LET ME TELL YOU/DETECTIVE STORIES   YZ18
STORK
        THE STORK   FG
STORM
        THE DUST STORM OR I'VE GOT TEXAS IN MY LUNGS   5
STORY
        SHORT SHORT STORY/LIONS/LIBRARY   E
STRANGE
        THE STRANGE CASE OF CLASHING CULTURES/ANGLOPHILE/BUFFALO   7
        THE STRANGE CASE OF MR. BALLENTINE'S VALENTINE   Z4
        THE STRANGE CASE OF MR. DONNYBROOK'S BOREDOM   BWZ4
        THE STRANGE CASE OF MR. FORTAGUE'S DISAPPOINTMENT/INNISFREE   Z4
        THE STRANGE CASE OF MR. GOODBODY OR A TEAM THAT WON'T BE BEATEN, CAN'T BE BEATEN/CLICHES   D1
        THE STRANGE CASE OF MR. NIOBOB'S TRANSMOGRIFICATION/MOTORIST/FOURLANED-HIGHWAYS/TRUCKS   Z2
        THE STRANGE CASE OF MR. O'BANION'S COME-UPPANCE/CLINICAL/SKEPTIC   Z5
        THE STRANGE CASE OF MR. ORMANTUDE'S BRIDE/MARRIAGE/UNDERSTANDING   BYZ29
        THE STRANGE CASE OF MR. PALLISER'S PALATE/GOURMET COOKING   BZ3
        THE STRANGE CASE OF MR. PAUNCEFOOT'S BROAD MIND   Z2
        THE STRANGE CASE OF MR. WOOD'S FRUSTRATION/BEING FIRST   Z6
        THE STRANGE CASE OF MRS. MOODUS'S SECOND HONEYMOON/LYSISTRATAGEMS   A
        THE STRANGE CASE OF PROFESSOR PRIMROSE/ABSENTMINDED/HARVARD   D
        THE STRANGE CASE OF THE AMBITIOUS CADDY/GOLF   Z4
        THE STRANGE CASE OF THE BAFFLED HERMIT/OLIPHANT   D1
        THE STRANGE CASE OF THE BLACKMAILING DOVE/DAINGERFIELD   Z4
        THE STRANGE CASE OF THE BLIGHT THAT FAILED/GREAT-AUNT/WRATH   6
        THE STRANGE CASE OF THE CAUTIOUS MOTORIST/SCHWELLENBACH   Z5
        THE STRANGE CASE OF THE DEAD DIVORCEE/MINT JULEP   Z4
        THE STRANGE CASE OF THE ENTOMOLOGIST'S HEART/BUGS   Z3
        THE STRANGE CASE OF THE GIRL O' MR. SPONSOON'S DREAMS/RUN-OVER   Z4
        THE STRANGE CASE OF THE IRKSOME PRUDE/VIRTUES/VICES   Z14
        THE STRANGE CASE OF THE LOVELORN LETTER WRITER/MISS DIX/DALLIANCE/LOVE   Z5
        THE STRANGE CASE OF THE LUCRATIVE COMPROMISE   WZ6
        THE STRANGE CASE OF THE PLEASING TAXI-DRIVER   Z4
        THE STRANGE CASE OF THE RENEGADE LYRIC WRITER/SINGERS   Z3
        THE STRANGE CASE OF THE SILVER SPOON/DOCTORS   D
        THE STRANGE CASE OF THE SOCIETY GIRL'S NECK/TANTRUMS   D
        THE STRANGE CASE OF THE TSAR'S SUPERIORITY COMPLEX/BULGONIA   4
        THE STRANGE CASE OF THE WISE CHILD/PENDLETON BIRDSONG/FATHER   D1
        A STRANGE CASEMENT OF THE POETIC APOTHECARY/ADJECTIVES   7
STRANGERS
        FAMILY COURT/RELATIVES/FUN/STRANGERS   EGYZ89
STRAWBERRIES
        TASTE BUDS, EN GARDE/FROZEN STRAWBERRIES   A
STRAWBERRY
        HAND ME DOWN MY OLD SCHOOL SLIDING PADS OR THERE'S HINT OF STRAWBERRY LEAVES IN THE AIR   5
STRAWBRIDGE
        POOR MR. STRAWBRIDGE/DRAWBRIDGE   Z14
STREET
        WHAT STREET IS THIS, DRIVER?/SIXTH-AVENUE EL/NEW YORKER   2
STREETS
        HI-HO THE AMBULANCE-O/STREETS/WHEELS/FEET   Z5
STRIVE
        A THOUGHT ON THE MANNER OF THOSE WHO STRIVE TO ACHIEVE THE MANNER CALLED HEMINGWAY/WRITERS   C
STRONG
        A MINT OF PHRASES OR, A TEAM IS AS STRONG AS ITS BENCH/ORATORS/ELOQUENCE   7
STYLITES
        I ADMIRE SAINT SIMEON STYLITES   A
SUBLET
        APARTMENT TO SUBLET-UNFURNISHED/HOUSE/MURRAYS   BFG89
SUBSIDIES
        ONE FROM ONE LEAVES TWO/FARMING/SUBSIDIES   D1

THEE
    LITTLE PRETTY PENNY, LET'S SQUANDER THEE/MILLIONAIRES/WEALTH   A
    BOTANIST, AROINT THEE! OR, HENBANE BY ANY OTHER NAME   A
    PAPERBACK, WHO MADE THEE? DOST THOU KNOW WHO MADE THEE?/PAPYRUS-BACK   A
THEIR
    STICKS AND STONES MAY BREAK THEIR BONES, BUT NAMES WILL LOSE A SPONSOR/BASEBALL   A
    I'LL WRITE THEIR NUMBER DOWN WHEN WE GET HOME/WORDS/SOCIAL-LIFE   Z2
    THEIR STOMACH IS BIGGER THAN YOUR EYES/GRANDFATHER'S JOURNAL   A
THEM
    I KNOW YOU'LL LIKE THEM/OUT-OF-TOWN GUESTS/FRIENDS   YZ18
    NEVER WAS I BORN TO SET THEM RIGHT/VEXATION   A
    TO A SMALL BOY STANDING ON MY SHOES WHILE I AM WEARING THEM   CGY9
THEME
    SUCH AN OLD THEME, BUT SUCH FRESH DISTRESS/CULTURE   C
THEN
    TRY IT SUNS. AND HOLS. IT'S CLOSED THEN/RESTAURANT   Z6
    WHEN YOU SAY THAT, SMILE! OR ALL RIGHT THEN DON'T SMILE/UPHILL FIGHTS   FYZ18
THERE
    DOWN THE MOUSEHOLE, AND WHAT SCIENCE MISSED THERE/MARRIAGE/APOLOGY   WZ2
    TWO GOES INTO TWO ONCE, IF YOU CAN GET IT THERE/SQUARE PEG/ROUND HOLE   5
    IS THERE A DOCTOR JOHNSON IN THE HOUSE?/MEMORY   K
    IT WOULD HAVE BEEN QUICKER TO WALK OR DON'T TELL ME WE'RE THERE ALREADY/TAXI/PAYING   Z6
    IS THERE AN OCULIST IN THE HOUSE/WAR   7
    THERE ARE MORE WAYS TO ROAST A PIG THAN BURNING THE HOUSE DOWN/CIGARETTE LIGHTERS   Z3
    THERE IS NO DANGER LINE/SCIENTIST/EXPERIMENT   D
    THE EDUCATION OF ATHELNY JONES OR, ARE THERE MORE RADIOS IN HACKS THAN HACKS IN RADIO/FRENCH
        /TAXIS   6
    THERE ONCE WAS AN UMPIRE WHOSE VISION   A
    IMPRESSIONS OF SUBURBIA BY ONE WHO HAS NEVER BEEN THERE OR, ALL I KNOW IS WHAT I SEE IN ADS   7
    THERE WAS A YOUNG GIRL OF MILWAUKEE   A
    THERE WAS A YOUNG MAN FROM NEW HAVEN   A
    IF THERE WERE NO ENGLAND, 'COUNTRY LIFE' WOULD INVENT IT/HOUSES   A
    THERE WERE GIANTS IN THOSE DAYS OR MAYBE THERE WEREN'T/ANECDOTES   Z3
    PRIDE GOETH BEFORE A RAISE, OR AH, THERE, MRS. CADWALLADER-SMITH!/SOCIALITES/POISE   FZ8
    THERE'S A LAW, ISN'T THERE? OR I CAN CALL YOU NAMES BUT DON'T CALL ME NAMES/LIBEL   5
THERE'LL
    THERE'LL ALWAYS BE A WAR BETWEEN THE SEXES/HUSBANDS/WIVES   Z6
THERE'S
    THERE'S A LAW, ISN'T THERE? OR I CAN CALL YOU NAMES BUT DON'T CALL ME NAMES/LIBEL   5
    THERE'S A HOST BORN EVERY MINUTE/WEEKENDS/GUESTS   D1
    IN DULUTH THERE'S A HOSTESS, FORSOOTH   A
    THERE'S ALWAYS AN UBBLEBUB/MATCHMAKING/PARTIES   Z2
    HAND ME DOWN MY OLD SCHOOL SLIDING PADS OR THERE'S HINT OF STRAWBERRY LEAVES IN THE AIR   5
    THERE'S MORE TIME AT THE TOP, OR I WANT TO SEE MR. MURGATROYD/EXECUTIVES/ASSISTANTS   D
    I ALWAYS SAY THERE'S NO PLACE LIKE NEW YORK IN THE SUMMER/COTTAGES   Z6
    SONGLAND REVISITED OR, THERE'S NO PURITY LIKE IMMATURITY/POPULAR SONGS/AGE/YOUTH   A
    THERE'S NOTHING LIKE INSTINCT, FORTUNATELY/YOUTH   Z39
    DON'T LOOK NOW, BUT THERE'S SOMETHING BEHIND THE CURTAIN/ADVENTURE/AGING /GREENHORNS   7
    WHERE THERE'S A WILL, THERE'S VELLEITY/VOLITION/DICTIONARIES/WORDS   YZ4
    GOD BLESS THE GIDEONS OR THERE'S ALWAYS THE KING JAMES VERSION/HOTEL/BOOKS   A
THERMOS
    I WANT A DRINK OF WATER, BUT NOT FROM THE THERMOS/FATHERS/TRIPS   Z2
THESE
    THESE LADIES/SPANIARDS/DUENNA   E
    THESE LATINS/DUENNA   Y8
THEY
    WE HAVE MET THE SASSENACHS AND THEY ARE OURS; EVEN THE YEAR IS NOW MCMLXIV/MCLUHAN/MCKUEN   P
    NO CONFORMITY TO ENORMITY, THE BIGGER THEY ARE THE HARDER I FALL/CARS/STAMPS/BANKS   7
    AROUND THE HOUSE OR WHAT PARENTS THINK ABOUT WHEN THEY AREN'T THINKING ABOUT CHILDREN   9
    HUSH, HERE THEY COME/BACKBITERS/GOSSIP/FRANKNESS   Z18
    THEY DON'T READ DE QUINCEY IN PHILLY OR CINCY/MURDER   A
    THEY DON'T SPEAK ENGLISH IN PARIS/GERTRUDE STEIN   D
    GOODBYE, OLD YEAR, YOU OAF, OR WHY DON'T THEY PAY THE BONUS?/NEW YEAR'S EVE   DYZ8
    IS IT TRUE WHAT THEY SAY ABOUT DIXIE OR IS IT JUST THE WAY THEY SAY IT?/FLATTERY   5
    THEY WON'T BELIEVE, ON NEW YEAR'S EVE, THAT NEW YEAR'S DAY WILL COME WHAT MAY/HANGOVER   BZ5
THEY'LL
    HAVE YOU TRIED STAYING AWAKE? OR THEY'LL FIND A WAY TO STOP THAT, TOO/BED-BOARD   WZ3
THEY'VE
    A POTTED WATCH NEVER BOILS OR, MAYBE THAT'S WHAT THEY'VE BEEN TRYING PROVE/WRISTWATCH   7

THIEF
          DO YOU PLAN TO SPEAK BANTU? OR ABBREVIATION IS THE THIEF OF SANITY   Z6
THINGS
          REMEMBRANCE OF THINGS TO COME/FATHER/DAUGHTER/ADMIRATION/HUMILIATION   G89
THINK
          WHAT TO DO UNTIL THE DOCTOR GOES OR IT'S TOMORROW THAN YOU THINK/LIVING   WZ3
          FATHER, DEAR FATHER, GO JUMP IN THE LAKE OR, YOU'RE COSTLIER THAN YOU THINK/PARENTS/SUPPORT   Z5
          AROUND THE HOUSE OR WHAT PARENTS THINK ABOUT WHEN THEY AREN'T THINKING ABOUT CHILDREN 9
          OH, DID YOU GET THE TICKETS? BECAUSE I DON'T THINK I'LL GO, AFTER ALL/WOMEN/DECISIONS 4
          A MAN CAN COMPLAIN, CAN'T HE? (A LAMENT FOR THOSE WHO THINK OLD)   AW
          MY DEAR, HOW DID YOU EVER THINK UP THIS DELICIOUS SALAD?   DYZ18
          DO SPHINXES THINK?/FINGERNAILS/ELEVATORS   Z4
          LINES TO A THREE-NAME LADY/THINK   FYZ8
          A CAUTION TO EVERYBODY/AUK/MAN/FLY/WALK/THINK   Z5
THINKING
          IT WAS NOT I WHO POSED FOR RODIN OR WHY I FLUNKED PHILOSOPHY IV/THINKING/FRENCH   5
          AROUND THE HOUSE OR WHAT PARENTS THINK ABOUT WHEN THEY AREN'T THINKING ABOUT CHILDREN 9
THINKS
          A LADY THINKS SHE IS THIRTY/MIRANDA   BGYZ18
THIRD
          THE THIRD JUNGLE BOOK/PYGMY/POLYGAMY   Y2
          THIRD LIMICK/DOVER/COW/CLOVER/NUDISTS   Z3
          ONE THIRD OF A CALENDAR/WINTER/ILLNESS/CHILDREN   WYZ189
          ON WAKING TO THE THIRD RAINY MORNING OF A LONG WEEK END/HOUSE GUEST   Z3
THIRST
          WATER FOR THE GANDER/THIRST/CHILDREN   29
THIRTEENTH
          A TALE OF THE THIRTEENTH FLOOR/WALPURGIS NIGHT/DOUBLE-DAMNED   6
          THE THIRTEENTH LABOR OF HERCULES/SPHINX   Z5
THIRTIETH
          LINES TO BE SCRIBBLED ON SOMEBODY ELSE'S THIRTIETH MILESTONE/BIRTHDAY   Z4
THIRTY
          A LADY THINKS SHE IS THIRTY/MIRANDA   BGYZ18
          I'M SURE SHE SAID SIX-THIRTY/WAITING/WIVES   BZ2
          NOT GEORGE WASHINGTON'S, NOT ABRAHAM LINCOLN'S, BUT MINE/BIRTHDAY/THIRTY-EIGHT/CAREER Z2
THIS
          THE DAY OF THE LOCUST OR, WHOSE WEDDING IS THIS ANYWAY?/GUESTS   A
          HOW LONG HAS THIS BEEN GOING ON? OH, QUITE LONG/BETTING/HORSE-RACING   Z18
          WHAT THIS COUNTRY NEEDS IS MORE BROADMINDED BABIES   G
          MY DEAR, HOW DID YOU EVER THINK UP THIS DELICIOUS SALAD?   DYZ18
          TARKINGTON, THOU SHOULD'ST BE LIVING IN THIS HOUR/ADOLESCENCE   Z39
          THIS IS GOING TO HURT JUST A LITTLE BIT/DENTISTS   W4
          THIS IS MY OWN, MY NATIVE TONGUE/RADIO/ACCENTS   Z5
          SO THIS IS WASHINGTON OR DEAD MEN RESENT NO TALES/PROHIBITION   D
          LET ME BUY THIS ONE/RICH/MONEY   4
          ARE YOU SAVING THIS SEAT FOR ANYONE OR YES, BUT WHAT'S THE USE?/BUS   D
          IS THIS SEAT TAKEN? YES OR, MY NECK IS STICKING IN/CONVERSATION   Z3
          READ THIS VIBRANT EXPOSE/SLEEP/INSOMNIA   DY1
          THIS WAS TOLD ME IN CONFIDENCE/GOSSIP   Z4
          WHAT STREET IS THIS, DRIVER?/SIXTH-AVENUE EL/NEW YORKER   2
THOMPSON
          AS GAUGUIN SAID TO SADIE THOMPSON, YOU PRONOUNCE IT, I'LL PAINT IT/SAMOA   7
THORNE
          THE SELF-EFFACEMENT OF ELECTRA THORNE/ACRESSES   Z6
THOSE
          THERE WERE GIANTS IN THOSE DAYS OR MAYBE THERE WEREN'T/ANECDOTES   Z3
          LINES WRITTEN TO CONSOLE THOSE LADIES DISTRESSED BY THE LINES "MEN SELDOM MAKE PASSES"/
              GLASSES   EG
          PUT BACK THOSE WHISKERS, I KNOW YOU/NEW YEAR   Z2
          A THOUGHT ON THE MANNER OF THOSE WHO STRIVE TO ACHIEVE THE MANNER CALLED HEMINGWAY/WRITERS C
          A MAN CAN COMPLAIN, CAN'T HE? (A LAMENT FOR THOSE WHO THINK OLD)   AW
THOU
          ALL GOOD AMERICANS GO TO LAROUSSE OR, I DON'T PRETEND TO BE MOLIERE THAN THOU/FRENCH A
          ROLL ON, THOU DEEP AND DARK BLUE COPY WRITER-ROLL/HEMINGWAY/MOVIES   Z3
          ROLL ON, THOU DEEP AND DARK BLUE SYLLABLES, ROLL ON/METROPOLITAN OPERA/MILTON CROSS   A
          PAPERBACK, WHO MADE THEE? DOST THOU KNOW WHO MADE THEE?/PAPYRUS-BACK   A
          TARKINGTON, THOU SHOULD'ST BE LIVING IN THIS HOUR/ADOLESCENCE   Z39
THOUGHT
          THOUGHTS THOUGHT ON AN AVENUE/WOMEN/FASHION   BYZ2

VACANCY
     NATURE ABHORS A VACANCY/LEASES/RESIDENCE   3
VACATION
     TOMORROW, PARTLY CLOUDY/VACATION/RAIN   YZ29
     SEPTEMBER MORN/VACATION/TRAINS   GZ89
VAGUE
     SAID A COMMISSAR LOYAL BUT VAGUE   A
VAGUENESS
     WHO PUT THAT SPOKESMAN IN MY WHEEL?/VAGUENESS/NEWS SOURCES   A
VAILLIE
     CAPERCAILLIE, AVE ATQUE VAILLIE/BIRD SONGS   7
VALE
     VIVA VAMP, VALE VAMP/BUSTS/LIPSTICK/MASCARA   7
VALENTINE
     ONCE MORE, TO MY VALENTINE/LOVE   B
     TO MY VALENTINE/LOVE   BY2
     OLD DOCTOR VALENTINE FOR ONCE DREAMS OF WEALTH/BRA/PEPS-OO-LA-LA/BOUNCE   5
     OLD DOCTOR VALENTINE TO A COLLEAGUE/CURES/MEDICINE   5
     OLD DOCTOR VALENTINE TO HIS ONLY MILLIONAIRE/BILLS   5
     OLD DOCTOR VALENTINE TO HIS SON/LIVE/DIE   5
     OLD DOCTOR VALENTINE TO THAT KIND OF PATIENT/TELEPHONE   5
     I'M NO SAINT, AND I HAVE MY DOUBTS ABOUT VALENTINE, TOO/VALENTINES   A
     I ALWAYS SAY A GOOD SAINT IS NO WORSE THAN A BAD COLD/VALENTINE   F8
     THE STRANGE CASE OF MR. BALLENTINE'S VALENTINE   Z4
VALENTINES
     I'M NO SAINT, AND I HAVE MY DOUBTS ABOUT VALENTINE, TOO/VALENTINES   A
VALLEE
     REFLECTION ON GRATITIDE/VALLEE   E
VAMP
     VIVA VAMP, VALE VAMP/BUSTS/LIPSTICK/MASCARA   7
VANCE
     LITERARY REFLECTION/VANCE/PANCE   EZ18
VANITIES
     THEATRICAL REFLECTION/VANITIES/PANTIES   EZ8
VANITY
     HA! ORIGINAL SIN/VANITY   CYZ8
VARLET
     HO, VARLET! MY TWO CENTS' WORTH OF PENNY POSTCARD!/POST OFFICE/MAIL   Z6
VELLEITY
     WHERE THERE'S A WILL, THERE'S VELLEITY/VOLITION/DICTIONARIES/WORDS   YZ4
VENICE
     TRANSATLANTIC TRANSPORTS/LONDON/PARIS/SWITZERLAND/MALAGA/VENICE/MOSCOW/TAXIS   7
VERACITY
     REFLECTION ON VERACITY/PURITY/OBSCURITY   E
VERMONT
     KIPLING'S VERMONT/SUMMER/SUTTEE   Z5
VERNACULAR
     REFLECTION ON THE VERNACULAR/RECEIPTS/RECIPES/LAKE OSSIPEE   Z5
VERNAL
     THE ETERNAL VERNAL OR IN ALL MY DREAMS MY FAIR FACE BEAMS/SPRING   Z3
VERSA
     IT'S ALWAYS JUNE IN JANUARY, ALSO VICE VERSA/SUMMER   A
VERSE
     GEDDONDILLO/NONSENSE/VERSE   Y29
     MY DADDY/BABY/VERSE   FGZ8
VERSION
     GOD BLESS THE GIDEONS OR THERE'S ALWAYS THE KING JAMES VERSION/HOTEL/BOOKS   A
VERY
     VERY FUNNY, VERY FUNNY/SENSE OF HUMOR   Z3
     VERY LIKE A WHALE/LITERATURE/METAPHOR/SIMILE   DZ18
     LINES IN PRAISE OF A DATE MADE PRAISEWORTHY SOLELY BY SOMETHING VERY NICE THAT HAPPENED TO IT C
     VERY NICE, REMBRANDT, BUT HOW ABOUT A LITTLE MORE COLOR?/SONGS   A
     DADDY, I WANT A PET FOR MY VERY OWN, I PROMISE TO TAKE CARE OF IT   9
     THE VERY UNCLUBBABLE MAN/CLUBS   DZ8
VEXATION
     CIVILIZATION IS CONSTANT VEXATION/AMERICA/EUROPE/BARBARIANS   D
     NEVER WAS I BORN TO SET THEM RIGHT/VEXATION   A

VIBRANT
    READ THIS VIBRANT EXPOSE/SLEEP/INSOMNIA   DY1
VICE
    IT'S ALWAYS JUNE IN JANUARY, ALSO VICE VERSA/SUMMER   A
    PARSLEY FOR VICE-PRESIDENT   Z4
VICES
    THE STRANGE CASE OF THE IRKSOME PRUDE/VIRTUES/VICES   Z14
VIEW
    DON'T GRIN OR YOU'LL HAVE TO BEAR IT/HUMOR/POINT-OF-VIEW   Z14
VIEWER
    THE ARMCHAIR GOLFER OR, WHIMPERS OF A SHORTCHANGED VIEWER/TV   A
VII
    CALLING SPRING VII-MMMC/MYSTERIES/ROMAN-NUMERALS/PUBLISHERS   Z5
VILLAGE
    OUR CITY, OUR CITIZENS/VILLAGE/GOLD COAST/PRESS CAFE/THEATER   7
VINEYARD
    MARTHA'S VINEYARD   Z3
VIRGINIA
    FIRST FAMILIES, MOVE OVER!/VIRGINIA/SOUTHERN   Z4
VIRTUES
    THE STRANGE CASE OF THE IRKSOME PRUDE/VIRTUES/VICES   Z14
VISION
    AND HOW KEEN WAS THE VISION OF SIR LAUNFAL?/MYOPIA/GLASSES   WZ6
    A GOOD PARENT'S GARDEN OF VISION; THE DREAM; THE NIGHTMARE; THE AWAKENING/DAUGHTER   FGZ89
    THERE ONCE WAS AN UMPIRE WHOSE VISION   A
VISIT
    THE VISIT/DALLIANCE/MISTRESS/YACHT   Z5
    A VISIT FROM DOCTOR FELL/GUESTS   Z2
    A VISIT FROM SAINT INITIALUS/CHRISTMAS/TAXPAYER/POLITICS   D
VISITING
    SUPPOSE I DARKEN YOUR DOOR/VISITING/GUESTS   DYZ8
    MR. BARCALOW'S BREAKDOWN/TACT/VISITING   Z4
VISITOR
    A VISITOR FROM PORLOCK, BUT, ALAS, NO XANADU/TRUISMS/THOUGHTS   A
VISITORS
    VISITORS LAUGH AT LOCKSMITHS, OR, HOSPITAL DOORS HAVEN'T GOT LOCKS ANYHOW   WZ2
VIVA
    VIVA VAMP, VALE VAMP/BUSTS/LIPSTICK/MASCARA   7
VIVE
    VIVE LE POSTMASTER GENERAL/REPUBLICANS/DEMOCRATS   F8
VOICE
    I DIDN'T SAY A WORD OR WHO CALLED THAT PICCOLO PLAYER A FATHER?/HEARING/VOICE/LOUDNESS   Z5
    THE SCREEN WITH THE FACE WITH THE VOICE/MOVIES   Z2
    HOW CAN ECHO ANSWER WHAT ECHO CANNOT HEAR?/VOICE/WIFE   B7
    THE VOICE OF EXPERIENCE/LECTURES/HUSBANDS   BYZ29
VOICES
    I'LL HUSH IF YOU'LL HUSH/VOICES   D
VOLITION
    WHERE THERE'S A WILL, THERE'S VELLEITY/VOLITION/DICTIONARIES/WORDS   YZ4
VOLUBLE
    THE VOLUBLE WHEEL CHAIR/AGING   Z5
VOTING
    ELECTION DAY IS A HOLIDAY/VOTING   FZ8
    FELLOW CITIZENS, I LOVE YOU/POLITICIAN/VOTING   D
VOWEL
    FABLES BULFINCH FORGOT: NARCISSUS AND THE TREACHEROUS VOWEL/SPEAKING   A5
WAIT
    DON'T LOOK FOR THE SILVER LINING, JUST WAIT FOR IT/SERENDIPITY   Z5
    I CAN HARDLY WAIT FOR THE SANDMAN/DREAMS   WZ6
    DON'T WAIT, HIT ME NOW!/CRITICISM   BZ2
WAITING
    I'M SURE SHE SAID SIX-THIRTY/WAITING/WIVES   BZ2
    THOUGHTS WHILE WAITING FOR PRONOUNCEMENT FROM DOCTOR, EDITOR.../TIME   WYZ2
    WAITING FOR THE BIRDIE/PHOTOGRAPHERS   Y4
WAKING
    MR. MINIKIN'S WAKING NIGHTMARE/TRAVEL/MARRIAGE   A
    ON WAKING TO THE THIRD RAINY MORNING OF A LONG WEEK END/HOUSE GUEST   Z3
WALDORF
    PEACOCK ALLEY-OOP/WALDORF ASTORIA HOTEL   C
    UP THE WALDORF, DOWN ON THE FARM/FARMER/CITY DWELLER   D

WALK

      A CAUTION TO EVERYBODY/AUK/MAN/FLY/WALK/THINK   Z5

      IT WOULD HAVE BEEN QUICKER TO WALK OR DON'T TELL ME WE'RE THERE ALREADY/TAXI/PAYING   Z6

WALKS

      NATURE-WALKS OR NOT TO MENTION A DOPPING OF SHELDRAKES   Z6

WALPURGIS

      A TALE OF THE THIRTEENTH FLOOR/WALPURGIS NIGHT/DOUBLE-DAMNED   6

WALTER

      SAVONAROLA OF MAZDA LANE/WALTER WINCHELL   C

WALTZ

      THE WALTZ/CANDLES/GOWNS/LIVERY   r

      THE ORGAN-GRINDER/HURDY-GURDY/WALTZ   r

      THE WALTZ OF THE FLOWERS/BALLROOM/DANCE   r

WANDERING

      THE NYMPH AND THE SHEPHERD OR SHE WENT THAT-AWAY/WIVES/WANDERING-OFF   BZ6

WANDERLUST

      CHANGE HERE FOR WICHITA FALLS OR, HAS ANYBODY SEEN MY WANDERLUST?/TRAVEL   Z5

WANT

      I WANT A DRINK OF WATER, BUT NOT FROM THE THERMOS/FATHERS/TRIPS   Z2

      DADDY, I WANT A PET FOR MY VERY OWN, I PROMISE TO TAKE CARE OF IT   9

      I WANT NEW YORK   E

      YOU'VE GOT TO BE MR. PICKWICK IF YOU WANT TO ENJOY A PICNIC/PAPER   7

      THERE'S MORE TIME AT THE TOP, OR I WANT TO SEE MR. MURGATROYD/EXECUTIVES/ASSISTANTS   D

      I WANT TO SIT NEXT TO EMILY/CONVERSATION   D

WANTS

      PAPPY WANTS A POPPY/SLEEP   Z3

      EVERYBODY WANTS TO GET INTO THE BAEDEKER/TRAVELING/GEOGRAPHY   Z5

      WHO WANTS TO TRAVEL ALL OVER EUROPE AND SEE NOTHING BUT A LOT OF AMERICAN TOURISTS? I DO. 6

WAPITI

      THE WAPITI   FGZ18b

WAR

      THERE'LL ALWAYS BE A WAR BETWEEN THE SEXES/HUSBANDS/WIVES   Z6

      HEIL, HEILIGE NACHT/CHRISTMAS/WAR   2

      IS THERE AN OCULIST IN THE HOUSE/WAR   7

      JULY 4, 1941 - JULY 4, 1942/FIREWORKS/WAR   2

WARNING

      MIDSUMMER WARNING/SUNBURN/MOONLIGHT   Y2

      A WARNING TO FIANCEES/GOLFERS   D

      A WARNING TO WIVES/INSURANCE/MURDER   BDZ8

WARREN

      FOR DOCTOR WARREN ADAMS, WHO KINDLY BOUND THE AUTHOR FOR BEYOND HIS DESERTS/TATTOOED   2

WAS

      THE SNARK WAS A BOOJUM WAS A PRAWN/SANTIAGO   Z6

      THERE WAS A YOUNG GIRL OF MILWAUKEE   A

      THERE WAS A YOUNG MAN FROM NEW HAVEN   A

      THERE ONCE WAS AN UMPIRE WHOSE VISION   A

      NEVER WAS I BORN TO SET THEM RIGHT/VEXATION   A

      IT WAS NOT I WHO POSED FOR RODIN OR WHY I FLUNKED PHILOSOPHY IV/THINKING/FRENCH   5

      AS I WAS SAYING TO SAINT PAUL JUST THE OTHER DAY/OPSIMATHY/LIFE   7

      WHEN THE DEVIL WAS SICK COULD HE PROVE IT?/SYMPTOMS   WZ18

      I HAD NO IDEA IT WAS SO LATE/WATCHES/WOMEN/MEN   YZ18

      AND HOW KEEN WAS THE VISION OF SIR LAUNFAL?/MYOPIA/GLASSES   WZ6

      THIS WAS TOLD ME IN CONFIDENCE/GOSSIP   Z4

      A BIRTHDAY THAT NEVER WAS: A FEBRUARY FANTASY/JOHN WILKES BOOTH/LINCOLN/WASHINGTON   6

WASHINGTON

      UNTOLD ADVENTURES OF SANTA CLAUS/WASHINGTON/DELAWARE/REVOLUTION   x

      ALL QUIET ALONG THE POTOMAC EXCEPT THE LETTER G/WASHINGTON/KISSINGER/KIPLINGER   7

      LET'S NOT CLIMB THE WASHINGTON MONUMENT TONIGHT/MIDDLE AGE   WZ3

      SO THIS IS WASHINGTON OR DEAD MEN RESENT NO TALES/PROHIBITION   D

      WASHINGTON'S BIRTHDAY EVE   Y14

      NOT GEORGE WASHINGTON'S, NOT ABRAHAM LINCOLN'S, BUT MINE/BIRTHDAY/THIRTY-EIGHT/CAREER Z2

      A BIRTHDAY THAT NEVER WAS: A FEBRUARY FANTASY/JOHN WILKES BOOTH/LINCOLN/WASHINGTON   6

      WATCHMAN, WHAT OF THE FIRST FIRST LADY?/MRS. GEORGE WASHINGTON   CYZ8

WASN'T

      THAT'S FUNNY, WASN'T IT? NO, IT WON'T BE/COMIC ARTISTS/HUMOR   Z6

      THE CHRISTMAS THAT ALMOST WASN'T/NICHOLAS/LULLAPAT/HEROES   v

WASP

      THE WASP   Z29

WATCH

      A POTTED WATCH NEVER BOILS OR, MAYBE THAT'S WHAT THEY'VE BEEN TRYING PROVE/WRISTWATCH   7

WATCHED
        A WATCHED EXAMPLE NEVER BOILS/THUNDERSTORM   GZ189
WATCHERS
        WHICH CAME FIRST, OBEISANCE OR OBESITY/PLATE-WATCHERS/WEIGHT-WATCHERS   7
        THE CALENDAR-WATCHERS OR WHAT'S SO WONDERFUL ABOUT BEING A PATRIARCH?/AGE   Z5
        UP FROM THE EGG: THE CONFESSIONS OF A NUTHATCH AVOIDER/BIRD WATCHERS   WZ6
WATCHES
        I HAD NO IDEA IT WAS SO LATE/WATCHES/WOMEN/MEN   YZ18
        THE SABOTEUR/WATCHES   6
        ASK ME NO QUESTIONS/MOTHER/FATHER/WATCHES   D
WATCHMAN
        WATCHMAN, WHAT OF THE FIRST FIRST LADY?/MRS. GEORGE WASHINGTON   CYZ8
WATER
        WATER FOR THE GANDER/THIRST/CHILDREN   29
        I WANT A DRINK OF WATER, BUT NOT FROM THE THERMOS/FATHERS/TRIPS   Z2
        CAN I GET YOU A GLASS OF WATER? OR PLEASE CLOSE THE GLOTTIS AFTER YOU/COUGHING   Z6
WAY
        HEY, HEY FOR THE AMERICAN WAY/REPUBLICANS/DEMOCRATES   5
        IS IT TRUE WHAT THEY SAY ABOUT DIXIE OR IS IT JUST THE WAY THEY SAY IT?/FLATTERY   5
        HAVE YOU TRIED STAYING AWAKE? OR THEY'LL FIND A WAY TO STOP THAT, TOO/BED-BOARD   WZ3
        WHO'S GOING MR. PLATT'S WAY?/NEIGHBORS/CAR-SHARING   2
WAYS
        THERE ARE MORE WAYS TO ROAST A PIG THAN BURNING THE HOUSE DOWN/CIGARETTE LIGHTERS   Z3
WE
        LET'S NOT GO TO THE THEATER TONIGHT, OR WE COULDN'T GET SEATS ANYHOW/MANHATTAN   D8
        SHALL WE DANCE? BEING THE CONFESSIONS OF A BALLETRAMUS   7
        WHAT'LL WE DO NOW, OR I'M AFRAID I KNOW OR, GOOLD OLD JUST PLAIN CHARADES, FAREWELL/GAMES 2
        I'LL WRITE THEIR NUMBER DOWN WHEN WE GET HOME/WORDS/SOCIAL-LIFE   Z2
        HERE WE GO QUIETLY NUTS IN MAY   Z2
        WE HAVE MET THE SASSENACHS AND THEY ARE OURS; EVEN THE YEAR IS NOW MCMLXIV/MCLUHAN/MCKUEN P
        ON GRATITUDE WE STAND PATITUDE/THANKSGIVING   2
        THE PANDIT OR, PERHAPS WE WERE WRONG ABOUT THAT, BUT AS LONG AS WE'RE BEING FRANK   7
        WE WOULD REFER YOU TO OUR SERVICE DEPARTMENT, IF WE HAD ONE/APPLIANCES   Z3
        WE DON'T NEED TO LEAVE YET, DO WE? OR, YES WE DO/MARRIAGE   29
WEALTH
        OLD DOCTOR VALENTINE FOR ONCE DREAMS OF WEALTH/BRA/PEPS-OO-LA-LA/BOUNCE   5
        THE SONG OF SONGS/WEALTH/DISTRIBUTION   4
        THE TERRIBLE PEOPLE/WEALTH/MONEY   FYZ18
        LITTLE PRETTY PENNY, LET'S SQUANDER THEE/MILLIONAIRES/WEALTH   A
WEARING
        TO A SMALL BOY STANDING ON MY SHOES WHILE I AM WEARING THEM   CGY9
WEATHER
        IT'S NEVER FAIR WEATHER/SEASONS   DZ189
        WEATHER CLEAR, TRACK FAST, HORSES PHOOIE!/BETTING   D
        WHAT'S IT LIKE OUTSIDE? OR ITS ALWAYS FAIR WEATHER UNLESS SOMEBODY SAYS IT ISN'T   O
        SEPTEMBER IS SUMMER, TOO OR IT'S NEVER TOO LATE TO BE UNCOMFORTABLE/HOT WEATHER   Z3
WEBSTER
        TO EE IS HUMAN/DICTIONARIES/MR. WEBSTER/MR. MERRIAM   Z6
WEDDING
        THE DAY OF THE LOCUST OR, WHOSE WEDDING IS THIS ANYWAY?/GUESTS   A
        TIN WEDDING WHISTLE/LOVE/MARRIAGE   BYZ29
        EVERYBODY LOVES A BRIDE, EVEN THE GROOM/WEDDING   5
        HERE USUALLY COMES THE BRIDE/JUNE/WEDDING   Z3
WEDNESDAY
        WE'LL ALL FEEL BETTER BY WEDNESDAY/MONDAY/WEEKENDS   3
        WEDNESDAY MATINEE/THEATER/WOMEN   Z4
WEEK
        ON WAKING TO THE THIRD RAINY MORNING OF A LONG WEEK END/HOUSE GUEST   Z3
WEEKDAYS
        EVERY DAY IS MONDAY/WEEKDAYS   Z4
WEEKENDS
        THERE'S A HOST BORN EVERY MINUTE/WEEKENDS/GUESTS   D1
        WE'LL ALL FEEL BETTER BY WEDNESDAY/MONDAY/WEEKENDS   3
WEIGHT
        AND DON'T FORGET WEIGHT-LIFTING, SHOTPUTTING, AND THE LADIES' JUNIOR BACKSTROKE CHAMPIONSHIP 7
        WHICH CAME FIRST, OBEISANCE OR OBESITY/PLATE-WATCHERS/WEIGHT-WATCHERS   7
        CURL UP AND DIET/LADIES/WEIGHT   WZ4
WELL
        MOTHER ISN'T WELL/ENGLISH PRONOUNCIATION   7
        WHAT THE WELL-READ PATIENT IS TALKING ABOUT OR LOOK, MA, WHAT I GOT!/MEDICAL TERMINOLOGY WZ6
WE'LL
        WE'LL ALL FEEL BETTER BY WEDNESDAY/MONDAY/WEEKENDS   3

WENDIGO
    THE WENDIGO/CANNIBAL/ALGONQUIANS   WZ5
WENT
    AN EXILED IRAQI WENT BACK   A
    THE NYMPH AND THE SHEPHERD OR SHE WENT THAT-AWAY/WIVES/WANDERING-OFF   BZ6
WERE
    IF HE WERE ALIVE TODAY, MAYHAP, MR. MORGAN WOULD SIT ON THE MIDGET'S LAP/BANKER   A
    THERE WERE GIANTS IN THOSE DAYS OR MAYBE THERE WEREN'T/ANECDOTES   Z3
    IF THERE WERE NO ENGLAND, 'COUNTRY LIFE' WOULD INVENT IT/HOUSES   A
    PAJAMAS, HUH? OR DRESSES WERE SO NICE/PANTS   C
    THE PANDIT OR, PERHAPS WE WERE WRONG ABOUT THAT, BUT AS LONG AS WE'RE BEING FRANK   7
WE'RE
    THE PANDIT OR, PERHAPS WE WERE WRONG ABOUT THAT, BUT AS LONG AS WE'RE BEING FRANK   7
    WE'RE FINE, JUST FINE/HEALTH/ILLNESS/GLOWING COMPLEXION   AW
    IT WOULD HAVE BEEN QUICKER TO WALK OR DON'T TELL WE'RE THERE ALREADY/TAXI/PAYING   Z6
WEREN'T
    THERE WERE GIANTS IN THOSE DAYS OR MAYBE THERE WEREN'T/ANECDOTES   Z3
WEST
    DOCTOR FELL AND POINTS WEST/TICKET-WINDOW/TRAINS   Z2
    MAE WEST   D
WESTERN
    ONE WESTERN, TO GO/BLANCH/RANCH   A
WET
    THE DOG/WET   7
WE'VE
    YOUR LEAD, PARTNER, I HOPE WE'VE READ THE SAME BOOK/BRIDGE/CARDS   Z6
WHA
    EVERYTHING'S HAGGIS IN HOBOKEN OR, SCOTS WHA HAE HAE/ROBERT BURNS   Z5
WHALE
    VERY LIKE A WHALE/LITERATURE/METAPHOR/SIMILE   DZ18
    MUSEUM OF NATURAL HISTORY: TYRANNOSAURUS REX; PYTHON; ROCK ROOM; WHALE; HALL OF PRIMATES   N
WHAT
    AT LEAST I'M NOT THE KIND OF FOOL WHO SOBS; WHAT KIND OF FOOL AM I?   X
    A DAY ON A CRUISE OR, WHAT A DAY. WHAT A CRUISE./SHIPS   7
    EHEU! FUGACES OR, WHAT A DIFFERENCE A LOT OF DAYS MAKE/YOUTH/MIDDLE-AGE   WZ5
    WHAT ALMOST EVERY WOMAN KNOWS SOONER OR LATER/HUSBANDS   DYZ89
    WHAT'S IN A NAME? HERE'S WHAT'S IN A NAME OR I WONDER WHAT BECAME OF JOHN AND MARY   Z6
    HOW CAN ECHO ANSWER WHAT ECHO CANNOT HEAR?/VOICE/WIFE   BZ
    WHAT EVERY WOMAN KNOWS SOONER OR LATER/HUSBANDS   1
    MAYBE YOU CAN'T TAKE IT WITH YOU, BUT LOOK WHAT HAPPENS WHEN YOU LEAVE IT BEHIND/MONEY   Z5
    HOW TO BE MARRIED WITHOUT A SPOUSE; KIPLING OR WHAT HAVE YOU DONE WITH MR. HAUKSBEE/INDIA   BZ5
    WHAT THE WELL-READ PATIENT IS TALKING ABOUT OR LOOK, MA, WHAT I GOT!/MEDICAL TERMINOLOGY   WZ6
    HEARTS AND FLOWERS OR WHAT I KNOW ABOUT BOLIVAR BLACK/GENEROSITY/LOANS   DZ8
    WHAT I KNOW ABOUT LIFE   Z3
    IMPRESSIONS OF SUBURBIA BY ONE WHO HAS NEVER BEEN THERE OR, ALL I KNOW IS WHAT I SEE IN ADS   7
    WHAT IS BIBBIDI-BOBBIDI-BOO IN SANSCRIT?/FRENCH   Z5
    BABY, WHAT MAKES THE SKY BLUE/CHILDREN/INGENUOUS/PARENTS   19
    THEY WON'T BELIEVE, ON NEW YEAR'S EVE, THAT NEW YEAR'S DAY WILL COME WHAT MAY/HANGOVER   BZ5
    WATCHMAN, WHAT OF THE FIRST FIRST LADY?/MRS. GEORGE WASHINGTON   CYZ8
    AROUND THE HOUSE OR WHAT PARENTS THINK ABOUT WHEN THEY AREN'T THINKING ABOUT CHILDREN   9
    DOWN THE MOUSEHOLE, AND WHAT SCIENCE MISSED THERE/MARRIAGE/APOLOGY   WZ2
    WHAT STREET IS THIS, DRIVER?/SIXTH-AVENUE EL/NEW YORKER   2
    IS IT TRUE WHAT THEY SAY ABOUT DIXIE OR IS IT JUST THE WAY THEY SAY IT?/FLATTERY   5
    A POTTED WATCH NEVER BOILS OR, MAYBE THAT'S WHAT THEY'VE BEEN TRYING PROVE/WRISTWATCH   7
    WHAT THIS COUNTRY NEEDS IS MORE BROADMINDED BABIES   G
    WHAT TO DO UNTIL THE DOCTOR GOES OR IT'S TOMORROW THAN YOU THINK/LIVING   WZ3
    LOOK WHAT YOU DID, CHRISTOPHER/COLUMBUS/AMERICA   FZ8
    DO, DO, DO WHAT YOU DONE, DONE, DONE BEFORE, BEFORE, BEFORE/APPLAUSE/AMATEUR THEATER   YZ2
    WHAT, NO OYSTERS?   Z2
    WHAT, NO SHEEP?/SLEEP-INDUCERS   WZ6
    GOOD RIDDANCE, BUT NOW WHAT?/NEW YEAR'S EVE   WZ39
WHAT'LL
    WHAT'LL WE DO NOW, OR, I'M AFRAID I KNOW OR, GOOD OLD JUST PLAIN CHARADES, FAREWELL/GAMES   2
WHAT'S
    MA, WHAT'S A BANKER? OR HUSH, MY CHILD   DZ18
    WHAT'S HECUBA TO HIM? A ONE-MINUTE CLOSE-UP/TV REPORTING DISASTERS   A
    WHAT'S IN A NAME? SOME LETTER I ALWAYS FORGET/SPELLING   Z5
    WHAT'S IT LIKE OUTSIDE? OR ITS ALWAYS FAIR WEATHER UNLESS SOMEBODY SAYS IT ISN'T   O

WHAT'S
    ARE YOU SAVING THIS SEAT FOR ANYONE OR YES, BUT WHAT'S THE USE?/BUS   D
    WHAT'S THE USE?/WOMEN/PANTS   Y18
    WHAT'S IN A NAME? HERE'S WHAT'S IN A NAME OR I WONDER WHAT BECAME OF JOHN AND MARY   Z6
    WHAT'S SAUCE POUR L'OIE IS SAUCE POUR L'ETAT C'EST MOI/FRENCH   M
    THE CALENDAR-WATCHERS OR WHAT'S SO WONDERFUL ABOUT BEING A PATRIARCH?/AGE   Z5
    WHAT'S THE MATTER, HAVEN'T YOU GOT ANY SENSE OF HUMOR?/PRACTICAL JOKES   YZ18
WHEEL
    THE VOLUBLE WHEEL CHAIR/AGING   Z5
    DETROIT, SPARE THAT WHEEL!/AUTOMOBILES/HORSEPOWER   6
    WHO PUT THAT SPOKESMAN IN MY WHEEL?/VAGUENESS/NEWS SOURCES   A
WHEELBARROW
    UP FROM THE WHEELBARROW/MACHINERY   Z4
WHEELS
    HI-HO THE AMBULANCE-O/STREETS/WHEELS/FEET   Z5
WHEN
    JUST HOW LOW CAN A HIGHBROW GO WHEN A HIGHBROW LOWERS HIS BROW   7
    WHEN THE DEVIL WAS SICK COULD HE PROVE IT?/SYMPTOMS   WZ18
    WHEN THE MOON SHINES OVER AND OVER/RADIO   F
    AROUND THE HOUSE OR WHAT PARENTS THINK ABOUT WHEN THEY AREN'T THINKING ABOUT CHILDREN   9
    I'LL WRITE THEIR NUMBER DOWN WHEN WE GET HOME/WORDS/SOCIAL-LIFE   Z2
    MAYBE YOU CAN'T TAKE IT WITH YOU, BUT LOOK WHAT HAPPENS WHEN YOU LEAVE IT BEHIND/MONEY   Z5
    WHEN YOU SAY THAT, SMILE! OR ALL RIGHT THEN, DON'T SMILE/UPHILL FIGHTS   FYZ18
WHERE
    TELL ME NO FIBLETS, WHERE ARE THE GIBLETS/GRAVY/TURKEY DINNER   A
    WHY THE POSTMAN HAS TO RING TWICE OR, YELLOW ENVELOPE, WHERE HAVE YOU GONE?/TELEGRAMS   Z5
    WHERE THERE'S A WILL, THERE'S VELLEITY/VOLITION/DICTIONARIES/WORDS   YZ4
WHICH
    WHICH CAME FIRST, OBEISANCE OR OBESITY/PLATE-WATCHERS/WEIGHT-WATCHERS   7
    EIPILOGUE TO MOTHER'S DAY, WHICH IS TO BE PUBLISHED ON ANY DAY BUT MOTHER'S DAY   Z4
    IN WHICH THE POET IS ASHAMED BUT PLEASED/DAUGHTER/FATHER   DGYZ89
    WHO DID WHICH? OR WHO INDEED?/KNOWLEDGE/FACTS   WZ3
WHILE
    WHILE HOMER NODDED: A FOOTNOTE TO THE ILIAD/ZEUS/ANTISCRUPULOS   A
    TO A SMALL BOY STANDING ON MY SHOES WHILE I AM WEARING THEM   CGY9
    PROGNOSTICATIONS ARE FOR THE BIRDS: LAY OFF ME, PLEASE, WHILE I EAT MY WORDS/FOOTBALL/COLTS   V
    THOUGHTS THOUGHT WHILE RESTING COMFORTABLY IN PHILLIPS HOUSE, MASSACHUSETTS GENERAL HOSPITAL   A
    THOUGHTS WHILE WAITING FOR PRONOUNCEMENT FROM DOCTOR, EDITOR.../TIME   WYZ2
    LINES TO BE EMBROIDERED ON A BIB OR, THE CHILD IS FATHER OF THE MAN, BUT NOT FOR QUITE A
        WHILE   Z39
WHIMPERS
    THE ARMCHAIR GOLFER OR, WHIMPERS OF A SHORTCHANGED VIEWER/TV   A
WHISKERS
    PUT BACK THOSE WHISKERS, I KNOW YOU/NEW YEAR   Z2
    WOODMAN, SPARE NOT THAT UNDERBRUSH/WHISKERS   D8
WHISTLE
    TIN WEDDING WHISTLE/LOVE/MARRIAGE   BYZ29
WHITE
    HOW TO TELL A QUAIL FROM A PARTRIDGE/BOB WHITE   D
WHO
    WHO UNDERSTANDS WHO ANYHOW?/MEN/WOMEN   Z4
    I DIDN'T SAY A WORD OR WHO CALLED THAT PICCOLO PLAYER A FATHER?/HEARING/VOICE/LOUDNESS   Z5
    WHO CALLED THAT PIED-BILLED GREBE A PODILYMBUS PODICEPS PODICEPS?/BIRD   A
    WHO CALLED THAT ROBIN A PICCOLO PLAYER/BIRDS   Z3
    I KNOW EXACTLY WHO DROPPED THE OVERALLS IN MRS. MURPHY'S CHOWDER/BORES   Z6
    LINES TO A WORLD-FAMOUS POET WHO FAILED TO COMPLETE A WORLD-FAMOUS POEM/MR. GUEST   FY189
    MERRY CHRISTMAS, YOU-ALL OR WHO FORGOT SAVANNAH?/CARDS/ARTISTS   5
    THE MAN WHO FRUSTRATED MADISON AVENUE/TV/COMMERCIALS   A
    IMPRESSIONS OF SUBURBIA BY ONE WHO HAS NEVER BEEN THERE OR, ALL I KNOW IS WHAT I SEE IN ADS   7
    SO THAT'S WHO I REMIND ME OF/RESEMBLANCE TO THE TALENTED   Z2
    WHO DID WHICH? OR WHO INDEED?/KNOWLEDGE/FACTS   WZ3
    FOR DOCTOR WARREN ADAMS, WHO KINDLY BOUND THE AUTHOR FOR BEYOND HIS DESERTS/TATTOOED   2
    THE BOY WHO LAUGHED AT SANTA CLAUS/JABEZ DAWES   29c
    A PRINCESS WHO LIVED NEAR A BOG/FROG   A
    PAPERBACK, WHO MADE THEE? DOST THOU KNOW WHO MADE THEE?/PAPYRUS-BACK   A
    IT WAS NOT I WHO POSED FOR RODIN OR WHY I FLUNKED PHILOSOPHY IV/THINKING/FRENCH   5
    WHO PUT THAT SPOKESMAN IN MY WHEEL?/VAGUENESS/NEWS SOURCES   A
    WHO SAYS IT'S SO NICE TO HAVE A MAN AROUND THE HOUSE?/HUSBANDS   A
    ROLL OVER AND PLAY ALIVE, WHO SAYS YOU CAN'T TEACH AN OLD DOG TIRESOME TRICKS/KIPLING/JOKE   5

WORLD
        REFLECTION ON A WICKED WORLD/PURITY/OBSCURITY   YZ8
        LEAVE ME ALONE, AND THE WORLD IS MINE/AUTOMOBILES/RADIOS   D
        EVERYBODY'S MIND TO ME A KINGDOM IS OR, A GREAT BIG WONDERFUL WORLD IT'S/PUNS   Z5
        LINES TO A WORLD-FAMOUS POET WHO FAILED TO COMPLETE A WORLD-FAMOUS POEM/MR. GUEST   FY189
WORM
        TURNS IN A WORM'S LANE/BETTING SPORTS   FYZ18
WORSE
        I ALWAYS SAY A GOOD SAINT IS NO WORSE THAN A BAD COLD/VALENTINE   F8
        HEARTS OF GOLD OR A GOOD EXCUSE IS WORSE THAN NONE/APOLOGIES/REMORSE   FYZ8
WORTH
        HO, VARLET! MY TWO CENTS' WORTH OF PENNY POSTCARD!/POST OFFICE/MAIL   Z6
        A CHUCKLING TYCOON OF FORT WORHT   A
WOULD
        IF THERE WERE NO ENGLAND, 'COUNTRY LIFE' WOULD INVENT IT/HOUSES   A
        IT WOULD HAVE BEEN QUICKER OT WALK OR DON'T TELL ME WE'RE THERE ALREADY/TAXI/PAYING   Z6
        THE SANKE, WITHOUT WHOM ADAM WOULD NEVER HAVE LOOKED AT THE LADY ONCE/KISSED   5
        WE WOULD REFER YOU TO OUR SERVICE DEPARTMENT, IF WE HAD ONE/APPLIANCES   Z3
        IF HE WERE ALIVE TODAY, MAYHAP, MR. MORGAN WOULD SIT ON THE MIDGET'S LAP/BANKER   A
WRAP
        JUST WRAP IT UP, AND I'LL THROW IT AWAY LATER/SHOPPING   BZ2
WRATH
        THE STRANGE CASE OF THE BLIGHT THAT FAILED/GREAT-AUNT/WRATH   6
WRISTWATCH
        A POTTED WATCH NEVER BOILS OR, MAYBE THAT'S WHAT THEY'VE BEEN TRYING PROVE/WRISTWATCH   7
WRITE
        I'LL WRITE THEIR NUMBER DOWN WHEN WE GET HOME/WORDS/SOCIAL-LIFE   Z2
WRITER
        THE STRANGE CASE OF THE LOVELORN LETTER WRITER/MISS DIX/DALLIANCE/LOVE   Z5
        THE STRANGE CASE OF THE RENEGADE LYRIC WRITER/SINGERS   Z3
        ROLL ON, THOU DEEP AND DARK BLUE COPY WRITER-ROLL/HEMINGWAY/MOVIES   Z3
WRITERS
        ARTHUR BISBANE/WRITERS/PLATITUDES   E
        A PARABLE FOR SPORTS WRITERS, SOCIETY COLUMNISTS, BOND SALESMEN AND POETS/PUBLISHING BOOKS FZ8
        ENCYCLOPEDIA BRITANNICA/WRITERS   C
        I'LL CALL YOU BACK LATER/WRITERS   C
        NOTE ON HUMAN NATURE/WRITERS   E
        A THOUGHT ON THE MANNER OF THOSE WHO STRIVE TO ACHIEVE THE MANNER CALLED HEMINGWAY/WRITERS C
WRITING
        LOVE FOR SALE/POETS/WRITING   D8
WRITTEN
        LINES WRITTEN TO CONSOLE THOSE LADIES DISTRESSED BY THE LINES "MEN SELDOM MAKE PASSES"/
                GLASSES   EG
WRONG
        I MAY BE WRONG/BENDER   E
        THE PANDIT OR, PERHAPS WE WERE WRONG ABOUT THAT, BUT AS LONG AS WE'RE BEING FRANK   7
        WRONG-HEADED/DISHONORABLE   E
WRONGS
        THE WRONGS OF SPRING OR, NO ALL FOOLS' DAY LIKE AN ALL OLD FOOLS' DAY/BIRTHDAY   A
XANADU
        A VISITOR FROM PORLOCK, BUT, ALAS, NO XANADU/TRUISMS/THOUGHTS   A
YACHT
        THE VISIT/DALLIANCE/MISTRESS/YACHT   Z5
YANKAKEE
        TUNE FOR AN ILL-TEMPERERED CLAVICHORD/YANKAKEE   Z5
YEAR
        MERRY N.R.A. AND HAPPY FISCAL YEAR/BUSINESS   F
        AND THREE HUNDRED AND SIXTY-SIX IN LEAP YEAR/SHAVING/BATHING   Z2
        WE HAVE MET THE SASSENACHS AND THEY ARE OURS; EVEN THE YEAR IS NOW MCMLXIV/MCLUHAN/MCKUEN P
        GOODBYE, OLD YEAR, YOU OAF, OR WHY DON'T THEY PAY THE BONUS?/NEW YEAR'S EVE   DYZ8
        PUT BACK THOSE WHISKERS, I KNOW YOU/NEW YEAR   Z2
YEARS
        I HAVE USED IT FOR YEARS/ADVERTISING/ENDORSEMENTS   F8
        THE SUNSET YEARS OF SAMUEL SHY/KISSING   A
YEAR'S
        GOOD RIDDANCE, BUT NOW WHAT?/NEW YEAR'S EVE   WZ39
        THEY WON'T BELIEVE, ON NEW YEAR'S EVE, THAT NEW YEAR'S DAY WILL COME WHAT MAY/HANGOVER   BZ5
        GOODBYE, OLD YEAR, YOU OAF, OR WHY DON'T THEY PAY THE BONUS?/NEW YEAR'S EVE   DYZ8

YOU